INFINITE

SOLUTIONS

A SOLUTION TO EVERYTHING

ONE WORLD. ONE FLAG. ONE CONSTITUTION.

ZERIT

TEKLAY

THE HIGHEST LEVEL OF SUCCESS IS WHEN SOMEONE, WITH A TEAM OF OTHERS, SOLVES MAJOR GLOBAL CRISISES SUCH AS WARS, FAMINE, CRIME AND CIVIL UNREST IN A GLOBAL LEVEL.

"The only solution that will end World wars from not starting is when all countries become equally super powerful."

"Why do we get sick? We get sick because of types of food we eat, we get sick because of the types of drinks we drink, we get sick because of the types of news we see and hear, we get sick because of sleeping too much or sleeping too little. We get sick because of weak immune systems and malnutrition."

"World War is the biggest problem of our World today. Solving a major big World War is not only the duty of Governments, but it is also everyone's duty and responsibility. So let us prevent any major World War from happening before it happens by means of peaceful approach and diplomacy instead of by Arms, Nuclear bombs and Cyber attacks. Let us guide each TV news or Social Media platforms not to generate and circulate hatred among nations against nations, and let us also guide ourselves not to generate and circulate hatred among ourselves and among nations. Without any discrimination any people of any country, my heart goes out and aches with any people of any country whose heart is aching in the midst of on Going Wars and Terrors. Let working for peace be the duty and responsibility of each one of us. Together let us succeed on preventing a major World War from happening by our words and by our deeds."

Zerit Teklay's dream for this book is that the Purpose Statement and the noble ideas written in this book will be carried from generation to generation until they become true. Zerit's mission s to one day take flight to the United Nations Geneva Convention, to represent the people of the world, and share the solutions he has written in this book. Let anyone who reads this book fulfill that mission, not to represent a specific country, but to represent the people of the whole world. Zerit only hopes that he is not running short of time to prevent a major World War Three. Let the dreams of this book be translated into all the languages, carried to all the lands, to all of the people of the world.

Amaz🌐xa
PEACE UNIVERSITY

ZERIT TEKLAY SEBHATLEAB

GLOBAL SOLUTION
THE HOME OF TRUE EDUCATION

Amaz🌍xa
PEACE UNIVERSITY

Eritrean-born, Dr. Zerit Teklay Sebhatleab, the founding father, CEO, and the President of Amazoxa Peace University, the home of true education, is dedicating his life to making a grand transformation in the world with his unorthodox, invaluable intellect, that can't be hacked or stolen.

Determined to unite the world, he has invented a step-by-step plan, which, if implemented, will foster world peace by eradicating war crimes, and also change the trajectory of the entire planet. While this mastermind's work is centered on Africa, his motherland, and the cessation of discrimination particularly with respect to race and gender, he has plans set for the rest of the world, with a system that allows only 7 Presidents, representing each continent,

Determined to unite the world, he has invented a step-by-step plan, which, if implemented, will foster world peace by eradicating war crimes, and also change the trajectory of the entire planet. While this mastermind's work is centered on Africa, his motherland, and the cessation of discrimination particularly with respect to race and gender, he has plans set for the rest of the world, with a system that allows only 7 Presidents, representing each continent, who are accountable to the Supreme Court of the United Countries of the World. His agenda aims to end the individualistic culture in our world today, and create a world where people aren't solely focused on themselves and their countries, but the entire world.

This is a must-read for everyone who is passionate about creating a better world for the next generation.

Amazoxa Peace University

the home of True education

Infinite Solutions
A Solution to
Everything

One World. One Flag. One Currency. One Constitution. One University. One Love

ZERIT TEKLAY

A K A YES, WE CAN PRRCW

About the Author and his big Dreams

ZERIT Teklay Sebhatleab is the author of this book.

The biggest dream of the Author of this book is to achieve his purpose statement "Amazoxa Peace University the home of true Education" definite purpose Statement Dreams come true one day. Besides The purpose statement of the Author Zerit Teklay Sebhatleab says, "Infinite Solutions: A Solution to Everything. One World. One Flag. One Constitution and one University. If not in his lifetime, the Author of this book hopes his Purpose Statement and the noble ideas written in this book to be carried on from generation to generation until said noble ideas become true. God forbid, if something unexpected happens to the Author of this book, his first mission would be to take a flight to the United Nations Geneva convention, representing the people of the world. If his first mission does not come true, let anyone who reads this book pick up his First mission of representing the people of the World. Let anyone who picks up this book not represent a specific country. Let anyone who reads this book represent the people of the entire world, not the people of a specific country. Whoever picks up the First mission of the Author of this book can refer to this book's ideas on the United Nations Convention meeting and public speaking. The Author does not represent any specific country agenda; he only exclusively represents the people of all countries' agenda. He does not represent any specific government agenda. Although the Author understands that humanity will not totally perish by governments' agendas of World wars and domination, the Author hopes not to run out of time on preventing a major World War three.

He hopes he does not get assassinated like Martin Luther King was assassinated before his dreams come true. If his dreams do not come true while he is alive today, let his dreams written in this book be taught in schools and Universities, and let this book be translated to all languages, even after he is long gone. Let his noble mission and ideas be carried on in all lands by all the peoples of the World. Let every person, all the people in social media, in the radio, every president of every country, every government official of every country, every teacher, every publisher, every athlete, every movie producer, every musician, every designer, every good and brave journalist of every country in the world pick this book up and talk about, write about and make a movie about this book . Let the noble ideas he has written in this book be talked about in all TV channels, radios, and social media platforms.

About the Author

Eritrean-born, Dr. Zerit Teklay Sebhatleab, the founding father, CEO, and the President of Amazoxa Peace University, the home of true education, is dedicating his life to making a grand transformation in the world with his unorthodox, invaluable intellect, which can't be hacked or stolen.

Determined to unite the world, he has invented a step-by-step plan, which, if implemented, will foster world peace by eradicating war crimes, and also change the trajectory of the entire planet. While this mastermind's work is centered on Africa, his motherland, and the cessation of discrimination particularly with respect to race and gender, he has plans set for the rest of the world, with a system that allows only 7 Presidents, representing each continent, who are accountable to the Supreme Court of the United Countries of the World. His agenda aims to end the individualistic culture in our world today, and create a world where people aren't solely focused on themselves and their countries, but the entire world.

This is a must-read for everyone who is passionate about creating a better world for the next generation.

About this book

This book is about:

Amazoxa Peace University is the home of true Education and the home of True Meaningful Success. This book Authored by Amazoxa Peace University the home of true Education CEO, Dr. Zerit Teklay SEBHATLEAB Teaches about:
True Education!
True Peace!
True Justice!
True Equal opportunities for all Human beings!
This book teaches Practical Conflicts Resolutions!
This book teaches about the World of Spy Intelligence Agencies: The World of spying and being spied on.
This book teaches about the comparison of True Practical Human Intelligence Over Artificial Intelligence!
This book teaches Emotional Intelligence! Intuitive Human Intelligence!
This book teaches about how to become your own Doctor and how to become your own role model.
This book teaches about Risk and Risk-Taking!
Amazoxa Peace University teaches about practical and Effective International Diplomacy.
This book teaches about Writing. This book teaches about the newest constitution of the world called" Amazoxa Global Constitution"
This book teaches about international diplomacy of how to send letters of Diplomacy to Presidents and Ambassadors.
This book is University of Inspiration, Motivation, and University of definiteness of Purpose.
This book teaches about New Philosophies of becoming your own life, Doctor.
This book teaches how to Secure your ideas, inventions and intellectual properties.
This book teaches about how to be the Champion of Peace.
This book in General is about the Establishment, the intellectual properties, Ideas, inventions of the Newest Practical true Education University called " Amazoxa Peace University the home of true Education.

Dr. Zerit Teklay Sebhatleab is the founding father, CEO and President of Amazoxa Peace University home of true Education, Amazoxa Peace University the of True Meaningful Success for the greater good of all human beings.

Under The leadership of Dr. Zerit Teklay Sebhatleab, Amazoxa Peace University today has Virtual offices all over the world.

The Vice President of Amazoxa Peace University the home of True Education is going to be determined soon in the near future.

Until unknown time Amazoxa Peace University the home of true Education Vice president will remain to be Unknown.

~"Dr. Zerit Teklay Sebhatleab Amazoxa Peace University the home of true Education First favorite quote says" Wisdom is the highest level of Education"~ Dr. Zerit Teklay Sebhatleab, Amazoxa Peace University the home of true Education Founding father and current President.

~"Dr. Zerit Teklay Sebhatleab Amazoxa Peace University the home of true Education Second favorite quote says, " Thinking and Acting Globally for the greater good of all the poor people in the world is the highest level of Success any ambitious human being can ever hope to achieve."~ Dr. Zerit Teklay Sebhatleab, Amazoxa Peace University the home of true Education Founding father and current President.

~"Dr. Zerit Teklay Sebhatleab Amazoxa Peace University the home of true Education Founding father and current President in one of his private speeches told us that " The Meaning and Purpose of his existence is to be the Number One Champion of Peace"~ Doctor Monica

Infinite Solutions: A Solution to Everything. One World. One Flag. One Constitution.
- ✓ Hardback ISBN: 978-1-7375372-9-8
- ✓ E Book ISBN: 978-1-7375372-7-4
- ✓ Audio book ISBN: 978-1-7375372-8-1

- ✓ eBook Amazoxa Peace University. Amazoxa the home of true Education ISBN: 978-1-7375372-5-0
- ✓ eBook www.amazoxa.com ISBN: 978-1-7375372-4-

3. Global solution Services for: Individuals, Businesses, Corporations and Governments worldwide

Printed in the United States of America

Library of United State congress Cataloging-in-publication Data: ZERIT Teklay Sebhatleab, Infinite Solutions: A Solution to Everything. One World. One Flag. One Constitution.

Book design by ZERIT Teklay

Acknowledgement

To all the people who have helped me unconditionally:

My parents who raised me - Tiebe Mebrahtu and Teklay Sebhatleab,

My circle of strong men and women, who always are there to lift me up - my friends.

Many thanks to Doctor Michael and Doctor Monica who helped me select the title of this book.

Many thanks to Hannah.

To my brothers and sisters who continue to be dedicated support systems in my life.

Many thanks to my brother F.T.S who helped me beyond in reviewing, proofreading, reorganizing, and rewriting ideas.

To the love of my life, my future wife to be.

Chapters

IMAGINATION

LOGIC will get you
from A to B.
Imagination will take
you everywhere.

~ Albert Einstein

"Life is very brief and truly short! In the end, it does not matter whether we own material stuff (homes, businesses, cars) or not, or whether we have millions of dollars in the bank or not. What truly matters is that we have done something good for the greater good of all the people from all countries of the world; that we have worked for global peace, global justice, and global prosperity. Thinking globally and acting globally are the greatest legacies we as human beings can ever hope to achieve to help all the people of the world and of all nations for generations to come."

- Zerit Teklay

LOGIC will get you from A to B.
Imagination will take you everywhere.

The world is a dangerous place to live; not because of the people who are evil, but because of the people who don't do anything about it.

The only source of knowledge is experience.

Everyone is a genius.
but if you judge a fish on its ability to climb a tree, it will live its whole life believing that it is stupid"

Imagination is more important than knowledge. Knowledge is limited. IMAGINATION ENCIRCLES THE WORLD.

Insanity:
Doing the same thing over and over again and expecting different results.

~ Albert Einstein

"POLITICS, RACE, & RELIGION ARE THE THREE MOTHERS OF CRIME"

~ZERIT TEKLAY~

A K A YES WE CAN PRRCW

COPYRIGHT © 2021 BY ZERIT TEKLAY
A K A YES WE CAN PRRCW
የዜሪ ጸሐፊን በእሴን ናይ ሞቀዳሕ
ሞባለ ክፍሓፀለ እዪ።

Politics is the first mother of Crime, and terrorism.

Colonization is the second mother of crime and terrorisim.

Poverty is the third mother of crime and terrorism.

~ZERIT TEKLAY

A K A YES WE CAN

The Golden rule:

"Do unto others as you would have them do unto you"

MATHEW (7:12)

HEALTH

ጥዕና

THE GREATEST WEALTH IS HEALTH.

እቲ ዝዓበየ ሃብቲ ጥዕና እዩ::

VIRGIL

"If you talk, you are just repeating what you already know before, but if you READ, LISTEN, AND OBSERVE, you will learn new things that are importa nt to you in your future life"

Nardos Mengsteab Teklay, Eritrean

"Courage. Kindness. Friendship. Character. These are the qualities that define us as human beings, and propel us, on occasion, to greatness."

— R.J. Palacio, *Wonder*

"No one ever attains very eminent success by simply doing what is required; it is the amount and excellence of what is over and above the required, that determines the greatness of ultimate distinction."

- Charles Adams

FOR:

My father **Teklay Sebhatleab**

My niece   Nardos Mengsteaab

For:

Eritrean MARTYRS freedom fighters
who died in War for Eritrean
independence 1961-1991

R.I.P Eritrean Martyrs

Introduction

This book is about:

How the formation of Global Universal Supreme Constitutions of the United Countries of the World will transform our world to be one world, under one flag, one currency and one constitution. This provision of the future world international constitution will keep international peace, international justice, international prosperity, international safety, and international security of one indivisible world of our planet called planet earth. There will be heaven on earth when this book's noble ideas start to be used by all nations of the World. The author of this noble book is full of noble ideas that are optimistic and ready to be used in the real world of all nations of our planet earth.

This material contains extraordinary and truly universal global thoughtful visionary ideas, proposals, demands and laws ready to be used by all nations to maintain international peace, international prosperity and international freedom for independence, international safety, and security of one peaceful, justice oriented, safe, secure, and prosperous world.

This book is written to document the Author of this book, Zerit Teklay's dreams of promoting the need for an international constitution which one day will come true in keeping international peace, international justice, international prosperity, and international equality of all nations in the world.

Chapter 1
Writing

~"Benjamin Franklin once said, either write something worth reading, or do something worth writing about. If Benjamin Franklin were alive today, what would he say on reading this book? Just like Benjamin Franklin said to write something worth reading, I hope you, the reader of this book, find this book to not only be a book worth reading,
but also, be a one-of-a-kind book of infinite solutions, forming one just and peaceful world, if interpreted without bias."~ Zerit Teklay

~"When it comes to publishing, I do not want my original ideas to be stolen by anyone or be reproduced by anyone who reads my ideas in my manuscript. If you do not want the ideas in your manuscript to be stolen, or to not be reproduced by idea thieves, do not send it to anyone via email. Encrypt your document with a password and be the only Editor and proofreader of your ideas. Do the editing and proofreading by yourself regardless of the results. Trust no one in the publishing industry."~ Zerit Teklay

~"There is nothing as joyful as authoring your book the way you want your book to be written, without being influenced by someone or the government's agendas. It is not the desire for my book to be best New York times seller that makes me happy, it is the fact that I write my book my way the way I want it, without the interference or influence of any one or any government. And that is truly what makes me incredibly happy. If you author your book your way, the way you want it, you will experience everlasting eternal joy and eternal happiness that you cannot buy with money." ~ Zerit Teklay

~"If you want to author an original book, turn of your TV, turn off your social media and turn off your radio. Do not read anything or listen to anything. If possible, do not speak with anyone until you finish your book, because words you hear on the TV or radio, or words you read on books will interrupt your thought process.

"When it comes to publishing, don't be distracted by random ideas that come in and out of your head. Avoid distracting ideas, and first focus on finishing what you have started. If you are working on the Glossary section of your book, stay focused on that part exclusively, and not on whatever idea that comes in and out of your head, no matter how good it sounds. Second, stay focused, and control your emotions; do not let your emotions distract your focus.

When you write, write only based on truth and facts. Avoid self-incriminating yourself with what you write or what you say, because anything you write or say might be held against you in the court of law. Be incredibly careful what you write on social media platforms. Do not write anything that promotes violence, hatred, animosity, discrimination, confrontation, and bullying.

Do not write anything based on lies. Let every word you use in your writings be for the worthy cause of the greater good of everyone in the world, regardless of their nationality. Let every word you write be like a good seed that grows in a very fertile land.

Chapter 2

Securing Your Ideas and writing

~"If you want to keep your ideas from being stolen, I think you are better of saving your ideas in your mind instead of saving them in your computer or your phone." ~ Zerit Teklay

~"There is only one thing hackers and intelligence spy agencies cannot do, and that is to hack the human brain. They cannot hack the human brain, as that is the only hack-proof place. Therefore, if you do not want your ideas to be intercepted, do not send your ideas to anyone by email. Also, do not save your ideas on your phone, laptop, or computer devices. Save your ideas in your mind because your mind is the only secure place to safe your ideas." ~ Zerit Teklay

~"If you suspect a government spy agency or a hacker is trying to hack your phone or computer device, don't send any precious ideas or intellectual idea by email, and don't store it in your phone or computer, because our activities on phones and computers are being tapped, watched and recorded by hackers and government spy agencies 24/7 and 365 days a year." ~ Zerit Teklay

Chapter 3

GOVERNMENTS

Governments are the most powerful organizations in the history of powers of the world. The Existence of Governments is an exceptionally good thing. The existence of governments is an exceptionally good thing because all governments have one exceptionally good thing in common. And that is all governments main purpose of existence is to maintain peace, order, justice, and Equal opportunity for all. Wethe people of private citizens must help all governments in the maintenance of peace, order, justice, and Equal opportunity for all by being an active participants Governments activity such as Voting on Presidential election days, by writing our ideas whichwe hope, and think will help governments in their role of maintaining peace, order, justice, and Equal opportunity for all. The main existence of Governments is not to engineer wars, create wars and train soldiers to kill innocent civilians. The needof the idea of being a soldier must not be to kill innocent civilians. Soldiers are the in the world to help Governments maintain peace, order, justice, and Equal opportunity for all.

Therefore, the good part of Existence of both Governments and Soldiers is an exceptionally good thing on the maintenance of peace, order,justice, and equal opportunity for all. The bad part of the Existence of Governments and soldiers is that Governments and Soldiers are the main Engine of all the past, present and future wars in the World. Therefore, it is the duty and responsibility of all of us we the private citizens of the world to help Governmentsand soldiers Stop from thinking about wars and going into wars by our words we write in books, by our words we spread on social media and by our deeds. I think the world without the existence of Governments, police force and soldiers would be the most un peaceful and disorderly world.

Therefore, let us we the private citizens we the people give thecredit Good Government deserve on influencing all bad Governments to be Good Governments of the people to the people by the people.

May there always be Good Governments in every country in the world so that there will one day be a World where Peace, order, Justice, and Equal opportunity for all to prevail everywhere in the planet earth where there is no peace, no order, no justice, andno equal opportunity for all.

The Author of this book Zerit Teklay's letter sent to President Joe Biden 46th President of United States and Kamala Harris 46th Vice President of United States, and all presidents and vice presidents of the World.

Hello Dear Mr. President Joseph Robinette Biden Jr.
Hello Dear Mrs. Vice President Kamala Devi Harris
Hello Dear Presidents and Dear Vice presidents of all countries of the world

Subject: Politics Separates us, Religion divides us, Race disconnects us, but being human beings connects us in a human level!

Amazoxa Peace University https://amazoxa.com The home of True Education. Amazoxa Peace University CEO, Zerit Teklay Sebhatleab

Subject 1:

I Zerit Teklay Sebhatleab would like to one day meet you and your vice President her excellency Mrs. Kamala Harris in person to exchange my ideas of how I Zerit Teklay Sebhatleab, a private citizen will play a role in Government's efforts on maintaining Peace, Order, Justice, and Equal Opportunities for all. Can You give me the clearance to meet you in person one day?

Subject 2: Dr. Zerit Teklay Favorite YouTube Video songs are

"IMAGINE" By John Lennon, "We are the champions" by Queens song, "Commander in chief song" by Demi Lovato, The Blacked Eyed Pease-Where is the love song by Song

Where Is the Love?
Artist
The Black-Eyed Peas
Album
Where Is the Love?

These songs are the most relevant songs to this book I Dr. Zerit Teklay Sebhatleab Authored. If it was not for the Systemic Corruption and Racial Discrimination in the world of Hollywood Grammy Awards racism and behind the scenes systemic corruptions, these songs would have been Awarded a Hollywood Grammy Awards If there was no systemic racism and systemic corruption in the world of Hollywood and Grammy Awards. I Dr. Zerit Teklay Sebhatleab in collaboration of some renowned World celebrities are working as a team to bring tangible change in the history of the Hollywood Grammy Awards world of Racial discrimination and behind the scenes systemic corruption of Hollywood Grammy Awards.

I Dr. Zerit Teklay Sebhatleab have Wrote a Song called "Politics Separates us, Religion divides us, Race disconnects us, but being human beings connects us as human beings in a human level.

I Dr. Zerit Teklay Sebhatleab by my free will am giving my song to My Favorite Artist Demi Lovato Who exceptionally stood up and Sang a Song on behalf of all the people suffering today. If it was not for the systemic racism and system behind the scenes corruptions in the world of Holly wood Grammy Awards, Exceptional Artist Demi Lovato of a song called "Commander in Chief" Would have been a Grammy award nominee every year. My other favorite Exceptionally talented Artists are the Black-Eyed Pease-Where is the Love Song Singers, performers, and directors. My number one Favorite English song called The Black-Eyed Pease-*Where Is the Love song? Would have been awarded a Grammy awards every year* If it was not for the systemic racism and system behind the scenes corruptions in the world of Holly wood Grammy Awards.

The Black-Eyed Pease- Where is the love Song is *a song by American hip hop group The Black-Eyed Peas. Which was released in June 2003 as the lead single from their third album, Elephunk. The song was written by will.i.am, apl.de.ap, Taboo, Justin Timberlake, Printz Board, Michael Fratantuno and George Pajon.*

I thought listening to these songs "Commander in chief song by Exception Artist **Demi Lovato** and "The Black-Eyed Pease song- where is the love by **will.i.am, apl.de.ap, and Taboo and singer J. Rey Soul**. Will help you introduce Equal Opportunity Justice of Hollywood Grammy Awards for all races. I hope you would do something about the injustices, discriminations, and behind the scenes system corruption of the world of Hollywood Grammy awards Nominations. Even though I dr. Zerit Teklay SEBHATLEAB understandyou have much bigger tasks of dealing with On Going Wars such as Ongoing War in Russia-Ukraine Wars, I think you can find few minutes of your day thinking about the systemic and behind the scenes system corruption in the world of Hollywood Grammy awards nominations. I hope you would do something about the Racial discrimination in Hollywood Grammy Awards during the term of your presidency.

Black Eyed Peas (also known as The Black-Eyed Peas) is an American musical group consisting of rappers **will.i.am, apl.de.ap, and Taboo and singer J. Rey Soul**. Originally an alternative hip hop group, they subsequently refashioned themselves as a more marketable pop-rap act.

I would love if you and your vice president her Excellency Mrs. Kamala Devi Harris don't mind watching the YouTube video mf my favorite songs called "Commander in chief "By my favorite Artist Demi Lovato, and my other favorite song called the Black Eyed peas-Where is the love? By The American Musical group called the Black-Eyed Peas, My other favorite song called "IMAGINE" by John Lennon. And my other favorite song called "We are the Champions" By QUEENS, **My Number one Eritrean Revolutionary song is called "Harbenya Aynebrin u Tariku eu Zweres, my other** Favorite Exceptional Eritrean Singers are Yemane Baryia, Abraham Afwerki, Feven Tsegay, Okbagabr Zuramo Hagerka, Tesfay Mahari Fihira, Senait Amine, Salem Welday Singer of a song called Abraham.
Favorite Exceptional Eritrean Singers are Yemane Baryia, Abraham Afwerki, Wedi Tukul, Kiflom Yikalo Tiblena Alena, Abrar Osman and Fistum Beraki Bahgi Aleni, Goitom Negassi (Sain Fkri, Tesiu Tezimiskir, Teum Nieru), Shiden Solomon, Wedi Gebru, Bereket Mengsteab, Veronica Solomon -Rahwa Kemets'eyu, Temesgen Yared- Arkanat, Wedi Tikabo, Zeresenay Ghirmay- Tezareb, Kiros Asfaha- Maet Were, Nipsey Hussle-Victory Lab, Tiffany Hadish, The Ariyam Sisters, Nyat Kidane- Eritreans in

Shimelba Camp Ethiopia, Melake Abraham, Mihreteab Michael Mama Tihamena Ala, ala Feven Tsegay, Okbagabr Zuramo Hagerka, Tesfay Mahari Fihira, Senait Amine, Salem Welday Singer of a song called Abraham.

Even though I know and understand neither you nor your vice president her Excellency Mrs. Kamala Harris Have never ever heard a Tigrigna Eritrean Revolutionary music, you have all the resources available to have the content my Favorite Eritrean Revolutionary song to be translated for you to English by Eritrean Native Language Translator. Long live Top Eritrean Revolutionary Song called "Harbenga aynebirn u Tariku eu zweres."

I Dr. Zerit Teklay Sebhatleab Strongly believe and understand on the power of Exceptional Music. Music is such a powerful thing which I Zerit Teklay Sebhatleab strongly believe and understand that listening to my favorite music I mentioned will help you, your vice president her excellency Mrs. Kamala Harris, and all the presidents and Vice presidents in the world in dealing with the UNHEALTHY TOXICIITY of the world of Politics and competition of Political Powers. I am the most curios person I ever know in the history of Curiosity. I am so interested and very curious what your and Vice President Mrs. Kamala Harris songs are? I am also curious what your thought is about Music?
 Subject 3: Even the laws of the United States does not allow a Naturalized American citizen to be the President of the United States, do you think even after 100 Years the United States law will change to allow a Naturalized American citizen to be the President of the United States? What does your vice president Kamala Harris think about this?

Subject 4: I would truly and dearly appreciate if you can connect me with former 44th United States President his excellency Mr. President Barack Obama. I really need his help to be the Champion of Peace in the history of the World.

Subject 5: I would like to let you know that I am so Grateful and thankful for United States of America for granting me a political asylum whereby I Today am A Naturalized American Citizen.

Subject 6:
Please be informed that Amazoxa Peace University is an Imaginary University which I am designing to build in every State in the United States and in Every Country in the World. Would you Mr. President Joe Biden commander in chief of this Great nation of the United States mind to take an Executive Action in Helping me to build Amazoxa Peace University in The United States by giving me Government grants for the project of Amazoxa Peace University. If you do this the World Attention will immediately divert from the news of the Art of Wars to the Good news of the Art of peace of the Construction of a new University called "Amazoxa Peace University" the home of True Education

My Name is Zerit Teklay.

I hope this letter reaches you in good health, and I hope you would find time to read and respond my letter. You both are the first president and vice president in the world with whom I am writing this letter. Eventually, I will be sending this letter and my book included to every president and every vice president of every country in the world. God forbid, but in the event that I unexpectedly get assassinated like Martin Luther was assassinated before I'm able to send this letter and my book to all presidents and vice presidents of the world, please send this letter to every president and vice president of every country in the world, including the President of Russia, Mr. President Vladimir Putin, President of Ukraine, Mr. President Volodymyr Zelensky, President of North Korea, Mr. President Kim Jong Un, President of South Korea, Mr. President Moon Jae-in, President of China, Mr. President Xi Ping , Prime Minister of Ethiopia, Mr. Prime Minister Abiy Ahmed, The people of Tigray Elected President of People's Liberation Mr. President Debretsion Gebremichael, and to the President of Eritrea, Mr. President Isaias Afwerki.

Also send this a copy of this book to all living presidents of all countries in the name of Universal Peace, Universal Justice, and Universal Prosperity. Please know that 91.91% content of this book is written based on true story, while 8.09 % of this book's content is based on fiction: an imaginary creation of my dream for our world to one day be a peaceful one under one Global Constitution, under one flag, under one Currency and under eight presidents of the eight continents of the world. This book will be turned into a movie.

God forbid, if something unexpected happens to me, I will be the main character on the movie production based on this book. If this book's ideas turn into a movie, it will influence millions and billions of people in the world to think and act in the realization of the noble dreams of global constitution and global presidential elections of eight president for each continent of the world. Please also know that English is my second language, and I am the only writer, editor, and proofreader of this book. Hence, my choice of words in this book may seem bossy and uncomfortable but know that this is not my intention. The second edition of this book will be edited and proofread by a professional book editor and proofreader whose first language is English. Nonetheless, it is okay for readers of this book to get out of their comfort zone for the better, safer, justice-oriented world of true genuine democracy.

In addition, please have the copy of this book be at the desks of the executive, legislative and judiciary branches of the United States Government as a reference point for the pursuit of true peace, true justice, and true genuine democracy to prevail whether it is here at home, or abroad.

If you would like to hire me, currently, I am looking for a job in any country's government. The position I am applying for is international diplomacy. I am simply curious if you have job positions of international diplomacy to be filled in. I would like to do something good in relation to restoring the peace in the world, whether it is in the lands of Ukraine, in the lands of Ethiopia or all lands of the earth, which are currently suffering from wars and war invasions. Included with this letter is my resume which I will send to all presidents and all vice presidents of the world. You both are the first president and vice president to receive my resume/book. Transparency is one of my greatest qualities. Why transparency? Well, transparency because transparency is the main solution to all the chaos, confusion, and wars in the world. My aim is to achieve the formation and implementation of global constitution. This is the biggest dream I can ever dream to achieve on the history of my life. I am so glad I am doing something good; something bigger than myself.

My second greatest quality is creative writing and producing creating contents based on truth.

Another of my biggest dreams I hope to achieve is that this book be taught at all schools and universities of all countries of the world. I dream for this book to be taught at former University of Asmara in Eritrea; to be taught in all prestigious universities such as Harvard University; and to be taught in all prestigious and non-prestigious schools and universities of all countries of the world.

I hope to be qualified to fill the job related to international diplomacy or United Nations Security Council positions so that I can carry out my dreams of working for the sake of international peace and International Justice.

If you do not mind, I would appreciate it if you got the word about this book out by writing me a review online, so that the success of this book begins its work in the real world.

If you have any questions, please contact me at my email address at zeritpprcw@gmail.com

May there be peace, justice, and prosperity in all lands of the world.

May there be true genuine democracy in all the lands and in all the seas of all autonomous independent countries of the world.

Sunday, March 13, 2022
Respectfully,
Zerit Teklay

Hello to his Excellency President of The United States M r . President Joe Biden and hello her Excellency Mrs. Vice President of the United States Mrs. Kamala Harris,

I hope you are well. Please know that we the Amazoxa Peace University and home of true Education have posted a letter addressed to you, to your Vice President and to all the Presidents and Vice presidents of all countries in the world.

To learn more about the letter please visit Amazoxa Peace University at www.amazoxa.com.

We the Amazoxa Team Board Members, and our Amazoxa Peace University The home of True Education CEO, Zerit Teklay Sebhatleab Wish you, your family, your co-workers, and your friends more success in your personal lives and work lives.

We have attempted contacting you to no avail or response. I hope this time we will get your response correspondence letter.

In Advance, We the Amazoxa, and our Amazoxa Peace University The home of True Education CEO, Zerit Teklay Sebhatleab Thank You for your time and consideration of responding this message when you can.

Warmest and best Regards,

Amazoxa Peace University The home of True Education CEO, Zerit Teklay Sebhatleab

Amazoxa Peace University the Home of True Education Board Members of public and Government Relations Committee

Hello to his Excellency President of the Federation of Russia Mr. President Vladimir Putin and hello to his Excellency Mr. Vice President of the Federation of Russia Mr. Dmitry Medvedev

I hope you are well. Please know that we the Amazoxa Peace University and home of true Education have posted a letter addressed to you, to your Vice President and to all the Presidents and Vice presidents of all countries in the world.

To learn more about the letter please visit Amazoxa Peace University at www.amazoxa.com.

We the Amazoxa Team Board Members, and our Amazoxa Peace University The home of True Education CEO, Zerit Teklay Sebhatleab Wish you, your family, your co-workers, and your friends more success in your personal lives and work lives.

We have attempted contacting you to no avail or response. I hope this time we will get your response correspondence letter.

In Advance, We the Amazoxa, and our Amazoxa Peace University The home of True Education CEO, Zerit Teklay Sebhatleab Thank You for your time and consideration of responding this message when you can.

Warmest and best Regards,

Amazoxa Peace University The home of True Education CEO, Zerit Teklay Sebhatleab

Amazoxa Peace University the Home of True Education Board Members of public and Government Relations Committee

Hello to his Excellency President of the Republic of China Xi Jinping and hello his Excellency Vice President of the republic of China Mr. Wang Qishan

I hope you are well. Please know that we the Amazoxa Peace University and home of true Education have posted a letter addressed to you, to your Vice President and to all the Presidents and Vice presidents of all countries in the world.

To learn more about the letter please visit Amazoxa Peace University at www.amazoxa.com.

We the Amazoxa Team Board Members, and our Amazoxa Peace University The home of True Education CEO, Zerit Teklay Sebhatleab Wish you, your family, your co-workers, and your friends more success in your personal lives and work lives.

We have attempted contacting you to no avail or response. I hope this time we will get your response correspondence letter.

In Advance, We the Amazoxa, and our Amazoxa Peace University The home of True Education CEO, Zerit Teklay Sebhatleab Thank You for your time and consideration of responding this message when you can.

Warmest and best Regards,

Amazoxa Peace University The home of True Education CEO, Zerit Teklay Sebhatleab

Amazoxa Peace University the Home of True Education Board Members of public and Government Relations Committee

Hello to his Excellency President of North Korea Kim Jong-un

I hope you are well. Please know that we the Amazoxa Peace University and home of true Education have posted a letter addressed to you, to your Vice President and to all the Presidents and Vice presidents of all countries in the world.

To learn more about the letter please visit Amazoxa Peace University at www.amazoxa.com.

We the Amazoxa Team Board Members, and our Amazoxa Peace University The home of True Education CEO, Zerit Teklay Sebhatleab Wish you, your family, your co-workers, and your friends more success in your personal lives and work lives.

We have attempted contacting you to no avail or response. I hope this time we will get your response correspondence letter.

In Advance, We the Amazoxa, and our Amazoxa Peace University The home of True Education CEO, Zerit Teklay Sebhatleab Thank You for your time and consideration of responding this message when you can.

Warmest and best Regards,

Amazoxa Peace University The home of True Education CEO, Zerit Teklay Sebhatleab

Amazoxa Peace University the Home of True Education Board Members of public and Government Relations Committee

Hello to his Excellency President of South Korea Mr. President Moon Jae-in

I hope you are well. Please know that we the Amazoxa Peace University and home of true Education have posted a letter addressed to you, to your Vice President and to all the Presidents and Vice presidents of all countries in the world.

To learn more about the letter please visit Amazoxa Peace University at www.amazoxa.com.

We the Amazoxa Team Board Members, and our Amazoxa Peace University The home of True Education CEO, Zerit Teklay Sebhatleab Wish you, your family, your co-workers, and your friends more success in your personal lives and work lives.

We have attempted contacting you to no avail or response. I hope this time we will get your response correspondence letter.

In Advance, We the Amazoxa, and our Amazoxa Peace University The home of True Education CEO, Zerit Teklay Sebhatleab Thank You for your time and consideration of responding this message when you can.

Warmest and best Regards,

Amazoxa Peace University The home of True Education CEO, Zerit Teklay Sebhatleab

Amazoxa Peace University the Home of True Education Board Members of public and Government Relations Committee

Hello to his Excellency President of Israel Mr. President Naftali Bennett

I hope you are well. Please know that we the Amazoxa Peace University and home of true Education have posted a letter addressed to you, to your Vice President and to all the Presidents and Vice presidents of all countries in the world.

To learn more about the letter please visit Amazoxa Peace University at www.amazoxa.com.

We the Amazoxa Team Board Members, and our Amazoxa Peace University The home of True Education CEO, Zerit Teklay Sebhatleab Wish you, your family, your co-workers, and your friends more success in your personal lives and work lives.

We have attempted contacting you to no avail or response. I hope this time we will get your response correspondence letter.

In Advance, We the Amazoxa, and our Amazoxa Peace University The home of True Education CEO, Zerit Teklay Sebhatleab Thank You for your time and consideration of responding this message when you can.

Warmest and best Regards,

Amazoxa Peace University The home of True Education CEO, Zerit Teklay Sebhatleab

Amazoxa Peace University the Home of True Education Board Members of public and Government Relations Committee

Hello to his Excellency President of Palestine Mr. President. Mahmoud Abbas

I hope you are well. Please know that we the Amazoxa Peace University and home of true Education have posted a letter addressed to you, to your Vice President and to all the Presidents and Vice presidents of all countries in the world.

To learn more about the letter please visit Amazoxa Peace University at www.amazoxa.com.

We the Amazoxa Team Board Members, and our Amazoxa Peace University The home of True Education CEO, Zerit Teklay Sebhatleab Wish you, your family, your co-workers, and your friends more success in your personal lives and work lives.

We have attempted contacting you to no avail or response. I hope this time we will get your response correspondence letter.

In Advance, We the Amazoxa, and our Amazoxa Peace University The home of True Education CEO, Zerit Teklay Sebhatleab Thank You for your time and consideration of responding this message when you can.

Warmest and best Regards,

Amazoxa Peace University The home of True Education CEO, Zerit Teklay Sebhatleab

Amazoxa Peace University the Home of True Education Board Members of public and Government Relations Committee

Hello to his Excellency President of The State of Eritrea Mr. President Isaias Afwerki and his Excellency Mr. Yamane Gebreab the head of political Affairs and presidential Advisor of his Excellency Mr. President Isaias Afwerki President of Eritrea.

I hope you are well. Please know that we the Amazoxa Peace University and home of true Education have posted a letter addressed to you, to your Vice President and to all the Presidents and Vice presidents of all countries in the world.

To learn more about the letter please visit Amazoxa Peace University at www.amazoxa.com.

We the Amazoxa Team Board Members, and our Amazoxa Peace University The home of True Education CEO, Zerit Teklay Sebhatleab Wish you, your family, your co-workers, and your friends more success in your personal lives and work lives.

We have attempted contacting you to no avail or response. I hope this time we will get your response correspondence letter.

In Advance, We the Amazoxa, and our Amazoxa Peace University The home of True Education CEO, Zerit Teklay Sebhatleab Thank You for your time and consideration of responding this message when you can.

Warmest and best Regards,

Amazoxa Peace University The home of True Education CEO, Zerit Teklay Sebhatleab

Amazoxa Peace University the Home of True Education Board Members of public and Government Relations Committee

Hello to his Excellency the People of Tigray Elected President of Tigray Mr. President Debretsion Gebremichael and his Excellency the Spokesperson of the Tigrayan People's Liberation Front Mr. Getachew Reda.

I hope you are well. Please know that we the Amazoxa Peace University and home of true Education have posted a letter addressed to you, to your Vice President and to all the Presidents and Vice presidents of all countries in the world.

To learn more about the letter please visit Amazoxa Peace University at www.amazoxa.com.

We the Amazoxa Team Board Members, and our Amazoxa Peace University The home of True Education CEO, Zerit Teklay Sebhatleab Wish you, your family, your co-workers, and your friends more success in your personal lives and work lives.

We have attempted contacting you to no avail or response. I hope this time we will get your response correspondence letter.

In Advance, We the Amazoxa, and our Amazoxa Peace University The home of True Education CEO, Zerit Teklay Sebhatleab Thank You for your time and consideration of responding this message when you can.

Warmest and best Regards,

Amazoxa Peace University The home of True Education CEO, Zerit Teklay Sebhatleab

Amazoxa Peace University the Home of True Education Board Members of public and Government Relations Committee

Hello to his Excellency Prime Mister of Ethiopia Dr. Abiy Ahmed and his excellency

I hope you are well. Please know that we the Amazoxa Peace University and home of true Education have posted a letter addressed to you, to your Vice President and to all the Presidents and Vice presidents of all countries in the world.

To learn more about the letter please visit Amazoxa Peace University at www.amazoxa.com.

We the Amazoxa Team Board Members, and our Amazoxa Peace University The home of True Education CEO, Zerit Teklay Sebhatleab Wish you, your family, your co-workers, and your friends more success in your personal lives and work lives.

We have attempted contacting you to no avail or response. I hope this time we will get your response correspondence letter.

In Advance, We the Amazoxa, and our Amazoxa Peace University The home of True Education CEO, Zerit Teklay Sebhatleab Thank You for your time and consideration of responding this message when you can.

Warmest and best Regards,

Amazoxa Peace University The home of True Education CEO, Zerit Teklay Sebhatleab

Amazoxa Peace University the Home of True Education Board Members of public and Government Relations Committee

Hello to his Excellency President of Ukraine Volodymyr Zelensky

I hope you are well. Please know that we the Amazoxa Peace University and home of true Education have posted a letter addressed to you, to your Vice President and to all the Presidents and Vice presidents of all countries in the world.

To learn more about the letter please visit Amazoxa Peace University at www.amazoxa.com.

We the Amazoxa Team Board Members, and our Amazoxa Peace University The home of True Education CEO, Zerit Teklay Sebhatleab Wish you, your family, your co-workers, and your friends more success in your personal lives and work lives.

We have attempted contacting you to no avail or response. I hope this time we will get your response correspondence letter.

In Advance, We the Amazoxa, and our Amazoxa Peace University The home of True Education CEO, Zerit Teklay Sebhatleab Thank You for your time and consideration of responding this message when you can.

Warmest and best Regards,

Amazoxa Peace University The home of True Education CEO, Zerit Teklay Sebhatleab

Amazoxa Peace University the Home of True Education Board Members of public and Government Relations Committee

Hello to his Excellency Prime Minster of Canada Mr. Justin Trudeau

I hope you are well. Please know that we the Amazoxa Peace University and home of true Education have posted a letter addressed to you, to your Vice President and to all the Presidents and Vice presidents of all countries in the world.

To learn more about the letter please visit Amazoxa Peace University at www.amazoxa.com.

We the Amazoxa Team Board Members, and our Amazoxa Peace University The home of True Education CEO, Zerit Teklay Sebhatleab Wish you, your family, your co-workers, and your friends more success in your personal lives and work lives.

We have attempted contacting you to no avail or response. I hope this time we will get your response correspondence letter.

In Advance, We the Amazoxa, and our Amazoxa Peace University The home of True Education CEO, Zerit Teklay Sebhatleab Thank You for your time and consideration of responding this message when you can.

Warmest and best Regards,

Amazoxa Peace University The home of True Education CEO, Zerit Teklay Sebhatleab

Amazoxa Peace University the Home of True Education Board Members of public and Government Relations Committee

Hello to his Excellency Prime Minister of United Kingdom Mr. Prime Minister Boris Johnson

I hope you are well. Please know that we the Amazoxa Peace University and home of true Education have posted a letter addressed to you, to your Vice President and to all the Presidents and Vice presidents of all countries in the world.

To learn more about the letter please visit Amazoxa Peace University at www.amazoxa.com.

We the Amazoxa Team Board Members, and our Amazoxa Peace University The home of True Education CEO, Zerit Teklay Sebhatleab Wish you, your family, your co-workers, and your friends more success in your personal lives and work lives.

We have attempted contacting you to no avail or response. I hope this time we will get your response correspondence letter.

In Advance, We the Amazoxa, and our Amazoxa Peace University The home of True Education CEO, Zerit Teklay Sebhatleab Thank You for your time and consideration of responding this message when you can.

Warmest and best Regards,

Amazoxa Peace University The home of True Education CEO, Zerit Teklay Sebhatleab

Amazoxa Peace University the Home of True Education Board Members of public and Government Relations Committee

Hello to his Excellency President of Ireland Mr. President Michael D. Higgins

I hope you are well. Please know that we the Amazoxa Peace University and home of true Education have posted a letter addressed to you, to your Vice President and to all the Presidents and Vice presidents of all countries in the world.

To learn more about the letter please visit Amazoxa Peace University at www.amazoxa.com.

We the Amazoxa Team Board Members, and our Amazoxa Peace University The home of True Education CEO, Zerit Teklay Sebhatleab Wish you, your family, your co-workers, and your friends more success in your personal lives and work lives.

We have attempted contacting you to no avail or response. I hope this time we will get your response correspondence letter.

In Advance, We the Amazoxa, and our Amazoxa Peace University The home of True Education CEO, Zerit Teklay Sebhatleab Thank You for your time and consideration of responding this message when you can.

Warmest and best Regards,

Amazoxa Peace University The home of True Education CEO, Zerit Teklay Sebhatleab

Amazoxa Peace University the Home of True Education Board Members of public and Government Relations Committee

Hello to his Excellency the incumbent prime minister of Australia Mr. Prime Minister Scott Morrison

I hope you are well. Please know that we the Amazoxa Peace University and home of true Education have posted a letter addressed to you, to your Vice President and to all the Presidents and Vice presidents of all countries in the world.

To learn more about the letter please visit Amazoxa Peace University at www.amazoxa.com.

We the Amazoxa Team Board Members, and our Amazoxa Peace University The home of True Education CEO, Zerit Teklay Sebhatleab Wish you, your family, your co-workers, and your friends more success in your personal lives and work lives.

We have attempted contacting you to no avail or response. I hope this time we will get your responsecorrespondence letter.

In Advance, We the Amazoxa, and our Amazoxa Peace University The home of True Education CEO, Zerit Teklay Sebhatleab Thank You for your time and consideration of responding this message when you can.

Warmest and best Regards,

Amazoxa Peace University The home of True Education CEO, Zerit Teklay Sebhatleab

Amazoxa Peace University the Home of True Education Board Members of public and Government Relations Committee

Hello to their Excellencies Presidents of The United Countries of the World of Africa "MOTHERLAND OF PLANET EARTH AFRICA"

I hope you are well. Please know that we the Amazoxa Peace University and home of true Education have posted a letter addressed to you, to your Vice President and to all the Presidents and Vice presidents of all countries in the world.

To learn more about the letter please visit Amazoxa Peace University at www.amazoxa.com.

We the Amazoxa Team Board Members, and our Amazoxa Peace University The home of True Education CEO, Zerit Teklay Sebhatleab Wish you, your family, your co-workers, and your friends more success in your personal lives and work lives.

We have attempted contacting you to no avail or response. I hope this time we will get your response correspondence letter.

In Advance, We the Amazoxa, and our Amazoxa Peace University The home of True Education CEO, Zerit Teklay Sebhatleab Thank You for your time and consideration of responding this message when you can.

Warmest and best Regards,

Amazoxa Peace University The home of True Education CEO, Zerit Teklay Sebhatleab

Amazoxa Peace University the Home of True Education Board Members of public and Government Relations Committee

Hello to their Excellencies Presidents of the European Union

I hope you are well. Please know that we the Amazoxa Peace University and home of true Education have posted a letter addressed to you, to your Vice President and to all the Presidents and Vice presidents of all countries in the world.

To learn more about the letter please visit Amazoxa Peace University at www.amazoxa.com.

We the Amazoxa Team Board Members, and our Amazoxa Peace University The home of True Education CEO, Zerit Teklay Sebhatleab Wish you, your family, your co-workers, and your friends more success in your personal lives and work lives.

We have attempted contacting you to no avail or response. I hope this time we will get your response correspondence letter.

In Advance, We the Amazoxa, and our Amazoxa Peace University The home of True Education CEO, Zerit Teklay Sebhatleab Thank You for your time and consideration of responding this message when you can.

Warmest and best Regards,

Amazoxa Peace University The home of True Education CEO, Zerit Teklay Sebhatleab

Amazoxa Peace University the Home of True Education Board Members of public and Government Relations Committee

Hello to their Excellencies Presidents of the Continent of Asia and Presidents of the Continent of South Latin America.

I hope you are well. Please know that we the Amazoxa Peace University and home of true Education have posted a letter addressed to you, to your Vice President and to all the Presidents and Vice presidents of all countries in the world.

To learn more about the letter please visit Amazoxa Peace University at www.amazoxa.com.

We the Amazoxa Team Board Members, and our Amazoxa Peace University The home of True Education CEO, Zerit Teklay Sebhatleab Wish you, your family, your co-workers, and your friends more success in your personal lives and work lives.

We have attempted contacting you to no avail or response. I hope this time we will get your response correspondence letter.

In Advance, We the Amazoxa, and our Amazoxa Peace University The home of True Education CEO, Zerit Teklay Sebhatleab Thank You for your time and consideration of responding this message when you can.

Warmest and best Regards,

Amazoxa Peace University The home of True Education CEO, Zerit Teklay Sebhatleab

Amazoxa Peace University the Home of True Education Board Members of public and Government Relations Committee

Hello to their Excellencies Commanders in chief of the NATO AND THE UNITED NATIONS.

I hope you are well. Please know that we the Amazoxa Peace University and home of true Education have posted a letter addressed to you, to your Vice President and to all the Presidents and Vice presidents of all countries in the world.

To learn more about the letter please visit Amazoxa Peace University at www.amazoxa.com.

We the Amazoxa Team Board Members, and our Amazoxa Peace University The home of True Education CEO, Zerit Teklay Sebhatleab Wish you, your family, your co-workers, and your friends more success in your personal lives and work lives.

We have attempted contacting you to no avail or response. I hope this time we will get your response correspondence letter.

In Advance, We the Amazoxa, and our Amazoxa Peace University The home of True Education CEO, Zerit Teklay Sebhatleab Thank You for your time and consideration of responding this message when you can.

Warmest and best Regards,

Amazoxa Peace University The home of True Education CEO, Zerit Teklay Sebhatleab

Amazoxa Peace University the Home of True Education Board Members of public and Government Relations Committee

Hello to his Excellency President of Afghanistan Mr. President Shah Hussain Murtazavi

I hope you are well. Please know that we the Amazoxa Peace University and home of true Education have posted a letter addressed to you, to your Vice President and to all the Presidents and Vice presidents of all countries in the world.

To learn more about the letter please visit Amazoxa Peace University at www.amazoxa.com.

We the Amazoxa Team Board Members, and our Amazoxa Peace University The home of True Education CEO, Zerit Teklay Sebhatleab Wish you, your family, your co-workers, and your friends more success in your personal lives and work lives.

We have attempted contacting you to no avail or response. I hope this time we will get your response correspondence letter.

In Advance, We the Amazoxa, and our Amazoxa Peace University The home of True Education CEO, Zerit Teklay Sebhatleab Thank You for your time and consideration of responding this message when you can.

Warmest and best Regards,

Amazoxa Peace University The home of True Education CEO, Zerit Teklay Sebhatleab

Amazoxa Peace University the Home of True Education Board Members of public and Government Relations Committee

Hello to his Excellency Prime Minster of Australia Scott Morrison,

I hope you are well. Please know that we the Amazoxa Peace University and home of true Education have posted a letter addressed to you all, to all your Vice President and to all the Presidents and Vicepresidents of all countries in the world.

To learn more about the letter please visit Amazoxa Peace University at www.amazoxa.com.

We the Amazoxa Team Board Members, and our Amazoxa Peace University The home of True Education CEO, Zerit Teklay Sebhatleab Wish you, your family, yourco-workers, and your friends more success in your personal lives and work lives.

We have attempted contacting you to no avail or response. I hope this time we will get your responsecorrespondence letter.

In Advance, We the Amazoxa, and our Amazoxa Peace University The home of True Education CEO, Zerit Teklay Sebhatleab Thank You for your time andconsideration of responding this message when you can.

Warmest and best Regards,

Amazoxa Peace University The home of True Education CEO, Zerit Teklay Sebhatleab

Amazoxa Peace University the Home of True Education Board Members of public and Government Relations Committee

Hello to his Excellency President of France Mr. President Emmanuel Macron,

I hope you are well. Please know that we the Amazoxa Peace University and home of true Education have posted a letter addressed to you, to your Vice President and to all the Presidents and Vice presidents of all countries in the world.

To learn more about the letter please visit Amazoxa Peace University at www.amazoxa.com.

We the Amazoxa Team Board Members, and our Amazoxa Peace University The home of True Education CEO, Zerit Teklay Sebhatleab Wish you, your family, your co-workers, and your friends more success in your personal lives and work lives.

We have attempted contacting you to no avail or response. I hope this time we will get your response correspondence letter.

In Advance, We the Amazoxa, and our Amazoxa Peace University The home of True Education CEO, Zerit Teklay Sebhatleab Thank You for your time and consideration of responding this message when you can.

Warmest and best Regards,

Amazoxa Peace University The home of True Education CEO, Zerit Teklay Sebhatleab

Amazoxa Peace University the Home of True Education Board Members of public and Government Relations Committee

Hello to his Excellency President of South Korea Mr. President Moon Jae-in

I hope you are well. Please know that we the Amazoxa Peace University and home of true Education have posted a letter addressed to you, to your Vice President and to all the Presidents and Vice presidents of all countries in the world.

To learn more about the letter please visit Amazoxa Peace University at www.amazoxa.com.

We the Amazoxa Team Board Members, and our Amazoxa Peace University The home of True Education CEO, Zerit Teklay Sebhatleab Wish you, your family, your co-workers, and your friends more success in your personal lives and work lives.

We have attempted contacting you to no avail or response. I hope this time we will get your response correspondence letter.

In Advance, We the Amazoxa, and our Amazoxa Peace University The home of True Education CEO, Zerit Teklay Sebhatleab Thank You for your time and consideration of responding this message when you can.

Warmest and best Regards,

Amazoxa Peace University The home of True Education CEO, Zerit Teklay Sebhatleab

Amazoxa Peace University the Home of True Education Board Members of public and Government Relations Committee

Hello to Their Excellency to All Presidents of all Asian Countries in the continent of Asia,

I hope you are well. Please know that we the Amazoxa Peace University and home of true Education have posted a letter addressed to you all, to all your Vice President and to all the Presidents and Vicepresidents of all countries in the world.

To learn more about the letter please visit Amazoxa Peace University at www.amazoxa.com.

We the Amazoxa Team Board Members, and our Amazoxa Peace University The home of True Education CEO, Zerit Teklay Sebhatleab Wish you, your family, yourco-workers, and your friends more success in your personal lives and work lives.

We have attempted contacting you to no avail or response. I hope this time we will get your responsecorrespondence letter.

In Advance, We the Amazoxa, and our Amazoxa Peace University The home of True Education CEO, Zerit Teklay Sebhatleab Thank You for your time andconsideration of responding this message when you can.

Warmest and best Regards,

Amazoxa Peace University The home of True Education CEO, Zerit Teklay Sebhatleab

Amazoxa Peace University the Home of True Education Board Members of public and Government Relations Committee

Hello to his Excellency President of Ukraine Mr. President Volodymyr Zelenskyy

I hope you are well. Please know that we the Amazoxa Peace University and home of true Education have posted a letter addressed to you, to your Vice President and to all the Presidents and Vice presidents of all countries in the world.

To learn more about the letter please visit Amazoxa Peace University at www.amazoxa.com.

We the Amazoxa Team Board Members, and our Amazoxa Peace University The home of True Education CEO, Zerit Teklay Sebhatleab Wish you, your family, your co-workers, and your friends more success in your personal lives and work lives.

We have attempted contacting you to no avail or response. I hope this time we will get your response correspondence letter.

In Advance, We the Amazoxa, and our Amazoxa Peace University The home of True Education CEO, Zerit Teklay Sebhatleab Thank You for your time and consideration of responding this message when you can.

Warmest and best Regards,

Amazoxa Peace University The home of True Education CEO, Zerit Teklay Sebhatleab

Amazoxa Peace University the Home of True Education Board Members of public and Government Relations Committee

Chapter 4

Global Constitution and Global Presidential Election

The Real Question is not……...? The Real Question instead is……?

The question is not whether going into a war is good or bad. The real question is whether the war is for independence or for the domination of superpowerism and dictatorship.

The real question is who suffers the most from causes of wars and sanctions. The innocent people, the soldiers involved in the war are the only ones who suffer the most during times of wars, sanctions, and confrontations. While the innocent people, and the soldiers involved in wars suffer the excruciating painful traumas of a war, the governments at war continue plan how to defeat the adversary by believing in their military might, nuclear bombs which ultimately kill innocent people who have nothing to do with their deeply seated competition of dirty political power of who becomes the superpower of the world while the economy of the world continue to crash and while inflation sky rockets at the gas pumps and at the food super markets.

While nothing happens for the executive commanders of the wars who watches the war virtually being in highly secure offices watching the war from television and give speech about it as if they actually were in the war zone themselves, innocent civilians who are victims of the war continue to suffer and die. We the people of the world must not side with any government involved in any war. We must side with the people of victims of wars who has nothing to do with the dirty political agendas of Governments involved in wars.

Whose fault is a war? A war is 100% governments faults, not the innocent people. governmentspower hunger and competition of controlling Strategic seas, and lands and other hidden agendasare why governments open wars they cannot get out so easily. It is too easy start a war than to startfor peace for today's Government's arrogance and ego.

Every human being including a five-year-old child understand a war is an unbelievably bad terrible thing the humanity suffers from ever since the ancient times of the past wars of the First world war, the second world war, and the cold war for the power hunger of who becomes the most superpower of the world.

and now in year 2022, the year this book is published the world is in so much suffering of superpower countries computing on who becomes the superpower of the world, one by sanctioning the other while the other reacts to the sanctions and remembering history of the past of glory and power. We the United Countries of the world does not side with any governments involved in wars. We are on the side of the people suffering on the ongoing wars in distinct parts of the world suchas civil wars in Ethiopia, wars in the lands of Ukraine. We the United countries of the world haveone solution for everything to end all the wars in the world once and for good.

And the solution is that:

ALL SOLDIERS OF THE INVOLVED PARTIES AT WAR TO SAY NO TO A WAR!

All soldiers to say no TO BOMBING INNOCENT CIVILIANS.

This solution is the greatest solution our world can ever hope to magically happen where no soldier of any country goes into a war of any kind. NO Soldiers practically means No wars!

No Nuclear powers practically means No Wars!

No   Technological   Drone   bombings

practically means no wars No retaliation

practically means No Wars

Let us give an example: Imagine a share ride company called Uber without Uber drivers. And also imagine a war commander without soldiers. Uber company without a driver does not exist. And also, a War commander with no soldiers cannot go into a war. Governments without soldiers are powerless. The true power is in the hands of the people and all the soldiers of the world.

The main engine of uber company is the uber drivers. And the main engine of all wars are governments who deceive innocent soldiers by the name of to defend and protect while the Actual truth is something else such that of Superpoerism and domination of the world.

If the uber drivers Stop driving for Uber for one year protesting the cheap price of uber basepay, Uber ride share cannot exist without a driver. If all the Uber Drivers in the World stop driving for uber for 1 year, Uber company will not exist without the main engine of the drivers, The same thing is true with wars. If all the soldiers of Marine, Army, air force refuse from going into wars, there will not be any wars in the history of the world for many generations to come.

In the year this book is published year 2022, the inflation has plunged than ever before in the history of the world where gas price is close to $5-6 per gallon because of the wars on going in the world. Millions of people are in suffering the rise of price of goods in groceries because of the ongoing wars caused by governments not by the innocent people who are the immediate victims of wars. Superpower countries need to realize the competition of power on who becomes the most superpower in the world will repeat the history of the first and second world can repeat itself if soldiersdo not say enough is enough to wars. A war is a vicious cycle that backfire to anyone involved.

Therefore, We the people must say no to wars, We the soldiers of all Governments must disobeyAll Governments who force us to go into Wars. why? Because the real power is not in the hands of the President of United States, the real Power is not in the hands of the President of Russia, thereal power is not in the hands of the President of China, the real power is not in the hands of the president of North Korea, the real power is not in the hands of the president of Eritrea, the real power is not in the hands of the Prime Minister of Ethiopia, the real power is not in the hands of the president of Afghanistan, the real power is not in the hands of the president of Iraq,

the real power is not in the hands of all presidents of the European Union, the real power is not inthe hands of the Leader of Tigray People Liberation Front, the real power is not in the hands of thepresident of Australia, the real power is not in the hands of the president of Iran, the real power is not in the hands of the president of Canada, the real power is not in the hands of all presidents of the United Countries of the World of Africa to soon be, the real power is not in the hands of Prime Minister of United Kingdom, The real power is not in the hands of the president of India and in general the real true power is not, has never been and will never be in the hands of any president of any country in the world.

1. THE TRUE REAL POWER IS IN THE HANDS OF WE THE PEOPLE.

2. THE REAL POWER IS IN THE HANDS OF WE THE SOLDIERS OF THE WORLD. 3. ALL GOVERNMENTS COMBINED ALL TOGETHER ARE NOT AS POWERFULL

AS WE THE PEOPLE.

4. ALL GOVERNMENTS COMBINED together are not as powerful as we the soldiers of the world.

Therefore, We the People And soldiers of United States, we the people and soldiers of the federation of Russia, We the people and soldiers of the Republic of China, We the People and soldiers of Eritrea, We the people and soldiers of Ethiopia, We the people and soldiers of Tigray, We the people and soldiers of Palestine, We the people and soldiers of Israel, We the people and soldiers of Afghanistan, We the people and the soldiers of Iraq, We the people and soldiers of the NATO member Countries, We the people and soldiers of Ukraine, We the People and soldiers of the European countries, We the people and soldiers of Canada, we the people and soldiers of all countries in the World Must Bravely and Courageously say NO TO GOING INTO A WAR. The evil root cause of all the wars in the world is engineered by Governments not by us we the innocent People and soldiers of the world. It is time for us We the most powerful of all We the people and We the soldiers to speak up and stand up on not taking any part in any role of a war. Governments without us we the people and soldiers of the world are Powerless and engineless like a parked Car with no engine.

Let all of us We the people and soldiers of the World Stop the Engine of Governments who running all the wars regardless of the mass massacre of innocent civilians and innocent soldiers.

Let us peacefully without any violence rise up, speak up to stop the ongoing

Wars in the World.

We the Amazoxa peace University are diligently and wisely doing our part in the diversion of the world attention from the Art of War to the Art of Peace.

The Art of peace is the core primary principle of we the Amazoxa peace University Board of members committee worldwide Engineered and designed by our Amazoxa Peace University CEO, Dr. Zerit Teklay Sebhatleab. Amazoxa Peace University CEO, Dr. Zerit Teklay is the sole founding father, Engineer, and Designer of the Art peace Core Principles of Amazoxa Peace University The home of True Education. Amazoxa peace University is founded and designed by our Amazoxa peace University CEO, Dr. Zerit Teklay. Until there would be Universal peace, Universal Justice, and Universal Prosperity in the World, We the Amazoxa peace University Board members worldwide and our Amazoxa peace University Worldwide will diligently help the world to be successful world of Universal Peace, Universal Justice, Universal prosperity, and Equal Opportunity for all for many generations to come.

We the main Engine of governments we the people and we the soldiers must act now in Saying NO to going into a war. Because if We the people and the soldiers of the World say NO to going into war, no innocent victims of a war innocent civilians civilians will die in the midst of war andterror.

Governments without us we the people are like a car without an engine.

Therefore, let us we all the people of the world hold governments accountable for all the war crimes they are committing on humanity. Let us always remember this: Politics Separates us, Religion divides us, Race disconnects us, but being human connects us as human beings.

We the Amazoxa Peace University, and our Amazoxa Peace University CEO, Dr. Zerit Teklay thank you for your support in all the ups and downs of our journey of chasing our dreams One Peaceful, just full and Prosperous World.

We the Amazoxa peace University, and Our Amazoxa Peace University CEO, Dr. Zerit Teklay wish you well and success in your personal and work life.

Many thanks and best regards,

Amazoxa peace University CEO, Dr. Zerit Teklay

Amazoxa Peace University Team Board Members Worldwide.

~"The creation of a global constitution can end dictatorship throughout the world. Under the Supervision of Global constitution, no country will ever again dictate for another country. The birthday of a Global constitution will lead to the end of global dictatorship, and the death day of global dictatorship will lead to universal true democracy, which will in turn lead to universal true peace, justice, and equality. Under Universal true democracy, there will no longer be World Wars ever again."~ Zerit Teklay

Chapter 5

How the World Betrayed a small African Nation called ERITREA.

Amazoxa Peace University CEO, Zerit Teklay Sebhateleab Most favorite book I S B N 0060780924 Authored by MICHELA WRONG is called "I did not Do It for you: How the World Betrayed a small African Nation ERITREA.

Politics

~"The question is not whether everything is politics.
The question is what in this life is not politics. In my view, I Zerit Teklay Sebhatleab Strongly believe and strongly understand that everything in this thing we call "Life": including marriage, Relationships, dating, friendship, business, or anything that involves written words, spoken words or body language is 100% Pure politics. ~ Zerit Teklay Sebhatleab

Chapter 6

Translation from Tigrigna language to English Language

POLITICS

Politics is an unproductive sterile field. Those who receive help from politics are very few. Whereas those who lose because of politics are so many.

If you love your life, do not allow your life to be on the line of anyone's politics. Do not use your life as collateral damage just so you can be a political ally to anyone.

Politics has been like a pandemic ever since time immemorial. For as long as time, there has not been a solution or a cure for the pandemic that is politics. Politics has always been, and still is like a pandemic that spreads. No one has found a solution or a cure for said disease to this day.

It is causing so much suffering, as it affects the lives of all the people in the world. Because of this disease, all the people and other living things in the world are in so much suffering. Peace is nonexistent in our world today because of politics.

Therefore, you must be careful, and check yourself, whether you have the disease of politics or not, because if you catch a disease that does not have a cure, what comes next to you is death.

To understand this, you must be free from the disease of politics, and this does not have a cure yet.

If you have the disease of politics pandemics, and if you are submerged in the wilderness of politics, to you, the above written may sound like a joke.

~ F.T.S ERITREAN~

ሰምበት **27** መጋቢት **2022** ዓ.ም

ናብ ኩቡር አምባሳደር ኤርትራ አብ ሕቡራት መንግስታት አሜርካ አቶ ብርሃነ ስሎሙንን

ናብ ኩሉኩም ስራሕተኛታት ኤምባሲ ኤርትራ አብ ሕብራት መንግስታት አሜርካን ናብ ኩሉኩም አብ መላእ ዓለም ዘሎኩም አምባሳደራት ሃገርና ኤርትራን አብ ስደት ዉርደት ትነብሩ ዘለኩምን ኤርትራዉያንየሕዋት።

ሸመይ ዘርኢት ተከላይ ይብሃል። አብ ስደት አብ ሕቡራት መንግስታት
አመሪካ ይነብር አለኩ።

ዝከበርካ አምባሳደር አቶ ስሎሙን ብርሃነ፡ ብመጀመርያ ስላምታይ ናዓካን ንኩሉኩም መሳርሕትካን አብ ኤምባሲ ኤርትራ አብ Washington DC ምሳኻ ድሶርሑ ስራሕተኛታትን ስላምታይ የቅርበልካ/የቅርበልኩም፡ አብ ሂወትካ/ሂወትኩም ሙሉእ ጥዕና ይምነየልካ/ይምነነልኩም። አብ ማዓልታዊ ስራሕካ/ስራሕኩም ድማ ዓወትን አሳልጦን ይምነየልካ/ይምነየልኩም። አብ ኩሉ ትገብርዎ ተበግሶ አብ **East African Geo Politics** ናይ ምብራቅ አፍሪቃ ሰላም ንክስፍን ዓወትን አሳልጦን ይምነየልካ/ ይምነየልኩም።

አዛ ድሶደልካ ደለኩ ደብዳበን መጽሓፊይን ንኩሎም አብዛ ዓለም ዘለዉ ፕረዝደንትታትን ምክትል ፕረዝደንትታትን በብቃንቋኣም ሰዲደሎም ከም ዘለኩ ከሕብረካ ይፈቱ። ኩሎም ፕረዝደንትታት ናይዛ ዓለም ንመጽሓፊይ ዝተፈላለየ ትርጉምከምዝህብዋ ዝተፋላለየ ቃንቃ ውን ከምደዉጹላ ይርዳአኒ እዩ። አቲ አገዳሲ ቀምነገር ግን መጽሓፊይ ዝተፈላለየ ትርጉምንርዲኢትን አዋህባ አይዋሃባ ዘይኮነስ፡ አቲ ቀንዲ ቀምነገር አብ ሙሉእ ዓለም ዘሎ ቤት ንባባትን አብ ቤትምህርትታትን ከም መምሃሪት መጽሓፍ ከትከዉን ይሰርሑሉ ምህላወይን ይዕወት ካአ ምህላወይን እዩ እቲ ቀንዲ ናይ ዓወት መጽሓፊይ ቀምነገር።

ስለዝኮነ እዛ መጽሓፊይ ሳንሱር ሓሊፋ አብ ሃገርና ኤርትራ ከም መ ምሃሪት መጽሓፍ ከትከዉን አብ ሃገርና ኤርትራ ከትዘርጋሕንክፍቀደላ ብትሕትና ይሓተካ።ብተወሳኪ ዉን አብ ሙሉእ ዓለም ዘሎ ኤምባስታትን ማሕበረኮማትን ኤርትራዉያን ከትዘርጋሕ ሰናይ ተበግሶን ተባዕ ሱጉምትን ከትወስድ ይምነ መታን ህዝበና ንቕሓቱ ከዕብን ስንሰለት ስደት ከብተከን።

- መጽሓፊይ ብብሰላም አብ ኢድካ አትያ ከተንብባን ሃናጺ ሓሳባት ከትበንን አብ ሃገርና ኤርትራ መጽሓፊይ ከትወዝርጋሕ ከፍቀደላን ዓቢ ተስፋን ምራልን አለኒ። ከልተ መጽሓፍ ሓንቲ ንዓካን ንኩሎም መሳርሕትካን ኤምባሲ ኤርትራን፡ ሓንቲ ድማ ንኩቡር ፕረዝደንት ሃገርና ኤርትራ ፕረዝደንት አቶ ኢሰያስ አፍወርቂ

  ናብ አድራሰሻ ኤምባሲ *1708 New Hampshire Ave, 20009 Washington DC ሱዲየን አለኩ። Amazon Ordertracking # is: 113-6149929-9185810 ደሰደትከዋ ከምዶበጽሐት ብ ናይ U S P S taracking number አራጋጺ ከምወለኩን መልሲ ካባኻ ይኩን ካብ ኤምባሲ ኤርትራ አብ U S A Washington ከምዛይመጽኒ ከሕብረካ ይፈቱ።*

ስለዚ ኣብ መልሲ ምስዳድንን ንኩሉ ትገብረለይ ምትሕብባር ኣቀዳም ከመስግነካ ይደሊ፡፡ መታን መጽሓፈይ ኣብ ሃገርና ንከትዝርጋሕ ከፍቀደላን መታን መጽሓፈይ ሙሉእ ዓወት ንከትዕወትን፡፡

ሰንሰለት ስደት ዉርደት ዘይዉዳእ ወለዶታት ዘጥፍእ ወሎን ስደት ኤርትራዊያን ይብተከልናኑ ሰንሰለት ስደት ኤርትራዊያንንከብተክ ናይ ኩሉ ኤርትራዊ ሓላፍነት ይኩንኑዝኮነ ሕቶ: ርእይቶ ወይ ምትብባዕ ከትበኒ እንተ ደሊካቀ. ተሌፎነይ +1 336-715-0541Email:zeritprrc@gmail.com

ዝኮነ ሕቶ: ርእይቶ ወይ ምትብባዕ ከትበኒ እንተ ደሊካቀ. ተሌፎነይ +1 336-715-0541

Email:zeritprrc@gmail.com
My Mailing

address is:

Amazoxa Peace

University the

Home of

TrueEducation

Zerit Teklay

P.O.BOX 22226

Nashvile,

TN 37202

United

States of

America

ዘርኢት ተከላይ

ዘልኣለማዊ

ዝከሪ

ንስዋእትና

ዓወት

ንሓፍሽ!

Victory to the people!

ናብ ኩቡር ፕረዝደንት ሃገርና ኤርትራ ኣቶ ፕረዝደንት ኢሰያስ ኣፍወርቂ

ሸመይ ዘርኢ.ት ተከላይ ይብሃል። ኣብ ስደት ኣብ ሕቡራት መንግስታት ኣመሪካ ይነብር ኣለኹ።

ዝከበርካ ኣቶ ፕረዝደንት ኢሰያስ ኣፍወርቂ: ብመጀመርያ ሰላምታይ የቅርበልካ: ኣብ ሂወትካ ሙሉእ ጥዕና ይምነየልካ። ኣብማዓልታዊ ስራሕካ ድማ ዓወትን ኣሳልጦን ይምነየልካ። ኣብ ኩሉ ትግብሮ ጾዕሪ ኣብ **East African Geopolitics** ናይ ምብራቅ ኣፍሪቃ ሰላም ንከሰፍን ዓወትን ኣሳልጦን ይምነየልካ።

ኣዛ ድሰደልካ ደለኩ ደብዳበን መጽሓፊይን ንኩሉኝም ኣብዛ ዓለም ዘለዉ ፕረዝደንትታትን ምከትል ፕረዝደንትታትን በብቃንቁኣም ሰዲደሎም ከም ዘለኩ ከሕብርካ ይፈቱ። ንኣማካሪካ ኩቡር ኣቶ የማን ገብርኣብን ንኩሉኝም መሳርሕትኻን መጽሓፊይ ከንብብዋ ኣካፍሎም። ነዛ ደብዳቤ ዉን ከንብብዋ ኣካፍሎም። ኣቲ ምንታይ ሲ ኣነ ይኩን ንስካ ዘልኣለማዉያን ነበርቲ ሰለዘይኮና። ዘልኣለማዊ ነባሪ መጽሓፍን ታሪከን እምበር ዘልኣለማዊ ነባሪ ሰብ ስለዘየለ: ሰለዚ ኣነ ኣብ ታሪክ ናይ ዓለም ጹቡቅ ታሪከ ከመዝገብ ተበጊሰን ኣብ ተግባር ኣብ ባይታ ይሰርሓሉን ይዕወትን ኣለኩ። ንስካ ዉን ነዚ ሰናይ ተበጉሶይ ብምርዳእ ኩሉ ዝካኣለካ ዘበለ ምትሕብባር ከትገብረለይን ከተታባብዓንን ይምነ።

ኩሎም ፕረዝደንትታት ናይዛ ዓለም ንመጽሓፊይ ብዓይኒ ትርጉም ኣልቦ ዝኮነ ፈረ ዘይሕፈሶ ጥርጣረ ከከምዝሪኣየዎን:ካብ ጥርጣረ ብምብጋስ ኣብ ልዕለይን ኣብ ልዕሊ ስድራቤተይን ናይ ስለያ መርበባቶም ከምዘዋፍሩ ይፈልጥን ይርዳኣንን እየ። ኩሎም ሰለይቲ ናዓይን ንኩቡራት ስድራቤተይን ከስልዩ ወይ ዉን ከጎድኡ ብኩሎም ኝፕረዝደንትታት ናይዛ ዓለም ዝላኣኩ ሰለይቲ ቱርጉም እዝ ደብዳቤይ መጽሓፊይን ሰናይ ተበግሶይን ስለዘርድኣም ኣብ ልዕለይ ይኩን ኣብ ልዕሊ ስድራቤተይ ጉድኣትከዉሩዱ ሕልንኣም ኣይከፍቅደሎምን እዩ። ኣነን መሳርሕተይን ድማ ነቲ ኩሉ ብሕጂ ዘጋጥመና ብቶንኮል ዝተነድቀ ዕንቅፋታትን ሽግራትን ሸርሕታትን ኣብ መላእ ዓለም ጨንፈራት ብምክፋት ሰለስተ ስጉምቲ ንቅድሚት ቅድሚ ዝኮነ ሓያል መንግስቲ ንከይድ ኣለና። መጽሓፊይ ናብ 193 ቋንቃታት ናይ ዓለም ተዘርጊሓ ትርከብ።

ዉን በጀካ ኣብ ሃገርና ኤርትራ መጽሓፊይ ኣብ ሙሉእ ዓለም ከትዘርጋሕ ተፈቅድላ ኣብ ዓለም ብኩሉ ቋንቁ ተዘርጊሓ ትርከብ። መጽሓፊይ ኣብ ሃገርና ኤርትራ ከትዘርጋሕ ዓቢ ባህጊ ኣለኒ።

ከሎም ኝፕረዝደንትታት ናይዛ ገዛ ከራይ ዝኮነት ዓለምና ንመጽሓፊይ ዝተፈላለየ ትርጉምን ቋንቃን ከምዝህብዋ ይርዳኣኒ እዩ።

ኣቲ ኣገዳሲ ቀምነገር ግን መጽሓፊይ ዝተፈላለየ ትርጉምን ርዲኢትን ቋንቃን ኣዋሃባ ኣይዋሃባ ዘይኮነስ: ኣቲ ቀንዲ ቀምነገር መጽሓፊይ ኣብ ሙሉእ ዓለም ዘሎ ቤት ንባባትን ኣብ ቤትምህርትታትን ከም መምሃሪት መጽሓፍ ከትከዉን ይስርሓሉ ምህላወይ እዩ። ይዕወት ካኣ ኣለኩ።

ሰለዝኮነ እዛ መጽሓፊይ ሳንሱር ሓሊፋ ኣብ ሃገርና ኤርትራ ከም መ ምሃሪት መጽሓፍ ከትከዉን ኣብ ሃገርና ኤርትራ ከትዘርጋሕንከፍቀደላ ብትሕትና ይሓተካ።

መጽሐፈይ ብሰላም ኣብ ኢድካ ኣትያ ከተንብባን ሃናጺ ሓሳባት ከተበንን ኣብ ሃገርና ኤርትራ መጽሐፈይ ከትዝርጋሕ ከፍቀደላንዓቢ ተስፋን ምራልን ከትበኒ ብዓል ሙሉእ ተስፋ እየ።

ስለዚ ኣቀዲም ቡዙሕ የመስግነካ መጽሐፈይ ኣብ ሃገርና ኤርትራ ንከትዝርጋይ ንከፍቀደላ ከትታሓባበረኒ። መጽሐፈይ ሙሉእዓወት ከትዕወት ኣብ ሃገርና ኤርትራ ከትዝርጋሕ መንገዲ ጽረገላ። መጽሐፈይ ኣብ ሃገርና ኤርትር ንከይትዝርጋሕ ማዕጾ ምዝርጋሕ ከይዕፅወላ ይምነንይምነን ይብህግን።

ታሪክ ከምዝምስከር ኩሎም ጀጋኑ ኤርትራዉያን ብሂወት ዘለዉን ብሂወት ዘየለዉን ንእስነቶም ንነጻነት ኤርትራ ሃገርና ዘወፈዮ፡ ንስካ ዉን ንእስነትካ ኤርትራ ናጽነታ ከትረከብ ስለ ዝጸዓርካ ንዝደከምካን ከየመስገንኩካ ከሓልፍ ኣይደልን ሕልናይ ኣየፍቅደለይን እዩ። ኣብ ሃገርና ድሕሪ ነጻነት ዘጋጠመ ዝታሓላለከ ሽግራት ከይድገም ግን ይላቦን ይምነን መታን ዘዝተወለደ ኤርትራዊ ናብ ፍቆዶ ስደት ዉርደት ከይጠፍእዉ። ወዲ ሰብ ዓድ እዩ ከብረቱ።

ቀ.ተሌፍነይ +1 336-715-0541   Email:

zeritprrcw@gmail.com

www.amazoxa.com Amazoxa Peace

University The home of true

Education CEO, Zerit Teklay Sebhatleab

My Mailing address is: P.O.BOX 22226 Nashvile, TN 37202 United States of America

ሰንሰለት ናይ ስደት ኤርትራዉነያን ንክብተክ ይምነ: ሰንሰለት ስደት ኤርትራዉያን ንክብተክ ኣብዛ መጽሓፍ ተጻሒፉ ዘሎ ኣብ ባይታ ኣብ ተግባር ከግበር ኣለዋ: ተዘይኮይኑ ዘዝተወለደ ኤርትራዊ ኣብ ፍቆዶ ስደት ከጠፍእ እዩ። ስለዚ መታን ሃገርና ኤርትራ ዝዓበየ ናይ ሰብ ከሳራ ናብ ስደት ምጥፋእ ከየጋጥማ እዛ መጽሓፈይ ዕላምኣ ኣብ ባይታ ከፍጸም ኣለዋ። ኣብ ከሉ ሰናይ ጉዉዘይ መጽሓፈይ ባህጋ ንክፍጸም ከትታሓባበረኒ ብትሕትና ይሓተካ።

ኣብ ሂወትካ ሙሉእ ጥዕና ይምነየልካ።ኣብ ኩሉ ንስለ ዓለምን ሰላም ምብራቅ ኣፍሪቃ ትገብሮ ጸዐሪ ኣወትን ኣሳልጦን ይምነየልካ።ዘይዉዳእ ሰንሰለት ናይ ኤርትራዉያን ስደት ዉርደት ምብታክ ናይ ነበሲ ወከፍ ኤርትራዊ ሓላፍነት ይኩን።

ዘሪኢት ተከላይ

ዘልኣለማዊ

ዝከሪ

ንስዋእትና

ዓወት

ንሓፍሽ!

Victory to the people!

ፖለቲካ

"ፖለቲካ ዉሑዳት ሰባት ዝረብሕሉ፡ቡዙሓት ሰባት ድማ ዝጠፍኡሉ
ፍረ ዘይሕፈሶ መካን ዓዉዲ እዩ፡፡

ስለዚ ንሄወትካ ትፈትዋን ተፍቅራን እንተኮንካ ጸግዒ ናይ ገዛእ ርእስካ ዳእምበር
ጸግዒ ናይ ፖለቲካ ክትከዉ እሕሊፍካ አይትሃባ፡፡

ፖለቲካ እቲ ካብ ቅድም እትሒዙ ከምኡ ዉን ክሳብ ሎሚ
ፈዲሙ መፍትሕን ፈዉስን ዘይተረከቦ ተላባዒ ሕማም እዩ፡፡

እዚ ሕማም እዚ ካእ እብ ዉሽጢ ቡዙሓት ሰባት ብምስፋር ንዓላምን ነቶም
እብእ ዘለዉ ፍጡራት ሰላሞም ክሊኡ እብ ስቅያት የንብሮም እሎ፡፡

ስለዚ በዚ ፈዉሲ ዘይቡሉ ቡርቶዕ ተላባዒ ሕማም ተለኻፊ ንኪይትከዉ ጥንቁቅ
ክትከዉ እለካ፡፡ እቲ ምንታይ ሲ ፈዉሲ ዘይቡሉ ሕማም እንተሓሚምካ እቲ ሰዒቡ
ድመጽእ ሞት ጥራይ እዩ ናዓካ፡፡

እዚ ንክትርዳእ ድማ ካብቲ ፈዉሲ ኣልቦ ዝኮነ
ሕማም ናይ ፖለቲካ ነጻ ክትከዉን እለካ፡፡

ምናልባሽ ግን በቲ ፈዉሲ ዘይቡሉ ሕማም ተጠቂዕካ እብ ናይ
ፖለቲካ ዓዘቅቲ ተሸሚምካ ከምዚ እብ ከምኡ ትብል እንተዳእ
ሃሊካ እዚ እብ ላዕሊ ተጸሒፉ ዘሎ ጽሑፍ ከም ላግጺ ወይ ዉን
ከም ግጉይ ስነሓሳብ ኮይኑ ክራኣየካ ይክእል እዩ ናዓካ፡፡"

~F. T. S, ERITREAN~

Chapter 7

Translation From Tigrigna Language to English Language

KNOWLEDGE

Even if you are one thousand times knowledgeable, if you do not know how to share it or how to make it known, your knowledge is nothing. You are not only not knowledgeable, but you are also someone who has meaningless knowledge, and this has led you to your own failures.

You may say I am Mr. I know everything, but if you are not applying your knowledge on things that do not help your growth, the hefty price and hefty time you have paid to get your knowledge become the reason of your failure instead of your success.

Make sure your knowledge makes you friends, not enemies. If your knowledge makes you enemies, you have just made your knowledge your own weapon of self-destruction.

ፍልጠት

"ሸሕ ግዜ ፈላጥ እንተኮንካ ነቲ ዘለካ ፍልጠት በየናይ
መንገዲ ከተካፍል ወይ ዉን ከተፍልጥ ዘይትፈልጥ
እንተኮንካ ነስካ ፈላጥ ዘይኮንካስ በቲ ፈሊጠዬ እትብሎ
ነገር ናይ ገዛእ ርእስካ ዉድቀት እትዓድም ኣምር ኣልቦ
ዝኮነ ፍልጠት ዝዉነን ፍጡር ኢካ"

"ፈላጥ እየ እንዳበልካ ንፍልጠትካ ኣብ ከጠቅመካ
ዘይክእል ነገራት ተዉዒሎ እንተዳአ ኮንካ ነቲ
ቡዙሕ ግዝየን ዋጋን ከፊልካ ዘጥረካዬ ፍልጠትካ
ትጥቀመሉ ዘይኮንካስ ትወድቀሉ ኢካ ዘለካ"

"ፍልጠትካ ጸላኢ ዘይኮነ ፈተዉቲ ግዝኣሉ ኢካ
ኣፈልጥ እየ ኢልካ ብፍልጠትካ ጸላኢ ተጥሪ
እንተዳአ ከንካ ፍልጠትካ ፍልጠት ዘይኮነስ ገዛእ
ርእስካ እተጥፍኣሉ መሳርያ እዩ ናዓካ"

~F. T. S, ERITREAN~

Chapter 8

Translation From Tigrigna Language to English Language

LEADERSHIP

Before you think of being the leader of your people, and wanting to lead your people, verify that you do not have even one single enemy among the people you are thinking of leading.

If you find out that you have enemies, defeat your enemies with love, diplomacy, and peace. Never engage in war, hatred, animosity, or retaliation in a bid to defeat your enemy.

A powerful leader of the people does not live abroad. A powerful leader is someone who stays in his motherland or returns to his motherland to lead his people by courageously saying, "Let there be justice and peace for the people." A powerful leader fights a good fight peacefully to bring justice and peace to his people. A powerful leader does not promote wars and oppression. A powerful leader is someone who does not kill innocent people of other countries, so that innocent people of his country do not get killed in retaliation. A powerful leader is someone who leads his people in peace.

Do not revolt against others so that you would not be a victim of retaliation. Wars can only end when the vicious cycle of endless retaliation is ended.

~ Zerit Teklay~
A K A YES, WE CAN PRRCW

መሪሕነት

" ቅድሚ ህዝቢ ከትመርሕ ምሕሳብካን
ምድላይካን ኣብዛ ዓለም ዋላ ሓደ
ሰብ ጸላኢ ከም ዘይብልካ ኣረጋግጽ"

"ጸላኢቲ ኣንተ ሃልየሙካ ንጸላኣትካ ብኪናትን
ብጽልእን ብሕነ ምፍዳይን ዘይኮነስ ብሰላምን
ብፍቅርን ብልዝብን ጸላኣትካ ሳዓር"

'ሓያል መሪሒ ህዝቢ ደባሃል ኣብ ስደት ኮይኑ ዘይኮነስ ኣብ ሃገሩ ኮይኑ ብትብዓት ሰላምን
ፍትሕን ይንገስ ኪናትን ጭኮና ህዝብን ይልግስ ብምግባል ንስለህዝቢ ደቃሰ ኣዩ"።
ሓያል መሪሒ ዝባሃል ኩሉ ንጹህ ህዝቢ መታን ሰላም ክረኸብ ከምቲ ህዝቡ ከቆተል ዘይደሊ፣
ንካልኣት ንኑጹህ ህዝቡን ንካልኣት ንጹሃት ህዝቢ ዘይቆትል ንህዝቡ ፈተዉቲ ዘብዝሕኣዩ።
'ሓያል መሪሒ ኑጹህ ህዝቡ ከይቆትል ናይ ካልኣት ኑጹሃት ህዝቢ ዘይቆትል ኣዩ"

"ሕነ ምፍዳይ መጀመርያ ኣምበር መወዳእታ
ሰለዘይብሉ መወዳእታ ዘይብሉ ሕነ ኣብ ልዕሌካ
ከይፍደየካ መወዳእታ ዘይብሉ ሕነ ኣብ ልዕሊ
ካልኦት ሰባት ኣይትፍደ"

~Zerit Teklay~
A K A YES WE CAN PRRCW

Chapter 9

Super Powerism

Super powerism is the root cause of dictatorship

~"Super powerism is, has always been and will always remain the main parent of all the past and present forms of dictatorships. Countries who accuse other countries' leaders of being dictators need to stop doing that while they themselves are still the greatest dictators our world has ever seen. I think that admitting and realizing this is the wisdom which will save humanity. It will also help humanity defend itself from perishing due to World Wars. Future World wars can be prevented by the formation of one Global Constitution, by which no country will ever dictate to another country, and when superpower countries realize that to be a superpower is to be a dictator. Every person in this world must figure out a solution to the problem of Super powerism.

Superpowerism is more of a problem than it is a solution. The desire to be a superpower leads to endless problems than solutions - same with under powersim. Moderate powerism is the equalizer/solution of the two problems of Superpowerism and Under powerism. All countries need to act on preventing another major World War; wars which have always been caused by the pursuit of who becomes a superpower of the World.

Likewise, we as the people of all countries must live in harmony by objecting the foreign policy of all governments, allowing them to interfere in other autonomous countries' internal affairs.

Chapter 10

The world of Spying and being spied on

~"Private or Government Spy agencies are there to spy on people going undercover, using cyber, powerful satellite surveillance cameras, bugs, unmarked cars, unmarked ships, unmarked helicopters, unmarked drones, unmarked plain clothes, artificial wigs, new haircut, and fake passports. The greatest tragedy in the world of spying and being spied on is that sometimes private or government spy agencies spy on the wrong person, wrong place, and wrong smartphone or computer device, and this results in a tragic catastrophic failure of apprehending, arresting, torturing, or killing the wrong person for all the wrong reasons. You can be an ordinary citizen who has done nothing wrong all your life, but once you get blackmailed or extorted by suspicion, you will be targeted, and be followed by private or government spy agencies 24/7. Just always do the right thing, do not worry. Let whatever is going to happen to happen, including the worst-case scenario of you being wrongfully incarcerated or assassinated by the private or government spy agencies. God forbid if this was going to happen to me, at least, I have written about it in this book. Oftentimes, I imagine how wonderful life would be if there was nothing like private or government spy agencies; a life where no one spies on no one else."~ Zerit Teklay

Chapter 11

Brain drains and Brain Washing Tragedy

Social media news, TV news, and radio news, conspiracy theories news, primary goal of Governments Briefings news, financial news, Political news, sports news, and medical news are the main agents that are shaping the mindset of everyone who hears or sees them?

Governments are the highest and most powerful forms of organizations. All governments' briefings have one primary goal in common, and that is the fact that they are designed on behalf of their country first, not designed on behalf of all countries of the world. The people in government or the people in journalism are not the primary cause of all the wars, chaos, and confusion in the world today; rather, it is the set system of governments and the set systems of journalism.

Nowadays, government representatives and even everyone speaks about things happening in the world as if they are physically present while it is happening, not realizing that everything is spoon-fed to them by their intelligence agencies which could be corrupt. Moreover, we the ordinary citizens must realize that all TV news, governments news, social media news is spoon-fed to us for the sole aim of brainwashing us. Just as government leaders like presidents do not verify the truthfulness of information provided to them by their intelligence agencies, we as individuals also do not verify the information released by TV or social media news outlets. Make no mistake on trusting the news. Before you can feel you trust what you hear in the news, verify.

Thus, like I mentioned earlier, if you genuinely want to express an original idea or write an original idea, you are better off not watching TV, listening to the radio, having social media accounts and listening to governments briefings, because all news channels have one thing in common that you are not aware of, and that is a hidden agenda that helps the system of the political party they support or the country of their birthplace. True journalism is, telling the truth without bias for any country or political affiliations. I may be wrong - which I doubt I am - but true journalism is now dead. However, not all hope is lost. This book is leading the path for pure truth. The author is aware that some parts of this book will offend big superpower countries, because this book is written based on truth and the facts. The author is also aware that any of the Superpower countries governments who read this book can target him as an enemy for exposing the truth. All governments have one thing in common, and that is, eliminating anyone whom they assume is a threat, even when he or she is not a threat at all.

In my opinion, television means "tell a vision," Not necessarily "tell the truth." In clearer terms, it means, "tell a vision of what they want you to hear, not the actual truth." This is not to mean that you should hate anyone working with the government or anyone working in journalism. Like you and I, they are just doing their job to make a living. The real enemy is not the people, it is the system.

Do not hate other countries' citizens based on what you hear in the news or based on their religion. Let there be no hate towards any people of any country in the world. It is the duty of each one of us not to allow hate to be circulated among people based on what is being said or written on TV and social media news.

Chapter 12

Presidents' true color, Future Global Presidential election of the 8 Continents our planet Earth, formation of Continental Foreign Policies of the eight continents

~ 'If you want to find out the true color of any president of any country, first understand why he is the way he is and why he does and says what he says. A good president does not create enemies with his words and deeds. A good president does not give an executive order to destroy other countries' lands with drones, missiles, and bombs. A good president does not send spies to other countries to exploit their natural resources. A good president does not take part in any form of corruption. A good president does not commit espionage, and never betrays his motherland. A good president does not abandon his country in times of war and confrontation. A good president is someone who always treats other people's countries and lands the same way he wants the people of his land to be treated. A true and patriotic president does not only stand for his country, but also stands for the people of all nations of the world. A true president does not hate any people of any country, even when he cannot stand the systems of governments of those people. A true president never sanctions any autonomous country, A true president elected by the people also never invades another autonomous country. A true president does not build military bases abroad, for the sake of not violating the rights of the people in foreign countries. A true president does not use brainwashing mechanism to expand his powers all over the world. The question is not whether there has ever been such a perfect president in the world or not. No president of any country in this world is perfect. There is no such a thing as a perfect president and there will never be. However, there will always be a better president who thinks and acts for global peace, global justice, and global prosperity. There will come a time when this book's noble ideas of the need to form a global constitution in the world will be implemented. Even if it takes 250 years for our world to understand this book's visions and noble ideas, so be it. The wait will be worth it, as long as there will be 8 presidents who represent the seven continents of our planet earth: the president of the continent of Africa, the president of the continent of Europe, the president of the continent of North America, the president of the continent of South America, the president of the continent of Australia, the president of the continent of Asia, and the president of the outer space and other planets above and below our planet earth. The proposed presidential election of the eight continents is drafted to be held every two years, where the people of each continent will vote to elect their president. There will no need for any spying intelligence agency to spy on other countries because by then, there will be eight continents' governments and eight presidents.

Foreign Policy: By 250 years or even less, there will only be 8 Foreign Policies whereby each continent will have one continental foreign policy. By then, eight presidents of the eight continents will have an annual presidents' meeting in Geneva, Switzerland. These eight presidents of the eight continents will take an oath to not engage in any type of war, invasion or colonization and exploitation of other continents' natural resources. This is the only way for our world to finally get a break from wars, crimes, poverty, and greed. Let it be the duty of every human being to take part in the journey of Formation of Global constitution of the eight continents. Global Constitution and Global Presidential election manuals are being written and are to be published in the second edition of this book. In the event that something happens before he publishes the second edition of this book, let the idea of formation of Global constitution and Global presidential election of the 8 continents live on the minds of all the people who read this book. The author hopes that this book be in the public libraries and homes.

Chapter 13

Domestic Terrorism Tragedy of January 6, 2021, U.S Capital attack tested American Democracy.

History shows that nothing like the January 6, 2021, attack has happened in American soil in the history of the United States of America in the last 230 years, or even more. The world saw the most respected and powerful U S Government Capital humiliated and disrespected by its own people whose ideals are supposed to be based on the stars spangled banner. The broken justice system has done nothing but arrest the insurrectionists, meanwhile, it still has not persecuted the big tycoons who brainwashed them to attack the capital by words and corruption. The greatest failure of the systems of government is that the rich and powerful presidents are immune from going to prisons, even when there is hard evidence that they have committed a crime. It is sad how the unfair the justice system is; it is sad to see that the law protects only the rich and the powerful, while it continues to put millions of ordinary people behind bars, sometimes, even for the crimes they did not commit. The justice system has sadly failed repeatedly to persecute the rich and powerful, who have the access and resources to hire the best lawyers in the world. The solution to this problem is that no violence of any form needs to be tolerated. Violence is violence. The word "violence" has the same meaning in the English dictionary. The greatest tragedy in the history of America is that of the right of civilians to bear arm…

The entire world saw civilians fully armed with Guns and Arms during the January 6 attack of the U.S. Capital. If the founding fathers who designed the law of the right to bear arms could come back from the dead to witness January 6 attack, I think they would have gathered in the situation room of the U S Capital and repealed the right to bear arms. Because of the right to bear arms, today, the United States is the number one country with the highest gun violence, and the largest prison system in the world.

Repealing the law of the right to bear arms is the only solution that can prevent another January 6 attack from happening in America or elsewhere where the right to bear arms exists. No country with laws should promote gun and arms violence. The one solution we can think of is for the American people to begin on a fresh slate by organizing a new third political party whose key role is to be an official mediator of the Republican party and the Democratic party, especially in times of domestic terrorism crises such as the January 6 attack. We implore every American to not take part in any act of violence. It is time for American Democracy to wake up and come together by narrowing the division of the hidden political war between the Democratic party and

Republican party. Let the United States Government pass a law which can be called "Article 6 Anti Domestic Terrorism Act," giving the Supreme Court of the United States the power to oversee Domestic and International Terrorism. The Supreme court is less bias and less corrupt than individual government employees working in all branches of government. At times, these branches of government commit corruption by covering up or inciting violence by using words that promote violence and hatred among people for the personal gain of political power.

Chapter 14

Big problems

Poverty, injustice, greed, loneliness, the bad side of technology, excluding the good side of Technology, teenage pregnancy, the laws that govern abortion, some online platforms, organized gangs' Mafia crimes , distribution of illegal drugs, alcohol addiction and sex addictions, pornographic addictions, prostitution, domestic violence, wars, assassination, professional killing by governments, government's corruption, conflict of interest, cyber-attacks, fraud, domestic and international terrorism, superpower countries' interference in foreign countries, overthrowing legitimate and autonomous countries, sanctions, invasions, and so on, are the greatest evil acts our world has been suffering from and is still suffering from.

We have written some of the solutions in this book's "Articles" section and throughout this book, so that governments can consider their implementation in the laws of all countries.

We are still writing the solutions to these problems and other problems to be published in the second edition of this book.

Chapter 15

Our Missions, Concerns and demands are:

- Send this book to all former presidents who are alive today and all current live presidents of all nations of the world.
- Translate this book to every language currently spoken in the world today.
- Our conflict resolution principle is only by reconciliation and open discussion. In our laws and principles, overthrowing any legitimate government by using violent force/coup d'état is illegal.

According to the supreme law of all nations' visionary constitution, conflict resolutions are handled by reconciliation and peaceful discussions.

- Participate in all United Nations meetings, NATO meetings and Future United Countries of the World of Third World Countries meetings.
- Ending the systematic exploitation of natural resources of poor continents such as the continent of Africa.
- See and hear no wars in the world one day.
- Eradication of systematic discrimination based on color of skin and gender.
- Reform of job application forms such that ALL JOB APPLICATION FORMS do not require any discriminatory race or gender-based forms.

Chapter 16

MISCELLANEOUS

This Chapter is for anyone, book critics, commentators, and journalists by free will to criticize the content of chapter 16.

The author has intentionally written this chapter as is, to encourage anyone who intends to write a critique not to worry about how perfect or imperfect the writing is. Nothing in this world is perfect. No one in this world is perfect. Everyone has an imperfection, every book written has an imperfection from the point view of book critics.

My response to the critics is this:

Hello Hannah,

The magnificent work you have done in creating an amazing summary of the book has made me have a second thought; I want to have my book be edited by you.

This book will be turned into a movie. I have dreamed that the movie based on this book will influence all the presidents, and even ordinary citizens. I am such an adventurous and curious writer, I could have written the movie, Black Panther. It is my dream that the movie based on this book is produced by Marvel Studios and distributed by Walt Disney Studios Motion Pictures. I can imagine what good can happen when this book is made into a movie. Like the rocky movie by Sylvester Stallone, 1993, the fugitive movie by Harrison Ford and Tommy Lee, and Mohammed Ali movies, this book 91.91% is based on true story and facts; only 8.09 % of this book is my imaginary creation of adventure and curiosity for the greater good. I will be the main character in the movie of this book. The Rocky movie and the Mohammed Ali movie showed the world physical strength. This book's movie will show the power of human intelligence over artificial intelligence, and the power of creative writing with the definite purpose of creative writing, not only for the good of a specific country, but for the good of all the people of all countries of the world.

The power of my imagination of one world, under one universal flag, under one universal currency, under one universal global constitution is the greatest blessing our world can ever hope to achieve. No movie that promotes universal peace, universal justice, universal equality, universal prosperity, and universal happiness has ever been produced.

Super powerism needs not be encouraged or applauded. A country should never invade another country. All the people of the world must object the exploitation of natural resources from Africa by superpower countries. This book will be sent to every president in the world, so it is important that this book's ideals and creative solutions do not offend any country's president or citizens. If you find any repeating ideas, repeating concepts of the ideas in the book, please take them out. Please, also let every idea be in the form of chapters; one idea per chapter, with a chapter not exceeding two pages. But the size of the interior book format stays as it is - 8.5× 11 inches - unless you have a recommended paper size such that the words are not too clustered. This book must be unique, down to the paper size format. If you find any idea that is too emotional or even, too conflicting, please edit such that they are in agreement with one idea. I am pursuing my true dreams, which is, making a difference in the world; I desire a world of peace, justice, and prosperity for all. It is my hope that there are technological advancements in all continents, including the continent I was born in 1981 - Africa. Like Martin Luther King said, "I have a dream," I too have a much bigger larger dream. I want the continent of Africa and all other poor continents to be rich and prosperous. I would like a fair world without suffering and wars triggered by governments. Let no human being suffer because of wars engineered by governments.

All the ideas in this book are not meant to offend any country, government, or person. Besides, this book's ideas are meant to only attract friends not enemies.

I am my most emotional self when I write my ideas. I also know I am so truthful, such that my ideas are based on truth, and nothing else. Although I believe in the famous saying, "If you want to get anything done well, Do It Yourself," but the amazing, extraordinary way you designed my book's original cover design, and the way you've summarized my book description has made me humble enough to admit that "two heads are always better than one head." And I am thankful for the great customer service experience you have provided me during our conversations.

Besides, when I was about to publish, I realized it was important that the content of the book matches the cover. I have edited it the best way I can, but I would like my book to be edited and proofread by you, Hannah. I think editing and proofreading will be very necessary, especially since the book will also be in audio books and eventually made to be a movie.

In my entire book, there must not be any language of writing that does not reflect the message written on the back of the book. Any statement that contradicts the content of the back of the book must be out. There must not be conflict of ideas.

The 45th President of the United States once said we should forget the dreadful things that have happened in the past, and not hold any grudges based on history, and focus on present - doing good. I would not like my book to focus on all the bad things that have happened in the past. I would like my book to be edited with exclusive focus on the good things of the present and the positive prospects the future of the worlds. I want this book to reflect my ideas which are free from resentment and grudges.

· No bossy language must be included in any part of the book. Any demands or proposals are to be written respectfully, because the biggest dream of this book is to promote peace, justice, equality, and prosperity in all nations of the world. There must not be any perceived form of allyship toward any government or government agenda. The only form of allyship that will be entertained is one that is with the people. This is the goal of this book.

· Let this book cater to all audience, including adults and children. The solution to all the chaos, wars and domination of other countries' autonomy begins with the values we instill in our children as they are growing up. Let children read this book so they can envision and dream of a harmonious, discrimination-free, peaceful, and just world early on.

·

The interior paper format needs to be in epub file format version to be compatible with ingram spark paper format requirements, pdf version and Microsoft word version. Since I have a dream for this book to be taught in schools, I would love the book to be formatted such that it is reader-friendly, and the fonts on the book cover match the one in the interior. There must not be any accusation of any government in the entire book. All governments are innocent until proven guilty under the international constitution of Global Constitution designed in this book. The main point is to be neutral, without bias toward any country or government.

Freedom of Expression, Freedom of press and freedom of assembly
experiment one

- If the United States is truly the land of equal job opportunities, why are gender and race included in job application forms? Whether or not the United States is the land of equal job opportunities depends on who you are asking.

- If the United States was truly the land of opportunities, why does one's birth certificate matter in presidential elections?
- If the United States was truly the land of opportunities, why is the U.S. government not doing anything to stop companies from checking credit scores of job applicants? How long will job

discrimination based on last name continue? Is America really the land of equal job opportunities? It is important for the public to question the government, and demand that they provide unbiased answers, free of political correctness.

Respect every life, remember history, and cherish peace.

We are not politicians.

We are not philosophers.

We are not scientists.

We are free thinkers.

We are visionary compassionate human beings.

We are idea inventors.

We are developers of thoughtful ideas and laws.

We are book publishers who only selectively publish ideas worth publishing.

We do not want to be politicians.

We do not want to be philosophers.

We do not want to be scientists.

We do not want any titles.

> **Let the supreme law** of the land of the United Countries of the world be above all laws of all nations in the world. Let the Global supreme law be the supreme law of the United Countries globally,

with respect to checks and balances of the legislative, the executive and judiciary branches of United Countries of all Governments and all nations of the world.

- Treat other countries' soldiers like they are your soldiers and treat other countries' innocent civilians like they are your innocent civilians.

- Stop manipulating, brainwashing, and applying a system of modern colonization of divide, rule, and exploit.

- According to the Supreme law of the land, no country's soldiers should die if you all presidents were wise.

- According to the future Supreme International Constitution of the United Countries of the World to be, all wars are caused by the hunger for glory, and hunger for exploitation of other countries' natural resources. Stop all war crimes for the sake of humanity.

- Freedom of press experiment three

- Stop brainwashing soldiers by having them defend and protect systematic brainwashing schemes. We apologize for some of our hard-to-swallow truths that are somehow offensive in this book. English is our second language, so, it may not be interpreted as intended by readers whose first language is English.

Experiment four

- If there is any unclear statement in this book, please email us at zeritprrcw@gmail.com for clarification. How dishonest are the crimes governments commit in other countries? For how long superpower countries will be police officers of the world just for the sake of power and exploitation of natural resources.

- Will there be any president in the future who will pull all soldiers from military bases of the United Countries of the world. Only time will tell.

- Let the law of the land, the Constitution of the United Countries of the World, check and balance systemic employment discrimination by removing race and gender from job application forms.

- Let the law of the land, the constitution of the United Countries of the World intervene to stop the rich and powerful from getting richer, and the poor and middle class from getting poorer.

- Let the ideas published in this book be brought up in the office desk of any current or future sitting president of every country in the world.

Dedication to the dreams can come through the fulfilment and finishing of the 1997 Constitution of Eritrea to one day be fully implemented, so that Eritrean people can experience implementation of 1997 Eritrean constitution. Let no foreign country interfere with the Internal Affairs of Eritrean Constitution. Let the Eritrean people be free from foreign interference in regard to the implementation of Eritrean constitution.

Please note that some part of the writing is to assess whether or not America really is the land of freedom of press, rightful assembly and freedom of expression?

We are exercising our rights to freely write as the founding fathers of this country U S wished. May our literary work never get interrupted by political correctness.

Every Country loses
In bloody civil war and terror.

Treat other countries' citizens the same way you want your country's citizens to be treated.

Do not kill anyone or other countries people, so that your country people will not be killed out of retaliation or revenge.

We are the people, by the people to the people.
Ambassadors for a peaceful, just, and safe World.

Where there is war, there will not ever be peace.
Where there is illegal invasion of foreign countries, there will always be terrorism.

Do not kill to avoid being killed.
Do not terrorize to avoid being terrorized.
Do not torture to avoid being tortured.
Do not kidnap to avoid being kidnapped.
Do not hijack other people's possessions to keep your possession from being hijacked.
Do not discriminate to avoid being discriminated against.
Do not hack to avoid being hacked.
We can outsmart any kind of artificial intelligence.
Do not lie to avoid being lied to.
Do not cheat to avoid being cheated on.
Do not steal to avoid being stolen from.
Do not harm any human being to avoid being harmed.
Do not dictate to anyone.
Do not dictate to any country.
Remember the famous saying, "What goes around eventually comes back around, pointing at you."

Root causes of all past wars and current wars are:

- Retaliation.
- Power Hunger.
- Glory.
- Gold.
- God.

- Colonization.
- Nonetheless, the exploitation of natural resources is the main parents/causes of all past and current wars.

Who are we?
We are not politicians. We are peace mediators, justice preservers, and idea, law, and policy inventors.
We do not own guns!
We do not own weapons of mass destruction!
We own books of mass construction!
We own skills, equipment, and tools of mass construction!

We do not track!
We do not hack!

We are men and women from all walks of life of different races, genders and professions.

We are ex-presidents, ex-politicians, lawyers, doctors, nurses, philosophers, psychologists, scientists, inventors, nutritionists, engineers, artificial intelligence inventors, plane manufacturers, car manufacturers, ship manufacturers, bike manufacturers, drivers of taxis, Uber, trucks, buses, trains, motor bikes, commercial planes, and submarines. We are captains, pilots, and airport employees.

What don't we do?

We do not create enemies.
We create many powerful and powerful friends!

We do not kill!
We do not terrorize!
We do not torture!
We do not oppress!
We do not neglect the homeless!
We do not neglect victims of sexual abuse and sexual harassment!
We do not neglect victims of domestic violence!

We do not track!
We do not hack!
We do not discriminate!
We do not lie!
We do not steal!
We do not manipulate, but we outsmart!
We outsmart any technology!
We do not plant spy bugs in cars, shoes, clothes, or homes.
We are humble!
We do not participate in corruption!
We do not use credit cards or mortgages loans!
We do not care about credit score!
We choose to make our credit score bad, so we do not get accepted for any loans!

Taking loans is the lifeline of poverty, misery, and unhappiness!
We are the happiest because we do not have any loan, credit card or mortgage debt!
We buy everything in cash!
We are the bodyguards of equal wealth distribution!
We are the bodyguards of peace, justice, equal opportunity, good health, and good news!

Who Wins in A War?

No one wins in war.
Everyone loses in war.
No country win in war.
Every country loses in war.

What are the main parents of war?

The main parent of any war is endless cycle of retaliation, power hunger and greed.

What are our missions?

Our first mission is to change the last name of the future country, planet earth's, president from Yes, We Can. We will fulfill all the court order requirements to have our president's last name to be changed from Yes, We Can. We have a strong mindset that believes everything is possible.

Our second mission is to end the war in Ethiopia. Our third mission is to end war in Afghanistan. Our fourth mission is to open a discussion table to all the countries who are at war. Our fifth mission is to end all the natural exploitation of poor countries. Our sixth mission is to end systemic racism from our country, planet earth.

We are setting the bar of ending war higher than it has ever been in the history of ending wars.
We, the country, planet earth, will be on a mission to end the systemic and inhumane tragic phenomena is, the rich get richer, and the poor get poorer.

Our Problem Solving and Conflicts resolution Skills of Reconciliation and mediation

We have all the skills, noble ideas, and tools to end crime, violence, injustice and violent protests and violent revolutions.
We do not protest with violence. We protest by publishing our books, using two hundred skills and technological advancement trademarks of our own.

The details on how to end injustice, inequality, discrimination, and violence will be in our second edition of this book.

We have the solution to the problem that is racism. We will start with the United Countries of the World Racism issue which makes the United Countries of the World to be the land of Equal opportunities. If America was truly the land of opportunities, why is there a race and gender discrimination in Job application forms? Race and gender are in Job application forms in America to Systematically discriminate race and gender to what color of skin gets the job first.

Our one sentence solution to end job discriminations in America is to Erase Race and gender from any job application forms. Where there is race / gender discrimination in job application forms, there will always be Employment discrimination In America. The So-called Zip Code is another systematic racism. Oscar Awards and America's Got talent is also where racism happens. Is there systemic racism in America? Yes, there is and there has always been there will always be system racism in Oscar Awards and America got talent shows. E and circumstantial evidence research paper about the system racism in America is almost completed and will be published after Author of this

Racism is everywhere. Is America really the land of equal opportunities? No America is not the land of equal opportunities. America now is the land of dis-equal opportunities. If America was the land of true Equal opportunities, what does race, and gender must do business with to be in the Job Application forms. Plain simple Race and gender are in job application forms to discriminate. Do not put your race and gender in the job application forms not to be discriminated against based on your race or gender. We will work with United Countries of the World law makers to fix race and gender issues of discrimination in job application forms. We will give solutions to why race and gender must not be in job application forms. Race and gender must not be in any job application form.

Traps and main reasons
why the
Rich gets richer and the poor
get poorer and poorer.

1. Credit Cards
2. Credit Score
3. Mortgages and loans
4. Zip Code Discrimination
5. Power Hunger
6. Greed
7. Job Discrimination
8. Colonization
9. Corruption
10. Pride, gold, and Glory
11. Wars

Stop being police officers of the World. Focus on being the police officers of your own country only.

Leave foreign lands alone to be governed by their own people and their own government. Stop being police officers of the World.

We wish you Success in pulling every single Soldier and all weapons of mass destruction from all other foreign land.

All blank pages are for you to write down any laws that you think will make our world to be peaceful, just, and safer to live than it is now. On the blank pages, please go ahead and write down useful thoughtful laws that you think will make our world peaceful, just, and safer to live. Our contributions of other laws we are drafting   are classified on behalf of Global Peace, On Behalf Global Prosperity, On Behalf of Global Justice, on behalf all the people who are dying of civil wars started by foreign countries

The contents of all the blank pages are for you to write down any laws that you think will make our world to be peaceful, just, and safer to live than it is today. Our ideas are not to be found in any computer device, Smartphone device or in any paper.

They   are in the Un-hackable or un- traceable human brain
 His Noble Ideas found in his brain cannot be hacked by any Technology, cannot be copied, or reproduced. If he dies, all the noble Ideas, Artificial Intelligence Inventions, Philosophies will die with him, and all current African Presidents are getting all his inventions and policies to make Africa United Africa and Pan Africanism. He will transform the United Countries of the World of Africa in 3 years if he does not get assassinated like Martin Lowther king was assassinated.

Our Party will be called Planet Earth Non-Political party, Our Currency will be called Planet Earth Currency, Our Laws will be called Planet Earth Laws of the Planet Earth, and Our Flag will be World Map. The first continent which will be free from systemic Modern Colonization, and Modern Exploitation of Natural resources will be the Continent of Africa, his homeland continent where he was born in 1981 in a country in Africa called Eritrea.

We will give a new name to Africa. Africa eventually will be called the United Countries of the World of Africa under One Flag, One currency and One President and One Vice President and Chiefs of Staff.

We are the only solution left in planet earth to save soldiers and innocent civilians from dying in foreign
Lands.

We Plan to be in the next United Nations Geneva Convention Peace talks if you send us an invitation to our email at zeritprrcw@gmail.com. See you on the next United Nations Geneva convention for peace discussions of ending all the current Wars in foreign lands

Reserved for highly Classified Philosophies, Problem Solutions, Inventions, and noble Ideas of our future
Planet Earth Peace and justice Ambassador A K A Zerit Teklay

The First President who we will send this book will be 45th President of United States his excellency Mr. President Joe Biden. The second president whom we will send this book will be his excellency President of the State of Eritrea his excellency Mr. President Isaias Afwerki. And eventually we will send this book to every president of every legitimate country of the world. This book is our business card and the CV resume book of Zerit Teklay C V resume. This book is the largest resume book of dreams, aspirations of Zerit Teklay author of this book.

This book will be in every Country's President Office This book will be translated in every language in this entire planet.

Why is the Author selling this book $91.91 U S dollar?

Zerit Teklay Only and main Author of this book is selling it for $91.91 in the honor of Eritrea's Independence Day 24 May 1991, Eritrea Martyrs Day June 20th and in the honor of this Book Author Zerit's father Ato Teklay who was one the Eritrea's Chief of intelligence Fedayin Hero who did lots of masterpiece Intelligence Works during the Eritrean Struggle for Independence which costed him to be imprisoned by Dergi Until 1991. Zerit's Father was freed from Mariam Gibi Prison in Asmara Eritrea by Eritrean Freedom fighters Heros on May 24th, 1991.

To this book's Author Zerit, 24 May 1991 is not only Eritrea's Independence Day but also the day of Kidanemihret day 24 May 1991 when Zerit's late father was freed from Mariam Gibi Prison By his Eritrean freedom fighters Intelligence Heros. He was one of the first one they Freed from Mariam Gibi which happened to be Dergi Fascist Notorious Worst Political Prisoners Prison In entire Eritrea.

Zerit Teklay Will dedicate his life on
Advocating all Political Prisoners who are suffering in Every Countries
Prison Cells in the memory of his father Eritrean Former Top Fedayeen
(Intelligence Officer) during the Eritrean Struggle for independence who
recently died.

R I P to the honor of Zerit's Father Ato Teklay who died a few years ago.

Our Urgent concern

and Demand number 1

Stop the civil war in Ethiopia.

Why are Tigray soldiers, Ethiopian Soldiers, Eritrean Soldiers killing each other in bloody War and Terror while you all enjoy your lives giving political correctness speeches in T V, Radios being in the comforts of safety, prosperity and luxury of your safe homes and High-level offices.

Do not kill to be killed back

Do not continue to go to foreign countries not to have innocent people being killed by your hidden agendas of exploiting East Africa Geopolitics. Stop making the people of East Africa kill each other. Stop your dreams of the exploitation of indirectly controlling the Red Sea and The Bab emended channel of the red sea which is the number one strategic sea in the world. Stop brain washing the people of Ethiopia, Eritrea, the People of Tigray to kill each other so than you continue exploitation exploit their Natural resources while they kill each other.

Where there is a war there will always no be peace
Where there is illegal invasion of foreign countries, there will always be increased terrorism which can never be stopped by any Technology or by any type of Military Intelligence spying.

Extraordinary Vision

imagination of heroism, bravery, and Resilience on forming United Countries of the World of One Africa.

The African President will one day testify the Heroism, bravery, Resilience, Courage, wisdom of Author of this book A K A YES, WE CAN PRRCW peace and justice A ambassador A K A. Zerit. Save your energies, resources, and Intelligence on trying to extract High Skills information from him. He already started a project called the beginning of African Civilization in the United Countries of the World of Africa 2 years ago. Just protect him. Do not fake his death, do not poison his food, and do not orchestrate his Premeditated Suicide. Here in his book on behalf of his Future country United Countries of the World of Africa, he is confirming in advance that he will never commit suicide in case you hear Fake news of him committing suicide.

He is writing this highly classified information for all Intelligence agencies not to try to torture or break him to extract his two hundred intellectual property ideas of philosophy, Computer science, Medicine, Artificial intelligence, and so on. He will not be broken; he will not kill himself. If he died in prison the entire world will know he died of torture by Some Power-hungry governments.

We commend all Superpower NATO nations to all G 7 countries to do only the right thing as it is written in the law of the land. Do not hijack him illegally for torture of information extraction, do not spy on him, do not have him killed in fake car accidents or fake suicides, do not plan any spy bugs in his homes or cars. Do not hack his phone. Do not track his phone. He is no harm to no one or to no country. Let him stop you from harming foreign land countries people and exploitation of natural resources of his mother continent Africa-Eritrea where he was born in 1981

He does not have any microchips in his body. God for bit if anything happens to him, the world will lose the most valuable person who speaks more than ten languages proficiently. He has two hundred Self learned Valuable Technological, Medical, Nutritional and Intelligence skills that will make our Future United Countries of the World of Africa to be a peaceful, safe, disease free, prosperous United Countries of Africa. He goes everywhere with no need of bodyguards because he has no enemies but lots and lots of loyal friends and loyal chiefs of staff for the formation of the United Countries of the World of Africa. This book is his protection from any ill will legally troubles Superpower's countries may give him a tough time by pulling him over, by planting Spy bugs in his cars, homes, shoes, clothes, his Samsung TV and so on. Leave him alone to End two wars going on now: civil war in Ethiopia.

We the PRRCW are respectfully writing our concerns, demands and proposals to the 46th U S president Jeo Biden, and 46th U S Vice president Kamala Harris, and to all current living presidents of all nations of the world to respond to our demands, proposals, and ideas below:

- pertaining the end of De capto colonization, the end of modern Systemic Neo colonialism

- Pertaining pulling out Military bases from foreign lands.

- Pertaining Unlawful imprisonment of visionary activists and Revolutionary peaceful laws and Invention's developers such as ourselves.

- Pertaining systematic racism based on Credit Scores, Skin color and gender

- Pertaining Global De legalization and banning of the porno graphic industry which is the main source of human trafficking and little girls kidnapping. According to our many years of research and independent investigations, we found out that where there exist porn industry, human trafficking and little girl kidnapping will never end. So, to end human trafficking and little girls trafficking, Porno graphic industry must be closed globally by all nations. We commend all world leaders to unanimously close the pornography industry once and for good.

- Pertaining Illegal deportation and inhumane treatment of Asylum seekers in all nations who illegally deport asylum seekers.

- Pertaining the balance of powers among branches of the government executive branch, judiciary branch and legislative branches of all Governments to be under the Supreme law of the Land not over or above the supreme law of the land.

- Pertaining prevention of terrorism by not committing terrorism in foreign lands. September 11 was not meant to happen. Retaliation is why the September 11 tragic attack happened. We let the public know that the only way to prevent and end terrorism for good is TO PULL out all foreign country's Military bases from foreign lands. And to leave other countries alone.

- Pertaining the establishment of United Countries of the World Non-Political party which will be a Mediator party for Republican party and Democratic party of the United States

  Pertaining our demand to officially be the United Countries of the World Charities Auditing Agency. We have Plans lined up to end all the corruption happening in the name of charities

- Pertaining the formation of United Countries of the World Ending homelessness political party

- Pertaining our demand for his excellency President of Eritrea Mr. President Isaias Afwerki, President of Tigray Debretsion Gebremichael, Prime Minister of Ethiopia Dr. Abby Ahmed Ali, and East African presidents to join us on the Upcoming United Nations Peace talk in Geneva Switzerland to end the Civil War in Ethiopia once and for good.

- Pertaining the call to Action for ending homelessness worldwide

- Pertaining other miscellaneous issues, concerns, and conflicts resolution solutions

1. We commend The United Countries of the World Legislative branch to pass a new law that makes invasion of autonomous country illegal.

2. No branch of Government of the U S Government is above the supreme law of the land designed by the United States of the World Founding fathers.

3.   No person is above the law, everyone must obey the law. Even the Legislative must obey the laws of the land of our country, land of Justice.

4.   No judge at whatsoever level is above the law. No judge at whatsoever level can twist the law of the land the United Countries of the World international constitution to their own interests and gains.

The blank pages are for you to write down any laws that you think will make our world to be peaceful, just, and safer to
of the he is only to be found in the Office desks of all African Presidents. No African President will ever commit Treason against the United Countries of the World of Africa. All his books will be published half blank and half written. He will never save the content of his book blank pages in any computer, phone, or paper. All his blank page highly classified contents will be in his most asset, his Physical Human Brain. Do not waste your time, energy, and resources on trying to hack his H P laptop, His Samsung Galaxy, and his iPhone. He leaves all his devices vulnerable to be hacked because he put nothing worth hacking on his computer or phone devices.

You have enough food, enough Natural resources, and enough wealth. So do not be Jealous when the United Countries of the World of Africa becomes the First continent to be in the G 7 status. Soon the Phenomenon on G 7 countries will be updated to G 8 countries including our country United Countries of the World of Africa Which soon to be officially founded.

His noble ideas cannot be copied, cannot be analyzed, cannot be hacked, cannot be stolen, and cannot be outsmarted. If suddenly die by torture which he doubts by one of the Superpower countries, all his noble ideas, Artificial Intelligence skills inventions, philosophies will die with him, and all current African Presidents will be the direct beneficiaries of all his Inventions. He is the continuation of Great American Founding Fathers. If you kill him, you will kill all dreams American Founding Fathers Dreamed. So do not kill, Torture, follow or spy him. Leave him alone to fix the broken systems by challenging the law of the land Birth Certificate issue which gave the 44th former U S President Barack Obama lots of challenging time. He is the next Obama of America. He is the Main engine of preserving 44th U S President Barack Obama Legacies and unfinished business.

we will name our currency Planet earth Currency. $ 1 Planet Earth currency will be equal to $ 1 U S dollar. We will put the inequality of the power of currencies into a real time Test.

While we work in America, we will have Strong ties with all African Presidents in the formation of the United Countries of the World of Africa and the continuation of the African Civilization project which was started in 2018. Our Flag will be the Continent of Africa Map. The first continent which will be free from modern colonization, and modern systemic exploitation of Natural resources will be our new country to be our country United Countries of the World of Africa. Motherland of the United Countries of Africa Under one currency called Motherland Africa. $ 1 motherland Africa currency will be equal to $ 1 currency of every country in the world. The United Countries of the World of Africa will have one president and once vice president. United Countries of the World of Africa elections will be every 2 years to discourage dictatorship and tyranny of one man show. The United Countries of the World of

Africa will see a New President Every 2 Years. No president can repeat the term of presidency. Our United Countries of the World of Africa Immigration laws will be simple and one page long. Our laws are only reserved to the author of this book

Zerit Teklay a K A yeswecanredskincolorman and all current African Presidents.

We plan to be in the next United Nations Geneva convention peace talks if you send us a clearance

Invitation to our email at zeritprrcw@gmail.com

Or Contact Our Future United Countries of the World of Africa office found somewhere in the world.

See you in the next upcoming Peace talk Geneva convention in the topic of ending all foreign interferences of foreign lands which are the main parents of crime, revolution, terrorism, Civil unrest, and civil war.

Author of this book Zerit Teklay and all current African Presidents. All his classified Philosophies, War Solutions, Inventions of Artificial intelligence will not and will never be found in any computer system. So, if you are a spy, give up spying on his devices which have nothing worth of spaying or hacking. He is three steps ahead of any intelligence in this entire globe. Spy him, instantly out of not nowhere will be spayed upon and be put in his Obstacle for progress of the United Countries of the World of Africa Blacklist.

.

This book will be in every country's president's office as a friendly reminder of the capabilities vision of forming the United Countries of the World of Africa.

This book will be translated in every country's language with a specific ISBN for each country.

The main reason the Author of this book Zerit Teklay is selling it for $91.91 is for the honor of

Eritrean Independence Day 24 May 1991, and Day of Kidanemihret day 24 May 1991 when his father was freed From Mariam Gibi worst Dergi Regime prisons still found in Asmara Eritrea and in the honor of Eritrean War for Independence Fallen Eritrean Martyr Day of remembrance June 20th.

No Country is supposed to be colonized if it was not for power hunger and Greed.

Legal Briefing Case

Criminal

Acts being committed on our mother continent the

**Continent of
Africa**

1. Exploitation of Continent Africa Natural resource exploitation by manipulating African Presidents kill each other now realizing and understanding who their true enemy the case of the argument to Free Africa from Systemic Modern Slavery and modern Colonization.
2. African Presidents must order all foreign land charities to exit Africa as soon as possible.
3. African Presidents are waking up in slow progress in detecting the Spy so-called Charities and Nonprofit organizations which are the number one reason Africa has always been a poor continent.
4. Under the leadership of our United Countries of the World Party, All Invaders currently exploiting Africa's Natural Resources will eventually be in the international court of Law. Powerful countries will be held accountable for making Africa to be dark continent, for creating diseases and experiments in poor Africa will soon be short lived with our rising Global Political and Global Volunteer Intelligence Agency of peace, justice and

Equality of all planet earth human beings.

5.   **WAR** in Africa or Anywhere in the World is a Criminal Act. No one is supposed to die in a war.

Modern Systemic Colonization of Continent Africa is one reason rich countries became richer and weather while mother land Africa Suffer of Wars, Hunger, Disease, genocide, and corruption.

No Country is supposed to systematically be colonized and its Natural resources be exploited by rich countries which makes them richer and richer, and which makes

Our Future New Country to be United Countries of one Africa.

Message to Systemic Modern 21rst invisible colonizers and foreign lands Invaders
 Treat other countries the same way you want your country to be treated.

Do not continue to go to any foreign land if you do not wish to be invaded back
Do not Terrorize and any one or any country not to be terrorized back
Do not Spy on, track, or hack any one not to be spied upon, hacked, and tracked into
Pull all your soldiers from all foreign lands to make the United Countries of the World of Africa as rich as, as prosperous as, as technologically advanced as, as Just as and Peaceful as your own country.

Do not systematically make African people kill each other so that you focus on exploiting their rich Natural resources and they continue to kill each other not detecting who their common enemy is.

Be happy for the prosperity of the United Countries of the World of Africa by not invading its natural resources. Please do not brainwash corrupt African officials for your own
Gains.

Start practices honest politics

Enough Natural Resources of our mother continent Africa has been exploited for so many decades. Yet you cannot have enough. Until this year we are publishing this book, The year 2022 you are continuing to exploit poor countries for all their natural resources while your hidden agenda of charity work is making Africans kill each other.

The So-called United Nations is under your full control of command. We are the Second United Nations putting the United Nations in checks and balances by holding U N accountable

Systemic invisible Exploitation of United Countries of the World of Africa Natural Resources will soon stop with the intervention of our Non-Political party.
Enough Torturing and spying the Author of this book who will be three steps ahead of you if you intend to harm, torture him. he Have a dream for every country in the world to be as rich a country as yours.

We have so many Dreams for the United Countries of the World of Africa. So do not be an obstacle to our progress in making our future country to be our country United Countries of the World of Africa. If you can help us reach our goals as best as you can and however you can.

Wish us Success in reaching our goals of one United Countries of the World of Africa

Help us Ending all the systemic modern colonization and systemic Modern Natural Resources Extraction and exploitation of us soon to be our country United Countries of the World of Africa.

Give us a hand by not setting us to be divided on killing each other.

Do not interfere in our Continent Africa affairs. Please mind your business. Focus on solving Homelessness, Crime and violence in your country and we will focus on ours.

Do not continue to be the Policeman of the world so that your soldiers do not continue to die in foreign lands endlessly. Focus on solving your Gender and race Systemic Job application Racism in your country. We do not have racism in our future Discrimination free Prosperous, peaceful, just and United Countries of the World of Africa land of True Opportunities. Do not be Jealous of Africa's Bright future. Do not block the author of this book Zerit Teklay for his dreams not come true by putting him in to Prison, by Creating fake news of Suicide, do not poison his food, do not send him spy girlfriends, or spy so called friends. Please know that until his Dream of forming the United Countries of the World of Africa, he will be his own only best friend, trusting only himself. Do not kill him in fake Car Accident or fake suicide. Do not pull him over pretending to be a police officer to hijack or force him. His Top Martial Art Skills. If you pull him over pretending to be a police officer, he will call 911 on you to confirm the validity of your badge. If you are any spy, an Intelligence agent assigned to follow him, you already lost your case. Because he will sacrifice his own life on behalf of the idea of the formation of the United Countries of the world of Africa. All rights reserved. He will not be complying with you on sharing his Intellectual

properties only reserved to African Presidents. You cannot kill him like you killed 16th U S President Abraham Lincoln
You cannot kill him like you killed 35th U S president J F Kennedy was killed.

You cannot kill him like Martin Luther king was killed
You cannot kill him like Malcolm X was killed.
You cannot kill him like Doctor Sebi Was killed.
you cannot kill him like Nipsey Hustle was killed. you cannot kill him like George Flayed was killed.
You cannot kill him like Muammar Gadhafi was killed.
He is no harm to any one or to any country in this world.

You can kill his physical body, but you will fail to kill this book. This book has already been in Action in the minds of millions of people all over the world. Even if you kill him physically, the legacy of this book will be carried on to one day a United countries of the World of Africa to be formed in the real world even if it may take the next 100 years from today.
You may kill his physical body, but the legacies of this book of the Formation of Global Constitution of eight presidents of eight continents legacy will be in the minds of billions of all people of the world.

Why Us?

Why is our non-political organization the most valuable and Unique nonpolitical organization in the World today?

Because we call ourselves as We the people of planet earth!

 Because we do not such a thing called my country your country your labeling discrimination! We think globally not individually.

Country name labeling and discrimination.

Because in our new country to be Country
Planet earth, we do not discriminate against job applicants based on their race or gender.

Because in our beloved country planet earth,
We do not have Zip Code based systemic modern racism.

we do not create any enemies. Therefore, we do not need soldiers.
Because we have no soldiers to die in
Foreign land wars they do not comprehend and understand.

Because in our Country, our wives and
Girlfriends do not wear makeup and they do not have to wear High hill shoes in offices. They are naturally beautiful inside out. Everything we, our wives and
Girlfriends do saves time & energy and resources. We will be working to open a new revolution on the greatest fall of Cosmetics and Make up companies. Let women restore natural beauty their confidence and natural self-esteem by just not having to spend thousands of hours on make ups and thousands of dollars on trying to wear make up to look artificially beautiful. All women who women who get in our job interviews will not need high hills shoes. It is not the high hills shoes women wear brings greatest value, it the fact that a woman's practical intelligence of solving problems on promoting a better world is our only requirement for any job application with us.

Our No makeup global revolution, global Justice, global peace, global prosperity and global safety and international security of one world, one flag, one, currency and one global international constitution will prevail to enlighten all women of the world who have lost confidence of natural beauty.

Because in our country planet Earth, we
Do not discriminate against our people based on their credit scores.

Because we do not get trapped in the
Systemic trap of Credit card companies who get richer and richer. We do not use credit cards at all.

- We enlighten society to wake up and start a personal revolution of no more using credit cards and loans.

Because we do not get trapped in the systemic trap of so-called Personal loan, Car loan, Mortgage loans and business loan. Our past loans and credit cards were only for experimental purposes. After we pay off the past credit cards and loans, we will publish another book based on tangible evidence of how we become financially free by paying off all our credit cards and loans debt. We have officially closed all our credit cards to be an example to society to wake up and exit from the traps of credit cards and loans.

We do not pay any loan interests because we have zero loans. Loans are one of the main causes why the rich get richer, and the poor get poorer and poorer.

What is our solution to make the poor get Richer? We have the following two simple solutions

Solution one. do not get into the trap of
Credit cards and loans debt. Pay off all your Credit card debts and loan debts and sign a divorcee agreement with yourself to never again apply for credit cards and loans. If you practice Solution 1, you are on your way to be financially free from any loan or credit debt.

Solution two. make a deliberate decision to make your credit score to be awfully bad and poor credit score. By doing that,
you do not have to worry about thinking of Loans. They systematically trap your mindset bay fooling you the better your credit score, the better of you are. The truth is if your credit score gets bad, rich people, rich banks lose millions of profits they were supposed to make of your loan interest rates. Be grateful if your credit score is bad because your credit score being bad saves you from financial ruin of getting loans. Do not be brain washed by the credit score systematic brainwash. Be wise and make your credit score to be unbelievably bad so that you will no longer get any loans for the rest of your life which will make you be financially free from loans. Only wise people will apply this highly classified valuable information deliberately ruining your credit score to be financial free. This part will not make loan and credit card companies happy because they do not want you know the hidden agenda and evil scheme behind the idea of loans and credit cards.

Solution 3: Do not work

paycheck to paycheck. If you find yourself working paycheck to paycheck, remember the greatest tragedy of you as employee being easily replaceable. There is a famous saying which says "Anyone who works paycheck to paycheck is one paycheck away to be a homeless and one paycheck away to be jobless. If not two hundred skills, have skills of thinking about being an employer mind set, not an employee mind set.

Solution 4 Own your own

business with legal business entity called LLC taxed as S corporation

Solution 5 Invest on Index stocks, Stocks, bonds, options, real estate

Dedication
To

- To the Author's Father Teklay Sebhatleab
- To the Author's mother Tiebe Mebrahtu
- To the Author's brothers and sisters
- To the Author's family and friends
- To the Author's Colleagues and chiefs of staff
- To all Eritrean Freedom fighters who died on behalf of the independence of Eritrea
- To independence and Eritrea's Independence Day May 24, 1991
- To Eritrea's Martery's 's day June 20th
- To all American freedom fighters who died on behalf of the Independence of United States of America.
- To July 4th United States Independence Day
- To all the past freedom fighters for independence who died on behalf of the independence of their country

- To Thomas Jefferson, Benjamin Franklin, John Adams, Roger Sherman, Robert Livingston

- To United Countries of the World international constitution Law of the Land

- To Eritrea's 1997 Constitution
- To the United Countries of the World of Africa progress of forming a one United countries of the world of Africa: Under One United African Currency. Under One United African Flag. Under one United African Constitution for the United Countries of Africa.
  :

- No government is above the law

- No Government official is above the law

- No Person is above the law

- Everyone must obey the law

- American Revolutionary war April 19, 1775, September 3, 1783

- United States Independence Day July 4th, 1776

Dedication to United Countries of the World international constitution Preamble

Note that the source of the Constitution of Eritrea published in Tigrigna and English is from the 1997 Eritrea's Constitution
Ratified by the State of Eritrea

The Future Supreme law of our planet earth
Land Constitution of United Countries of the World ready to one day be used by all nations of our planet earth to keep international peace, International Justice, International Prosperity, and International Security of our world land of our planet earth.

Note about friendship not mixing with dirty politics:

"You do not kill enemies with hate

You kill enemies with love and human compassion

If you do not want to have no enemies throughout your life journey, do not side with politicians, be on the side of the people and you will not have enemies all your life." ~ Zerit Teklay.

The Author Zerit once told us, He has no hate to any people of any country in the world. He says it is not the people, but Governments are the main reason for all the past and current wars and terrorisms. Zerit at one of his private speeches mentions how diversity in friendship can make a person wiser than smarter. In his speech he mentions all his friend from other countries who has nothing to do the dirty and filthy politics and dirty politicians. The main cause of war and peace in our world of war and terror is not committed by people instead all the war and terror in the world today is engineered by governments who are supposed to protect, serve, and defend human beings.

Our Conflict and civil wars resolution noble ideas, solutions of holding war criminals accountable and inventions our independently created Mass construction Artificial intelligence and cyber security intellectual properties

We will play historic role in keeping international peace, International Freedom of Expression and International freedom of speech, international freedom of Press, International freedom of assembly, International Justice, International prosperity, international safety, and international security of one peaceful and Justice oriented one world under one flag, one currency, one constitution and one love.

Every intellectual property we invent is to be found nowhere in any device. Our intellectual properties are saved in our human brain which is the main engine of all the Artificial intelligence and cyber security creations.
We cannot be hacked or be traced. We will make history in creating a peaceful and just world we imagined in this book.

Our dreams are big. And one day our dreams will come true. Because dreams do really come true eventually whether it takes 30 years or 245 years.
This book will eventually be in revolutionary history books to tell history of progress, reform, peace, justice, equality, liberty and change for the overall good of all society and all human beings.

We would like the public of the world to know, we are taking an initiative to send this book to all responsible War criminals and de capot colonization, systemic modern Neo colonizers war and colonization criminals to stop their manipulative hidden agenda of Modern colonization.

Dear Systemic Neo and de cap to modern systemic colonial powers, please stop exploiting Natural Resources of Poor continents such as Africa by creating divide, rule of Indigenous people and exploit their Natural resources. Poor continents such as continent African leaders need to wise up to end modern colonization.

The modern colonial powers are much worse than the Corona virus Pandemic which has suddenly changed how we live our lives.

The systemic colonial, neo colonial and de capot colonial powers are like the Corona virus to the progress and prosperity of the Continent Africa-Eritrea where the Author of this book was born in 1981.

African Leaders urgently need to unite to find New Political Vaccine to free Continent Africa from Neo colonialism, modern systemic colonialism and systemic de capot colonialism.

Civil wars and social unrests among poor continent African Leaders are caused by foreign countries who are systematically, technologically, politically, and psychologically super advanced.

We need to form United Africa Intelligence Agency to detect neo colonialist, de capot colonialist, and modern systemic modern colonialist powerful countries from not interfering in our continent Africa Internal Affairs. hunger for power, glory, gold, God are the main reasons why colonial powers will always systematically neo colonize and de capot colonize Poor continents such as continent Africa.

Enough are enough Colonialist countries. Your days of systemic colonization are numbered. Leave mother land Africa alone. Do not continue to brainwash African leaders to continue kill each other by civil wars and border wars.

When and if implemented

Our intellectual ideas, policies, laws written in the book will one day keep international peace, international justice, international prosperity, international freedoms of speech, freedoms of press, freedoms of lawful assembly, International Liberty, international true democracy, international safety, international security of one World, one flag, one currency, one constitution and one love.

This book is one of the most transparent books you will ever enjoy reading. Because we authored this book with bravery, courage, heroism and without fearing any consequences of unlawful imprisonment for authoring our heroic book based on truth.

We cannot be arrested for writing such a revolutionary book, because we know and understand the Supreme law of land of all laws of all nations of the world.

We are using our rights designed by the Founding fathers of the Supreme laws of all nations.

We humbly consider ourselves the sons and daughters of the Founding fathers of Supreme laws of lands who gave us the bill of rights and liberty to express our ideas, laws, and policies without fearing any unlawful imprisonment and unlawful torture.

So, please make sure our book Author who have big ideas and aspirations does not get unlawfully imprisoned for writing the truth about war crimes, war criminals, about systemic Racism, systemic de capot colonization, systemic modern colonization, and modern systemic zip code-based racism and systemic evil Neo colonization, and the new revolution of the great fall of Credit Cards and loan companies.

Our understanding of all Supreme laws of all lands and all nations of the world is our main assurance and guard against unlawful arrests, unlawful imprisonment and unlawful torture that can potentially happen for writing and exposing the secrets and exposing highly classified   systemic modern crimes committed by war criminal countries and War criminal commanders of all war's criminal acts.

This book will peacefully revolutionize American and World history for the better, safer, and just world of Tranquility and true freedom and liberty to life and pursuit of happiness.

The title other title of our book which is in publishing progress is called:

Dedication to No Government, no government official or No person is above the law.

Everyone must obey the law.

In our book we have written our demands and concerns for 46th U S president Jeo Biden, and 46th U S Vice president Kamala Harris to respond to our demands, proposals, and ideas:

- pertaining the end of De capot colonization, the end of modern Systemic Neo colonialism

- Pertaining pulling Military bases from all over the world of foreign lands

- Pertaining Unlawful imprisonment of visionary activists and Revolutionary peaceful laws and Invention's developers such as ourselves.

- Pertaining systemic racism based on Credit Scores, Skin color and gender

- Pertaining Global De legalization and banning of the porno graphic industry which is the main source of human trafficking and little girls kidnapping. According to our many years of research and independent investigations, we found out that where there exist porn industry, human trafficking and little girl kidnapping will never end. So, to end human trafficking and little girls trafficking, Porno graphic industry must be closed globally by all nations. We commend all world leaders to unanimously close the Pornography industry once and for good. We commend the citizen of the world to not support the porn industry by not watching any porn in the name of all the victims of the pornographic industry.

- Pertaining our demand for his excellency President of Eritrea President Isaias Afwerki, President of Tigray Debretsion Gebremichael, Prime Minister of Ethiopia Dr. Abby Ahmed Ali to join us on the Upcoming United Nations Peace talk in Geneva Switzerland to end the Civil War in Ethiopia once and for good.

- Pertaining the call to Action for ending homelessness worldwide

- Pertaining other miscellaneous issues, concerns, and conflicts resolution solutions

According to the Supreme laws of all nation's lands Constitution, we have rights to hold any branch of government in check and balance to not abuse power, to not committing War Crimes in the name of to defend and protect by invading other countries autonomous foreign lands. Invading other countries autonomy is a criminal act.

To have a good night sleep every day,
Do the right thing every day.

Your conscious will thank you every day of your life if you do the right thing every day of your life for the rest years of your lifetime.

Guaranteed you will have good night sleep for the rest of your life by just consistently doing the right thing every day.

Re-Read this book to stay focus on doing the right thing every day of your life journey.

Doing the right thing is not easy in our world which is tragically designed and engineered by of Greed, Glory hunger, Power Hunger, Poor continents Natural resource systemic exploitation hunger.

Re-place all Your Hungers of Greed, Glory hunger, Power Hunger, Poor continents Natural resource systemic exploitation hunger by doing the right thing hunger. By doing so you will have good night sleep every day of your life if you live in this temporary thing we call "Life"

To have a good night sleep every day,

Do the right thing every day.

Whenever you can, however you can participate

- Stopping systemic De capto colonization
- Stopping systemic Neo Colonization
- Stopping Systemic Modern Colonization
- Stopping Racism based on skin color and gender

- Stopping Unlawful imprisonment of political prisoners
- Stopping The Pornography Industry
- Stopping The Credit Cards and Loans Companies at least by not applying for credit card or loans. Stop the rich Credit card and loan companies get richer while you get poorer and poorer by applying for credit cards and loans.
- Stop Human Trafficking
- Stopping Deportation of Political Asylum seekers
- Stopping Prostitution and Prostitution brothels
- Stopping not to vote to any person who have history of War Crimes
- Stopping Invading foreign lands without the consent of the Indigenous people being invaded
- Stopping movie industry from making War movies, War documentaries, and porn movies.
- Stopping any alive world leader or president from committing War crimes.

- To 46th US President, Mr. President Joe Biden ,46th U S Vice President Kamal Harris
- To his Excellency President of Eritrea Mr. President Isaias Afwerki
- To Current Tigray TDF leader of Mr. President Debretsion Gebremichael, Prime Minister of Ethiopia Dr. Abiy Ahmed Ali
- To All current African Presidents
- To all Current Colonial Power presidents

- One Flag, One Currency, One Global International constitution visionary idea
- United Countries of the World of the World future global Constitutional 27 Article
- Testing Freedom of expression and freedom of press Experiment number

- Future United Countries of the World of the World Universal 5 Global constitutional laws and Articles
- United Countries of the World of the World Global Preamble
- Miscellaneous facts about us
- Partial United Countries of the World Constitution
- Credit Cards, loans, and credit score systems Trappe of why the rich get richer and the poor and middle class get poorer and poorer
- Our Demands and concerns
- Experiment one
- Our Action plans, ideas, and practical Homelessness solutions
- The rise of new revolution of United Countries of the World of the world Homelessness ending honest Non-Political party
- Charities investigation of funds misuse
- the U S constitution.
- Why are we Unique?
- What is our solution to make the poor get richer and richer instead of the poor getting poorer and poorer?
- The criminal acts of Natural resources exploitations of continent Africa and the rise of United Countries of the World of Africa Combating Systemic de capto colonization, systemic neo colonization and modern invisible systemic colonization of poor continent Africa soon to be rich continent Africa by our commitment to make Continent Africa to be the next G 8 countries.
- The State of Autonomous and independent Eritrea constitution of 1997 in Tigrigna language which is the official language of Eritrea and Eritrean Government.
- The State of Autonomous and independent Eritrea constitution of 1997 in English Language

- The United Countries of the World international constitution Supreme law of the land Amendments.
- Dedications
- Eritrean freedom fighters including the author of this book late father Teklay Heroism, resilience, bravery, and sacrifice on behalf of Eritrea's Independence
- We hope to meet at the next Geneva peace talk convention about ending the civil war in Ethiopia. We are honest non-Politicians Peace Mediators among nations which are in civil war currently. Ethiopia is currently in a merciless bloody civil war, horror, and unrest. Enough of civil war is our call to Action for Eritrea, Tigray, and Ethiopia to seize fire and end the civil war before Continent Africa Gets into Continent Africa Continental War 1. Learn from World War One and World War 2 African leaders. Do not kill each other African leaders. Be Wise and Save Continent Africa from civil wars Continent of Africa War 1. No African Country wins a War on motherland Africa. Every African country in Africa is losing in wars and always will lose in unlawful wars African presidents do not understand. African Presidents, please focus on ending civil wars instead of continuing killing your people in civil wars. Wise Up African Presidents. Make history on making Continent Africa to be peaceful, justice oriented, and a safe, secure, and prosperous continent.
- Some Blank page in this book is reserved for you or your kids to write whatever you or your kids want to write about, about something you care, or your kids care about, and which is dear to you and your kids.
- Author of this book, late father Mr. Teklay was one of Eritrea's freedom fighters for independence Chief of intelligence Fedayin Hero during the Eritrean struggle for independence. The author is carrying on the legacy of his father to preserve the independence of Eritrea to forever be an Autonomous independent country for all generations to come. Our best

Wishes for All the Upcoming Eritrea's Independence days to be celebrated every 24 May of every year.

We the United Countries of the World:

We are anonymous human beings from many nations and many occupations will anonymously and silently will be protecting and defending the preservation of Independent Eritrea to forever be an independent and Autonomous country. We will do so with silence whereby all our strategies to be found nowhere in any computer system, device, or paper. Our extraordinary Resources, two hundred inventions reserved for Eritrea and the continent of Africa will make Eritrea the next Singapore no matter how long it takes. We will not make useless Noise on Any social Medias. We work in silence on preserving and defending independent countries to continue to be independent and Autonomous, and our work speaks for itself.

- We are anonymous human beings from many nations and many walks of life. We wish all the people including the people of Tigray to be in peace. No one can defeat any people who fight for independence and Autonomy. The people of Eritrea fought 30 years bloody war in fighting against former colonialist Ethiopia. Geopolitics of East Africa is always in turmoil Because of the evil systemic manipulation of Superpowers powers indirect power presence in East Africa, the civil war in Ethiopia is actively being exploited by western modern evil colonizers which have brain washed African leaders and presidents for many years. Until now Indirect and systemic Brain washing of African leaders by evil colonial powers of 21rst century is still going on. that is why Africa with all its rich wealthy Natural resources is still the poorest continent because of the superpower indirect form of colonization of the United Countries of the world of One United Africa.

- We are pro Freedom for Independence of countries. Let the people of any country be free from indirect modern slavery and modern colonization.

- Let there be peace in the Entire continent of Africa. Enough is enough. Civil War is not a solution. Let the Civil War in Ethiopia involving the countries of Eritrea, Tigray and Ethiopia end this war and terror of civil war in Ethiopia by reconciliation and open discussion.

- We are inviting to the next United Nations Geneva peace talk convention to all the three president His excellency President of Eritrea Mr. President Isaias Afwerki, current president of Tigray Mr. President Debretsion Gebremichael, Prime Minister of Ethiopia Dr. Abiy Ahmed Ali.

- **Another example is** for example, the British tried to colonize Nepal, but the mountainous terrain that the Nepalese were used to was insurmountable to the British army. Similarly, several powers have tried to colonize Afghanistan, but its rugged terrain and tribalistic culture have made colonization impossible. Now Afghanistan is a Free Independent country after 20 years of foreign modern colonization in the name of dishonest to protect and defend political correctness.

- We admire Executive action of 46th President of United States of America his excellency Mr. President Joe Biden for making history on pulling all troops from Afghanistan as he promised. We found out 46th President of the United States of America his excellency Mr. President Joe Biden is one a kind of president who says what he means and who does what he says. This and his nomination of first African American United States Supreme Court Judge Ketanji Brown Jackson is the greatest blessing the American people land of the free witness true democracy and equal opportunities.

- Because of the executive order of 46th president of United States to free the peoples of Afghanistan to be free, today Afghanistan is a free country free from any foreign interference. When it comes to foreign policy, let all the upcoming U S presidents follow the examples of 46th President of the United States his excellency Mr. President Joe Biden,

- Although we do not side neither with democrats nor the republicans, every election day of the United States, although we vote based on results not on promises not kept. We vote based on the foreign policies candidates have not because of what they say on the re hearse tv interviews or empty promises.

- We salute you Mr. President Joe Biden for doing the right thing. and in advance, we gladly would like to tell you that we will vote for you to win the second term to be the president of the United States for 8 years. You have our millions of votes not because you are a democrat or not, because the results you bring in making not only America a great country, but also the world in general. We value your mind set of global justice and equal opportunities for all. We honor your heroic and Historic extraordinary executive action liberating Afghanistan from modern systemic Neo colonialism. We wish all upcoming presidents follow your Example. Dear American people: please remember this…when you vote to any president…. vote not based on what a candidate say but based on the actions.

- United Countries of the world Global Preamble

We the People of the planet earth, in Order to form a more   perfect Union,   establish   Justice,   ensure   International Tranquility, provide for the common defense, promote the general Welfare, and secure the Blessings of Liberty to all people in the world and all people of the world Posterity, do ordain and establish this Constitution.
The constitution of the United Countries of the World

was originally written in 2018, ratified in 2021, and in operation since 2021.

The United Countries of the World international constitution is the world's newest constitution to be in the history of the world. Its first three words – "We the People" – affirm that the governments of the United Countries of the World exist to serve all world human beings' citizens. The supremacy of the people through their elected Presidents is recognized in Article I, which to elect seven presidents from the seven continents of our world planet Earth.

- United Countries of the World global anthem is in progress of being invented.
- We are borderless with no entry visa needed.
- We come from different races, professions, and all levels of society.
- World flag is our official flag to be
- No employment discrimination based on race and gender exist in our employment job application form
- No credit score check needed
- Ownership of guns or weapons of mass destruction is illegal by United Countries of the World international constitution Article 1
- We, The Yes, We Can United Countries of the World Non-Political party are Anti Current War Criminals and War Crimes happening throughout the World.

- We are committed to maintaining international peace and promoting social progress, better living standards and human rights of all world countries

- We are publishing this book on behalf of Global peace, Global justice, and Global prosperity, on behalf of the wellbeing of every human being and on behalf all countries which are at bloody, merciless civil wars and Unrest. And on behalf of all the political asylum seekers starting such as
  Eritrean Political asylum seekers.

- We are publishing our books for campaign of Preserving Global Peace, Preserving Global Justice, Holding Global War Criminals Accountable
- We are publishing our books for Holding Global Corruption criminals accountable, Holding Global terrorist Criminals accountable, Holding Global Sex and Human Traffickers criminals accountable, Holding Sexual Harassment Abusers accountable, Holding Foreign Lands Invaders criminals accountable, Holding the Continent of Africa Natural Resources Exploiters Criminals disguised in name of charities Accountable. Ending Global Hunger and Global prosperity are core missions our honest nonpolitical party.
- We are publishing for Eritrea and its struggles to be addressed to all world nations that one day Eritrea 1997 constitution to be implemented even though its implementation makes take time due to the Geo-political Unrest of East Africa. We will send this book to his Excellency President of Eritrea Mr. President Isaias Afwerki to peacefully implement the Constitution of Eritrea to be fully implemented in the grounds of Eritrea and its people and by its government without the interference of foreign powers.
- In our laws, we members of the United Countries of the World do not commit any crimes of overthrowing any Government by Force. We are pro peace full change. We do not own guns and we do not kill any human being
- Zerit Teklay AKA Yes, we can be honest non -politician is the sole founder of the United Countries of the World Constitution. He is Self-Made Honest non-politician

  Philosopher, Inventor and founding father of Yes, we can unite countries of the world international constitution

- Our United Countries of the World international constitution is in progress of being written, re written, and the entire Universal constitution of our glob will be published in the second edition of this book
  Series.

- We are drafting a case to hold Anti War Criminals accountable, War Crimes and foreign lands invasion and Exploitation of African Natural Resources by the Western countries. We publish all our cases of United Countries of the World versus any country's crimes in our books to be read by all world citizens.

- We are the Yes, We Can United Countries of the World global organization.

- Our Commander in chief of our Global Nonpolitical party AKA name is The Yes, we can be honest non-Politician free thinker and visionary ideas inventor. He is also known by his legal name Zerit. He speaks ten languages; he is the founding father of our party called The Yes, we can United Countries of the World global Organization

- the inventor of an Artificial Intelligence Equipment of mass construction which the world will never see until our Global Non-Political party dreams and aspirations will come true.

- His Artificial intelligence invention of mass construction will always surpass all Artificial intelligence inventions currently in use in our today's world of Artificial intelligence and cyber-Security.

- Only poor continents who need it the most will be the only direct beneficiaries of all our ideas and inventions. We dream to eradicate poverty, dictatorship, and tyranny in poor continents such as

Africa. Our ideas cannot be hacked or traced, because we save our ideas in our brain not in our devices. Live smart and wise not to be harmed.

- We welcome all people of the world from all occupations to join our newly formed United Countries of the World global organization. We welcome all Political scientists, philosophers, psychologists, Artificial Intelligence Inventors, Computer scientists, Current live presidents of all countries, Public Servants, governments employees, pilots, Navy seal, Marine corps, Air force, Airport employees, diplomats, Taxi drivers, truck drivers, bus drivers, train drivers, Nasa Drivers, Space Satellite station owners, commercial and passenger pilots, intelligence agents, over 3 million Homeless worldwide.

One of our Agenda on doing well to society without expecting anything in return is:

His noble ideas to end homeless in our globe are the most valuable and precious ideas the world will be glad to embrace eventually.

So, if you see any homeless human being, do not look down on him, do not despise him, and do not judge him.

Help him or help her if you can help him or her however you can whenever you can wherever you go. Because no one was born homeless, no one was supposed to be homeless. Our Commander in chief will dedicate some of his life combating homelessness and War Crimes by travelling from east coast to west coast, from U S to Africa and all countries one country at a time. List of all the countries and cities where we the United Countries of the World we will operate are:

Streets Nashville Tennessee homeless street corners,

Manila Philippines, Streets of Enda Mariam Homeless Street in his home birth Eritrea, in the streets of Ethiopia Homeless corner streets, In homeless street corners of England, in Homeless Street corners of Uganda, Ukraine, United States, Afghanistan, Australia, Austria, Azerbaijan, Bangladesh, Bosnia and Herzegovina, Brazil, Burkina Faso, Cameron, Central American Republic, Chile, China, Colombia, Congo, Czech Republic

Denmark, Egypt, Estonia, Ethiopia, Eritrea, Finland, Germany, Ghana, Greece, Grenada, Guatemala,
Honduras, Hong Kong, Hungary, India, Iceland, Indonesia, Iran, Iraq, Ireland, Israel, Italy, Japan, Jordan, Latvia, Liechtenstein, Lithuania, Luxembourg, Mexico, Mozambique, Myanmar,
Netherlands, New Zealand, Nigeria, Norway, Pakistan, Peru, Philippines, Poland, Portugal, Romania, Russia, Servia, Slovenia, Somalia, South Africa, South Korea, North Korea, South Korea, South Sudan, Spain, Sudan, Sweden, Switzerland, Syria, Thailand, Togo, Turkey, Uganda, Ukraine, United Kingdom, Yemen, Vietnam, Zimbabwe, and Libya.

The rise of the United Countries of the World Homelessness Non-Political party is in progress.

After ending homelessness in Nashville Tennessee, we will make the biggest Homeless Non-Political party peaceful nonviolent protest America Has ever seen in the history of homelessness in America. The first biggest Homeless protest in American and World History. By our Short and easy to understand plans of action to End homelessness in America, there will be zero homeless in America in 365 days.

We have the solutions, Ideas, Practical Philosophies of Ending homelessness in America and other countries such as Eritrea in 365 days. America will be the first country to have zero homeless in the history of the world by the plans we have lined up.

In all our journey we will always be law-abiding citizens who obey all the supreme laws of the land.

Our top role Model Countries mentioned above have passed our 15 years through background checks that all these countries have clean backgrounds not colonizing or invading other autonomous countries. These countries mentioned above had to **fight back against attempts of Oppressive cruel colonial powers**. They had to fight back attempts at colonization. For example, United States and the American people fought to free their country from form British colonizer which colonized America from year 1607 to year 1783. Eritrea struggle for independence from year 1961 to year 1991 is the number 1 top role model country of Bravery, heroism, and Resilience history of Struggle for independence from the former oppressive Colonialist Ethiopia

Former oppressive Ethiopian Dictators Haile Selassie and Mengistu Hailemariam colonized Eritrea for over 30 years. But the Eritrean freedom fighters for independence fought for what is right to free their people and country from former Colonialist Ethiopia of Haile Selassie and Mengistu Hailemariam dictatorial colonization of Eritrea. After 30 years of extraordinary heroism, resilience, and bravery, Eritrean freedom fighters liberated their homeland Eritrea to be free from Oppressive dictatorship of Mengistu Hailemariam and Oppressive Dictatorship of Haile Selassie in 1991. **Eritrea today** is an independent country from May 24, 1991, until now in 2022 this book is being published.

Eritrea will forever be an autonomous independent country from generation to generation to come. No country, or No president will ever Annex Eritrea with any country without the consent of the People of Eritrea.

Chapter 17

Global Constitution Articles to be implemented in future World.

Constitution will be as follows:

Article 1

Ensures all governments are not above the supreme law.

Article 2

Run checks on whether all countries are fully abiding by the supreme law.

Under Article 2 supreme constitutional law of the United Countries of the world international constitution, the author of this book and the drafter of the United Countries of the World international constitution has selected the constitution of the United States of America, which is fully implemented and the Constitution of the State of Eritrea, which has never fully been implemented since May 23, 1997. When the constitution of the United countries of the world become an International Legitimate Constitution   of   the world, the United States of America constitution and the State of Eritrea's unfinished and unimplemented constitution will be the first two constitutions to be subject to checks and balances under United Countries of the World's Supreme law Court, article 2. By then, United States of America and all other countries who have Military bases in foreign lands will pull out all their military bases from all foreign lands according to the International Constitution.

Unimplemented constitution of the state of Eritrea will be fully implemented according to the International Constitution of Planet earth.

Article 3

The United Nations system of governance and administration will be replaced by the new rules and regulations based on the system and administration of the United Countries of the World.

Article 4

Banning and illegalization of guns and weapons of mass destruction ownership. Also, the right of bearing arms shall be repealed.

Article 5

Banning and global illegalization of making war movies.

Article 6

Global illegalization of foreign lands' invasion. By this provision, invading any autonomous, sovereign state is illegal.

Under article 6, all countries will and must pull out their military bases and soldiers from foreign lands.

Article 7

Global illegalization of systemic modern colonization, which is the act or process of settling among and establishing control over the indigenous people of an area.

Article 8

Shutting down of the pornography industry and shutting down of pornographic videos. Where there are

Pornographic videos, there will always be endless child pornography and endless Cruel human trafficking of innocent girls for the enslavement of the pornography industry. So, when and if Article 8 become law, there will not be human trafficking of innocent girls for pornography enslavement. The pornography industry will be globally closed. And all brothels worldwide will be closed for good.

Article 9

Global De legalization of dictatorship and
Tyranny. Under Article 9 any kind of dictatorship will be illegal.

Under article 9 our world will finally be free from dictators and oppressive governments

Article 10

This book content to be translated to every
Language currently spoken in the world

Article 11

Global De legalization of modern colonialism

Freedom of expression and Freedom of press Experiment number 5: Testing the waters of whether there is absolute Liberty of Freedom of expression and freedom of press is why we deliberately indicate some of our writings by saying "Experiment of freedom of expression and freedom of press number 5.

If the current colonial powers abolish colonialism modern Neo colonialism like they abolish slavery, our doors are open to make them our new allies. If today's modern colonization colonizers continue Neo colonizing other countries and continue to exploit natural resources of other countries, we will not have any alliance with them. We are transparent in our missions.

Article 12

Wi-Fi service to be available in every part in every corner of the entire world.

Article 13

Global De legalization of employment
Discrimination based on race and gender. Under article 13 all job application forms throughout the world will not have race and gender discriminatory criteria.

Article 14

Global De legalization of credit score system
Of systemic discrimination. Under article 14 our entire planet earth will be free from the system discriminatory systems of Credit Scores and Zip code systems of discrimination.

Article 15

Global De legalization of Credit cards and
Loans. The main reasons why the rich get richer, and the poor get poorer are Credit cards and loans. Therefore, Under Article 15 All Credit card and loan companies must cease to exist and must be delegalized by the supreme law on the planet earth constitution of the United countries of the World.

Article 16

Global Shutting down of the manufacturing
Of Guns and Weapons of Mass Destruction companies. By this article 16 all companies private or governmental guns Mass destruction manufacturing companies will be banned from producing and manufacturing any types of arms of mass destruction.

Article 17

Global De legalization of prostitution and
Prostitution brothels

Article 18

Global De legalization of overthrowing any legitimate government by violent force will be illegal. Under article 18 except the freedom for independence, overthrowing any legitimate
Government by force or by coup d etat   is a criminal act subject to criminal persecution under international court of law which will be based on Geneva Switzerland.

Article 19 Balance of Power Act world presidents' election.

Election of World president and World Vice president
Under article 19, 193
Countries
Of all the nation's presidents, there will be candidates for the World Presidential election. Under article 19, the World presidents will be elected only for two term for two years. The World Presidents of the eight continents will choose his or her vice president. The Vice president of the world will also only have a one-time vice-presidential term.

Article 20

Global De legalization of forced labor
And forced Military conscription

Article 21

Except anyone who has committed any crimes, all asylum seekers are approved to get asylum protection without any immigration interviews or immigration due process. Under article 21 supreme

Law of our planet earth immigration laws of the United Countries of the World every asylum seeker who has a clean background will be approved to get asylum protection. Under this International Immigration law, there will not be any forced involuntary deportations.

Article 22

Any country who starts or wage war
Against any other country will be subject to consequences of international constitution laws of violation of article 22

Article 23

Any person's
RETALIATION to any person out of resentment is Illegal. According to article 23, any person who causes any harm to any one by revenge and retaliation will be criminally prosecuted in the international court of law.

Article 24

Any country which wages war to another country out of retaliation, Animosity, exploitation of Natural resources will be criminally prosecuted under the International Universal law of Anti
Retaliation act, Article 24. No matter how powerful or mighty the country may be, no country is above the LAWS of Global International constitution laws.

Article 25

According to Article 25, overthrowing any government without the consent of the
People is criminal acts.
Any person   who overthrows any government shall be criminally prosecuted in the Supreme laws of the Global constitution.

Article26

the end of De facto colonization

De facto colonization is exploitation of other countries' land and exploitation of other countries People for economic gain of the colonizers. In other words, de facto colonization is a systemic modern colonization where other countries experience a de facto colonization, in which their lands and people are exploited for economic gain. Example of de facto colonization is that the colonizing power did not establish its government in that country. For example, for much of the twentieth century, Britain had the rights to all the oil under Iran's land. The British government did not officially rule Iran, but it did affect most of the government's policy because it owned the country's most valuable resource. Likewise, China was never colonized formally, but the Opium Wars were fought to ensure that British opium merchants had access to Chinese markets.

Article 27

Under Article 27 of the Supreme law of the Future United Countries of the World of the World, any country who directly or indirectly, systematically, or unsystematically interfere in the internal affairs of any country will be criminally prosecuted. under article 27 No Foreign country should interfere interferences in any autonomous country internal and external affairs. Any country who violates Article 27 will be prosecuted in our future United Countries of World Criminal Court which will be based on Geneva Switzerland.

Article 28

Anti-Systemic Birth Certificate Racism and discrimination Act,
Under Article 28, birth certificate-based racism and discrimination is a criminal act. Under article 28 any person elected and voted by the people will be a president of any country regardless of his or her birth certificate.
Article 28 challenge law makers of all nation to pass laws of this Article 28 of
Anti-Systemic Birth Certificate Racism and discrimination Act to be used in all Supreme laws of rule of laws of all nations and lands of the world.

Article 29

Anti-Character Assassination Criminal Act,

Under article 29, assassinating any person's character is a criminal act. Any person, any government official, or any government will be held accountable and will be criminally prosecuted in the global Supreme law of all lands for committing crimes of Character Assassination. Supreme Global law of all land's headquarters will be based in Geneva, Switzerland.

Article 30

Anti-Conspiracy theories Criminal Act,
Under article 30, any person, any government official, or any government will be held accountable and will be criminally prosecuted in the global Supreme law of all lands of all nations for committing crimes of conspiracy theories.

Article 31

Anti-false Accusations Criminal Act,

Under article 31, any person, any government official, or any government will be held accountable and will be criminally prosecuted in the global Supreme law of all lands of all nations for committing crimes of false accusations.

Article 32

Anti-Propaganda Criminal act,
Under article 32, any person, any government official, or any government will be held accountable and will be criminally prosecuted in the global Supreme law of all lands for committing crimes of propaganda. Supreme Global law of all land's headquarters will be based in Geneva,

Article 33

Anti-Black mailing Criminal act

Any person, any government official, or any government will be held accountable and will be criminally prosecuted in the global Supreme law of all lands for committing crimes of black mailing. Supreme Global law of all land's headquarters will be based in Geneva

Article 34

Anti-War movie production and Anti-War documentary productions criminal act...

According to Article 34, War movies, and War documentaries are the main catalysts of all upcoming wars including World War 3.

Any person, any government official or any government who encourages, takes part, or supports any War movie and War documentary productions will be criminally prosecuted in Global Supreme Court of law which will be based on Geneva Switzerland.

Article 35,

Anti-Police brutality criminal Act,
Any police officer who abuses power on brutality shooting, brutality chock holding, brutally beating any person will be prosecuted by the global Supreme law of all lands.

Article 36

Anti-violent words usage criminal act, of the words Kill, Gun, weapon, Bullet, hostage, Missiles, knife, murder, torture, assassinate criminal verbal languages.
All the miseries, problems, wars, crimes, corruptions, unhappiness, unrest in our world are caused by verbal usage of words such as "Kill you, murder you, torture you, Assassinate you and other violent verbal words.

Therefore, under Article 36, any person, any government official, any government, movie, and music industry who explicitly use words of violence such as killing, murdering, torturing, kidnapping, hijacking, terrorizing, Assassinating, will be criminally presented under the global Supreme law of all lands.

Article 37

Anti-Bad Nes Media, TV, and radio news criminal act,
All sad news will be subject to criminal persecution under article 37. We live in a very confused world where sad news is more appealing than good news.

Article 38

$7.7 billion U S Dollar Good News reward act for Television, Radio,

social Media Channels Under article 38, any TV station, Radio Station, Social media stations, News, and Magazine and YouTube channels which transmit only good news for the 30 years starting from year 2022 will   the winners of the Good News Academy Award of the United Countries of the world.

Good news TV stations, radio stations, and social media stations will be rewarded $7.7 billion after passing our Good News censorship background checks.

Eventually

Sooner or later We all the Human beings living in the world today inevitably each and EVERYONE of die. So let us live meaningful life of being the champions of Peace instead of being the champions of wars, Sanctions, Invasions, Colonization and competition of political powers.

Unfortunately mother nature death is the calling Equalizer of all human being which unexpectedly comes as a thief where by many of us including the author of this book who is 41 years old in year 2022, all current presidents, all War Criminals, all Current judges, all Dirty politicians, all Dirty lobbyist, all Dirty government official, all Dirty governments, all Dirty Dictators, all Dirty colonizers will be dead by at least year 2081 on mother nature's calling not realizing they keep leaving the world of injustice, wars, inequality behind them. This book hopes to all human being to do something about this book's provisions for the better world of tomorrow so that our children we leave behind live in a better world than we have. It is the duty of every human being pursue a dream of One World. One Flag. One Currency. One constitution which is a solution to everything written in this book. Let us not say "the famous saying which called "it is none of my business." Let us do something larger than ourselves in making our world to be a better place to live although no one lives forever. Let us remember an especially important truth which says" No one lives forever" and do something good to the world before we eventually be long gone like every huma being who is no longer alive today,

It is our business the business of each of us to leave our children a better world than it is today.

 if Governments do not pay attention to this book vision extraordinary warnings, wake up calls, reminders, and proposals. If government underestimate these books predictions, warnings, concerns, the world will be doomed to go back to the Stone Age where the entire world will experience horror and terror of Third World War between now years 2021 to year 2081. Prevention is better than cure. Preventing 3rd World War is wisdom of the few such as our intellectual properties of this book and other Intellectual properties we have saved in our brains. If we are alive, if our books live forever, Third Word War will be wisely prevented and avoided for good.

Article 40

Anti-Criminal act of Character Assassination of this book

Under article 40, any person, government official or government who commits the crime of character assassination in relation to this book will be criminally sued.

Whoever may try to oppress and defame the owner of this book, or even twist the author's words by making false legal allegations will be sued.

This book is written like a software code to defend itself and its ideas from being killed systematically. This book is three steps ahead in defending itself from all evils carried out by governments, oppressors, dirty politicians, dirty lobbyists, and dirty, greedy, systemic and modern colonizers. This book is our case book for keeping global justice, global peace, global safety, global security, and global prosperity. Let anyone who dreams to pursue Our vision of One World, One Flag, One Currency, and One Constitution use this book to promote global prosperity, global peace, and global justice.

Article 41

Under article 41, future supreme global rule of all laws of all lands, any person, spy agency, intelligence agency, government official, or government will be criminally persecuted for unlawfully hacking, tracking private citizens' smartphones, private citizens' laptops, and computer devices in the supreme global criminal court. Its headquarters will be in Geneva, Switzerland.

We do not save our intellectual properties and other important highly classified inventions in our phone devices and computer devices because after 20 years of research, we have found out that all the technological devices we use are 24/7 spied on and hacked without the consent of the people by dirty government spy agencies, intelligence agencies and national security agencies. We will not save our intellectual properties and two hundred inventions in any device until year 2081. We will not write our intellectual properties in any paper, notebook which can be stolen, lost, or destroyed. Our brain is our most un-hackable, untraceable asset where we will save all our intellectual properties and two hundred inventions until year 2081. Our intellectual properties and two hundred inventions will not be found anywhere in any device or notebook for the next 60 years until year 2081. We are 40 years ahead of any spy, intelligence agency or national security agency. All our books to be published, including this book, is written like a software code such that we are the only ones who can decode our books' content for the sake of reaching universal prosperity, universal justice, and universal peace. Our books cannot be analyzed or decoded by any spy, intelligence, or national security agency. Why are spy agencies everywhere anyway? In our future provisions, we imagine a spy-free world where no one must look over their shoulders on whether he or she is being followed or not. The people who work in spy and intelligence agencies are not the problem, the real problem is the set of messages their governments command them to execute. These people are just doing their job just to make a living like you and I, and to put a roof over their heads. One of the problems of spying or being spied on is that those who spy ask no questions on who they are following or spying on; they simply take orders given to them by their governments. We must not attack any person or people personally because like Justice Scalia United States Supreme Court judge once said, it is not the people who should be attacked; instead, it is the set of ideas.

The elimination of whoever the government suspects is a threat is the greatest human tragedy of our world today. The good governments need to be together in this, to ensure that ordinary citizens are not wrongfully targeted.

If the government instructs certain agents to kill, they kill without questioning systems of the government they work for and without question, and sometimes, they regret it. No one is supposed to be spied on if the world was fair, just, honest world. By year 2081, we should have a world of harmony and integrity, free of people looking over their shoulder and without being wrongfully targeted based on suspicions. Let us build our world in such a way that our children and grandchildren will love one another instead of being suspicious of one other.

Article 42

Anti-spy agencies, intelligence agencies, criminal illegal act of spying, tracking private citizens' smartphone devices, computer devices or private homes.

Under article 42

We will ethically trace all powerful spy agencies and intelligence agencies when they commit criminal unethical hacking and tracing of private citizens' smartphones, computers, and laptops without any prior warranty. We have artificial intelligence tools and skills privately created by us which will never be for sale. Our two hundred inventions and artificial intelligence skills will surpass all the artificial intelligence owned by spy agencies, intelligence agencies and national security agencies for the greater good of the world, just like all our inventions and innovations.

Under article 42, any spy agency, intelligence agency, or spy who commits crimes of unlawful spying, hacking of private citizens devices and other governments private emails will be criminally persecuted in the supreme global court in Geneva, Switzerland.

Article 43,

Role model non-Colonizer countries Alliance Act

Any country which directly, indirectly, or systematically collaborates with any current modern colonizer country will criminally be prosecuted under the supreme laws of all land's highest rules of law anti-modern Colonization Criminal act of Article 43.

Chapter 18

United States' Preamble and Portion of the United States of America Constitution

---

THE
CONSTITUTION
OF THE
UNITED STATES OF AMERICA

September 17, 1787

Preamble

We the people of the United States, in order to form a more perfect union, establish justice, ensure domestic tranquility, provide for the common defense, promote the general welfare, and secure the blessings of liberty to ourselves and our posterity, ordain and establish this Constitution for the United States.

The Insurrection Act of **1807** is a United States Federal law that empowers the President of the United States to deploy U.S. military and federalized National Guard troops within the United States in particular circumstances, such as to contain civil disorder, insurrection, or rebellion.

Transcript of the Proclamation

January 1, 1863

A Transcription

By the President of the United States of America:

A Proclamation.

Whereas, on the twenty-second day of September, in the year of our Lord, one thousand eight hundred and sixty-two, a proclamation was issued by the

President of the United States, containing, among other things, the following, to wit:

"That on the first day of January, in the year of our Lord, one thousand eight hundred and sixty-three, all persons held as slaves within any State or designated part of a State, the people whereof shall then be in rebellion against the United States, shall be then, thenceforward, and forever free; and the Executive Government of the United States, including the military and naval authority thereof, will recognize and maintain the freedom of such persons, and will do no act or acts to repress such persons, or any of them, in any efforts they may make for their actual freedom.

That the Executive will, on the first day of January aforesaid, by proclamation, designates the States and parts of States, if any, in which the people thereof, respectively, shall then be in rebellion against the United States; and the fact that any State, or the people thereof, shall on that day be, in good faith, represented in the Congress of the United States by members chosen thereto at elections wherein a majority of the qualified voters of such State shall have participated, shall, in the absence of strong countervailing testimony, be deemed conclusive evidence that such State, and the people thereof, are not then in rebellion against the United States."

Now, therefore I, Abraham Lincoln, President of the United States, by virtue of the power in me vested as Commander-in-Chief, of the Army and Navy of the United States in time of actual armed rebellion against the authority and government of the United States, and as a fit and necessary war measure for suppressing said rebellion, do, on this first day of January, in the year of our Lord one thousand eight hundred and sixty-three, and in accordance with my purpose so to do publicly proclaimed for the full period of one hundred days, from the day first above mentioned, order and designate as the States and parts of States wherein the people thereof respectively, are this day in rebellion against the United States, the following, to wit:

Arkansas, Texas, Louisiana (except the Parishes of St. Bernard, Plaquemines, Jefferson, St. John, St. Charles, St. James Ascension, Assumption, Terrebonne, Lafourche, St. Mary, St. Martin, and Orleans, including the City of New Orleans), Mississippi, Alabama, Florida, Georgia, South Carolina, North Carolina, and Virginia (except the forty-eight counties designated as West Virginia, and also the counties of Berkley, Accomac, Northampton, Elizabeth City, York, Princess Ann, and Norfolk, including the cities of Norfolk and Portsmouth), and which excepted parts, are for the present, left precisely as if this proclamation were not issued.

And by virtue of the power, and for the purpose aforesaid, I do order and declare that all persons held as slaves within said designated States, and parts of States, are, and henceforward shall be free; and that the Executive government of the United States, including the military and naval authorities thereof, will recognize and maintain the freedom of said persons.

And I hereby enjoin upon the people so declared to be free to abstain from all violence, unless in necessary self-defense; and I recommend to them that, in all cases, when allowed, they labor faithfully for reasonable wages.

And I further declare and make known that such persons of suitable condition, will be received into the armed service of the United States to garrison forts, positions, stations, and other places, and to man vessels of all sorts in said service.

And upon this act, sincerely believed to be an act of justice, warranted by the Constitution, upon military necessity, I invoke the considerate judgment of mankind, and the gracious favor of Almighty God.

In witness whereof, I have hereunto set my hand and caused the seal of the United States to be affixed.

Done at the City of Washington, this first day of January, in the year of our Lord one thousand eight hundred and sixty-three, and of the Independence of the United States of America the eighty-seventh.

By the President: ABRAHAM LINCOLN
WILLIAM H. SEWARD, Secretary of State.

Amendment I (1791)
Congress shall make no law respecting an establishment of religion or prohibiting the free exercise thereof; or abridging the freedom of speech, or of the press; or the right of the people peaceably to assemble, and to petition the Government for a redress of grievances.

Amendment II (1791)
A well-regulated Militia, being necessary to the security of a Free State, the right of the people to keep and bear Arms, shall not be infringed.

Amendment III (1791)
No soldier shall, in time of peace be quartered in any house, without the consent of the owner, nor in time of war, but in a manner to be prescribed by law.

Amendment IV (1791)
The right of the people to be secure in their persons, houses, papers, and effects, against unreasonable searches and seizures, shall not be violated, and no warrants shall be issued, but upon probable cause, supported by oath or affirmation, and particularly describing the place to be searched, and the persons or things to be seized.

Amendment V (1791)

No person shall be held to answer for a capital, or otherwise infamous crime, unless on a presentment or indictment of a grand jury, except in cases arising in the land or naval forces, or in the militia, when in actual service in time of war or public danger; nor shall any person be subject for the same offence to be twice put in jeopardy of life or limb; nor shall be compelled in any criminal case to be a witness against himself, nor be deprived of life, liberty, or property, without due process of law; nor shall private property be taken for public use, without just compensation.

Amendment VI (1791)

In all criminal prosecutions, the accused shall enjoy the right to a speedy and public trial, by an impartial jury of the State and district wherein the crime shall have been committed, which district shall have been previously ascertained by law, and to be informed of the nature and cause of the accusation; to be confronted with the witnesses against him; to have compulsory process for obtaining witnesses in his favor, and to have the Assistance of Counsel for his defense.

Amendment VII (1791)

In suits in common law, where the value in controversy shall exceed twenty dollars, the right of trial by jury shall be preserved, and no fact tried by a jury, shall be otherwise reexamined in any Court of the United States, then according to the rules of the common law.

Amendment VIII (1791)

Excessive bail shall not be required, nor excessive fines imposed, nor cruel and unusual punishments inflicted.

Amendment IX (1791)

The enumeration in the Constitution, of certain rights, shall not be construed to deny or disparage others retained by the people.

Amendment X (1791)

The powers not delegated to the United Countries of the World in the Constitution, nor prohibited by it to the States, are reserved to the States respectively, or to the people.

Amendment XI (1795/1798)

The judicial power of the United Countries of the World shall not be construed to extend to any suit in law or equity, commenced or prosecuted against one of the United States by citizens of another state, or by citizens or subjects of any foreign state.

Amendment XII (1804)

The electors shall meet in their respective states and vote by ballot for President and Vice-President, one of whom, at least, shall not be an inhabitant of the same state with themselves; they shall name in their ballots the person voted for as President, and in distinct ballots the person voted for as Vice-president, and they shall make distinct lists of all persons voted for as President, and of all persons voted for as Vice-President, and of the number of votes for each, which lists they shall sign and certify, and transmit sealed to the seat of the government of the United States, directed to the President of the Senate. The President of the Senate shall, in the presence of the Senate and House of Representatives, open all the certificates, and the votes shall then be counted. The person having the greatest number of votes for President, shall be the President, if such number be a majority of the whole number of electors appointed; and if no person have such majority, then from the persons having the highest numbers not exceeding three on the list of those voted for as President, the House of Representatives shall choose immediately, by ballot, the President. But in choosing the President, the votes shall be taken by states, the representation from each state having one vote; a quorum for this purpose shall consist of a member or members from two-thirds of the states, and a majority of all the states shall be necessary to choose. And if the House of Representatives shall not choose a President whenever the right of choice shall devolve upon them, before the fourth day of March next following, then the Vice-President shall act as President, as in the case of the death or other constitutional disability of the President. The person having the greatest number of votes as Vice-president, shall be the Vice-President, if such number be a majority of the whole number of electors appointed, and if no person has a majority, then from the two highest numbers on the list, the Senate shall choose the Vice-President; a quorum for the purpose shall consist of two-thirds of the whole number of Senators, and a majority of the whole number shall be necessary to a choice. But no person constitutionally ineligible to the office of President shall be eligible to that of Vice-President of the United States.

Amendment XIII (1865)
Section 1. Neither slavery nor involuntary servitude, except as a punishment for crime whereof the party shall have been duly convicted, shall exist within the United States, or any place subject to their jurisdiction.

Section 2. Congress shall have power to enforce this article by appropriate legislation.

Amendment XIV (1868)
Section 1. All persons born or naturalized in the United States, and subject to the jurisdiction thereof, are citizens of the United Countries of the World of the State wherein they reside. No State shall make or enforce any law which shall abridge the privileges or immunities of citizens of the United States; nor shall any State deprive any person of life, liberty, or property without due process of law; nor deny to any person within its jurisdiction the equal protection of the laws.

Section 2. Representatives shall be apportioned among the several States according to their respective numbers, counting the whole number of persons in each State, excluding Indians not taxed. But when the right to vote at any election for the choice of electors for President and Vice President of the United States, Representatives in Congress, the Executive and Judicial officers of a State, or the members of the Legislature thereof, is denied to any of the male inhabitants of such State, being twenty-one years of age, and citizens of the United States, or in any way abridged, except for participation in rebellion, or other crimes, the basis of representation therein shall be reduced in the proportion which the number of such male citizens shall bear to the whole number of male citizens twenty-one years of age in such State.

Section 3. No person shall be a Senator or Representative in Congress, or elector of President and Vice President, or hold any office, civil or military, under the United States, or under any State, who, having previously taken an oath, as a member of Congress, or as an officer of the United States, or as a member of any State legislature, or as an executive or judicial officer of any State, to support the Constitution of the United States, shall have engaged in insurrection or rebellion against the same, or given aid or comfort to the enemies thereof. But Congress may by a vote of two-thirds of each House, remove such disability.

Section 4. The validity of the public debt of the United States, authorized by law, including debts incurred for payment of pensions and bounties for services in suppressing insurrection or rebellion, shall not be questioned. But neither the United Countries of the World nor any State shall assume or pay any debt or obligation incurred in aid of insurrection or rebellion against the United States, or any claim for the loss or emancipation of any slave; but all such debts, obligations and claims shall be held illegal and void.

Section 5. The Congress shall have power to enforce, by appropriate legislation, the provisions of this article.

Amendment XV (1870)
Section 1. The right of citizens of the United Countries of the World to vote shall not be denied or abridged by the United Countries of the World or by any State on account of race, color, or previous condition of servitude.

Section 2. The Congress shall have power to enforce this article by appropriate legislation.

Amendment XVI (1913)
The Congress shall have power to lay and collect taxes on incomes, from whatever source derived, without apportionment among the several States, and without regard to any census or enumeration.

Amendment XVII (1913)
The Senate of the United States shall be composed of two Senators from each State, elected by the people thereof, for six years; and each Senator shall have one vote. The electors in each State shall have the

qualifications requisite for electors of the most numerous branches of the State legislatures.

When vacancies happen in the representation of any State in the Senate, the executive authority of such State shall issue writs of election to fill such vacancies, provided that the legislature of any state may empower the executive thereof to make temporary appointments until the people fill the vacancies by election as the legislature may direct.

This amendment shall not be so construed as to affect the election or term of any Senator chosen before it becomes valid as part of the Constitution.

Amendment XVIII (1919)

Section 1. After one year from the ratification of this article, the manufacture, sale, or transportation of intoxicating liquors within, the importation thereof into, or the exportation thereof from the United States territory subject to the jurisdiction thereof for beverage purposes is hereby prohibited.

Section 2. The Congress and the several States shall have concurrent power to enforce this article by appropriate legislation.

Section 3. This article shall be inoperative unless it shall have been ratified as an amendment to the Constitution by the legislatures of the several States, as provided in the Constitution, within seven years from the date of the submission hereof to the States by the Congress.

Amendment XIX (1920)

The right of citizens of the United States to vote shall not be denied or abridged by the United States or by any State on account of sex.

Congress shall have power to enforce this article by appropriate legislation.

Amendment XX (1933)

Section 1. The terms of the President and Vice President shall end at noon on the 20th day of January, and the terms of Senators and Representatives at noon on the third day of January, of the years in which such terms would have ended if this article had not been ratified; and the terms of their successors shall then begin.

Section 2. The Congress shall assemble at least once in every year, and such meeting shall begin at noon on the third day of January, unless they shall by law appoint a different day.

Section 3. If, at the time fixed for the beginning of the term of the President, the President-elect shall have died, the Vice President elect shall become President. If a President shall not have been chosen before the time fixed for the beginning of his term, or if the President-elect shall have failed to qualify, then the Vice President-elect shall act as President until a President shall have qualified; and the Congress may by law provide for the case wherein neither a President elect nor a Vice President-elect shall have qualified, declaring who shall then act as President, or the manner in which one who is to act shall be selected, and such person shall act accordingly until a President or Vice President shall have qualified.

Section 4. The Congress may by law provide for the case of the death of any of the persons from whom the House of Representatives may choose a President whenever the right of choice shall have devolved upon them, and for the case of the death of any of the persons from whom the Senate may choose a Vice President whenever the right of choice shall have devolved upon them.

Section 5. Sections 1 and 2 shall take effect on the 15th day of October, following the ratification of this article.

Section 6. This article shall be inoperative unless it shall have been ratified as an amendment to the Constitution by the legislatures of three-fourths of the several States within seven years from the date of its submission.

Amendment XXI (1933)
Section 1. The eighteenth article of amendment to the Constitution of the United Countries of the Worlds hereby repealed.

Section 2. The transportation or importation into any State, Territory, or possession of the United States for delivery or use therein of intoxicating liquors, in violation of the laws thereof, is hereby prohibited.

Section 3. This article shall be inoperative unless it shall have been ratified as an amendment to the Constitution by conventions in the several States, as provided in the Constitution, within seven years from the date of the submission hereof to the States by the Congress.

Amendment XXII (1951)

Section 1. No person shall be elected to the office of the President more than twice, and no person who has held the office of President, or acted as President, for more than two years of a term to which some other person was elected President shall be elected to the office of the President more than once. But this Article shall not apply to any person holding the office of President, when this Article was proposed by the Congress, and shall not prevent any person who may be holding the office of President, or acting as President, during the term within which this Article becomes operative from holding the office of President or acting as President during the remainder of such term.

Section 2. This article shall be inoperative unless it shall have been ratified as an amendment to the Constitution by the legislatures of three-fourths of the several States within seven years from the date of its submission to the States by the Congress.

Amendment XXIII (1961)

Section 1. The district constituting the seat of Government of the United States shall appoint in such manner as the Congress may direct:

A number of electors of President and Vice President equal to the whole number of Senators and Representatives in Congress to which the district would be entitled if it were a State, but in no event more than the least populous State; they shall be in addition to those appointed by the States, but they shall be considered, for the purposes of the election of President and Vice President, to be electors appointed by a State; and they shall meet in the District and perform such duties as provided by the twelfth article of amendment.

Section 2. The Congress shall have power to enforce this article by appropriate legislation.

Amendment XXIV (1964)

Section 1. The right of citizens of the United States to vote in any primary or other election for President or Vice President for electors for President or Vice President, or for Senator or Representative in Congress, shall not be denied or abridged by the United States or any State by reason of failure to pay any poll tax or other tax.

Section 2. The Congress shall have power to enforce this article by appropriate legislation.

Amendment XXV (1967)

Section 1. In case of the removal of the President from office or of his death or resignation, the Vice President shall become President.

Section 2. Whenever there is a vacancy in the office of the Vice President, the President shall nominate a Vice President who shall take office upon confirmation by a majority vote of both Houses of Congress.

Section 3. Whenever the President transmits to the President pro tempore of the Senate and the Speaker of the House of Representatives his written declaration that he is unable to discharge the powers and duties of his office, until he transmits to them a written declaration to the contrary, such powers and duties shall be discharged by the Vice President as Acting President.

Section 4. Whenever the Vice President and a majority of either the principal officers of the executive departments or of such other body as Congress may by law provide, transmit to the President pro tempore of the Senate and the Speaker of the House of Representatives their written declaration that the President is unable to discharge the powers and duties of his office, the Vice President shall immediately assume the powers and duties of the office as Acting President.

Thereafter, when the President transmits to the President pro tempore of the Senate and the Speaker of the House of Representatives his written declaration that no inability exists, he shall resume the powers and duties of his office unless the Vice President and a majority of either the principal officers of the executive department or of such other body as Congress may by law provide, transmit within four days to the President pro tempore of the Senate   and   the   Speaker   of   the

House of Representatives their written declaration that the President is unable to discharge the powers and duties of his office. Thereupon, Congress shall decide the issue, assembling within forty-eight hours for that purpose if not in session. If the Congress, within twenty-one days after receipt of the latter written declaration, or, if Congress is not in session, within twenty-one days after Congress is required to assemble, determined by two-third votes of both houses that the President is unable to discharge the powers and duties of his office, the Vice President shall continue to discharge the same as Acting President; otherwise, the President shall resume the powers and duties of his office.

Amendment XXVI (1971)
Section 1. The right of citizens of the United States, who are eighteen years of age or older, to vote shall not be denied or abridged by the United States or by any State on account of age.

Section 2. The Congress shall have power to enforce this article by appropriate legislation.

Amendment XXVII (1992)
No law varying the compensation for the services of the Senators and Representatives shall take effect, until an election of Representatives shall have intervened.

Chapter 19

The State of Eritrea's Unimplemented Constitution

The State of Eritrea's Unimplemented 1997 Constitution based on Autonomy and Independence

ERITREAN

CONSTITUTION

PREAMBLE

We are the people of Eritrea, united in a common struggle for our rights and common destiny, standing on the solid ground of unity and justice bequeathed by our martyrs and combatants. We are eternally grateful to the scores of thousands of our martyrs who sacrificed their lives for the causes of our rights and independence, during the long and heroic revolutionary struggle for liberation, and to the courage and steadfastness of our Eritrean patriots.

We are aware that it is the sacred duty of all Eritreans to build a strong and developed Eritrea on the basis of freedom, unity, peace, stability and security achieved through the long struggle of all Eritreans, which tradition we must cherish, preserve and develop. We realize that in order to build a developed country, it is necessary that the unity, equality, love for truth and justice, self-reliance, and hard work, which we nurtured during our revolutionary struggle for independence, and which helped us to triumph, must become the core of our national values. In appreciating the fact that for the development and health of our society, it is necessary that we inherit and improve upon the traditional community-based assistance and fraternity, love for family, respect for elders, mutual respect, and consideration.

Therefore, we are convinced that the recognition, protection and securing of the rights and freedoms of citizens, human dignity, equality will guarantee a balanced development; lay down the groundwork for satisfying the material and spiritual needs of citizens; usher in a democratic order that is responsive to the needs and interests of citizens, guarantee their participation and bring about economic development, social progress and harmony.

Noting the fact that the Eritrean women's heroic participation in the struggle for independence and solidarity based on equality and mutual respect generated by such struggle, will serve as an unshakable foundation for our commitment and struggle to create a society in which women and men shall interact on the bases of mutual respect, fraternity, and equality.

It is our desire that the Constitution we adopt will be a covenant between us and the government, structured by our free will and serve as a means for governing in harmony for the present and the future generation. We aim to bring about justice and peace, founded on democracy, national unity, and the rule of law.

Today... on this historic date, after active popular participation, approve and solemnly ratify officially, through the Constituent Assembly, this Constitution as the fundamental law of our Sovereign and Independent State of Eritrea.

CHAPTER I GENERAL PROVISIONS

Article 1: The State of Eritrea and its Territory

(1) Eritrea is a sovereign and independent State founded on the principles of democracy, social justice, and the rule of law.

142

(2) The territory of Eritrea consists of all its territories, including the islands, territorial waters, and airspace, delineated by internationally recognized boundaries.

(3) In the State of Eritrea, sovereign power is vested in the people, who shall exercise such power through their representatives, duly elected, pursuant to the procedures authorized by the provisions of this Constitution.

(4) The State that is to be established by a democratic process to represent the people's sovereignty shall have strong institutions, capable of accommodating people's participation and of serving as foundation of a viable democratic and political order.

(5) The State of Eritrea shall have a unitary government, divided into units of local government; the powers and duties of these units shall be determined by law.

Article 2: Supremacy of the Constitution

(1) This Constitution is the legal expression of the sovereignty of the Eritrean people.

(2) This Constitution enunciates the principles on which the State is to be based and guided by and determines the organization and operation of government. It is the source of government legitimacy and the guarantor for the protection of the rights, freedoms, and dignity of citizens and of just administration.

(3) This Constitution is the supreme law of the country and the source of all laws of the State; all laws, orders and acts contrary to its letter and spirit shall be null and void.

(4) All organs of the State, all public and private associations and institutions and all citizens shall be bound by and remain loyal to the Constitution and shall ensure its observance.

(5) Pursuant to the provisions of this Constitution and other laws, the conduct of the affairs of government and all organizations and institutions shall be accountable and transparent.

(6) This Constitution shall serve as a basis for instilling constitutional culture and for enlightening and ensuring that organizations of the State and citizens respect fundamental human rights and duties.

No government is or government official is above the law, no person is above the law. Everyone must obey the law

Article 3: Citizenship

(1) Any person born of an Eritrean father or mother is an Eritrean by birth.
(2) Any foreign citizen may acquire Eritrean citizenship pursuant to law.
(3) The details concerning citizenship shall be regulated by law.

Article 4: National Symbols and Languages

(1) The Eritrean Flag shall have green, red, and blue colors, with golden olive leaves located at the center. The exact description of the Flag shall be determined by law.
(2) Eritrea shall have a National Anthem and a Coat of Arms appropriately reflecting the

History and the aspiration of its people. The details of the National Anthem and the Coat of Arms shall be determined by law.

(3) The equality of all Eritrean languages is guaranteed.

Article 5: Gender Reference

Without consideration to the gender wording of any provision in this Constitution, all its articles shall apply equally to all genders.

CHAPTER II: NATIONAL OBJECTIVES AND DIRECTIVE PRINCIPLES

Article 6: National Unity and Stability

(1) As the people and government struggle to establish a united and developed Eritrea, within the context of the diversity of Eritrea, they shall be guided by the basic principle, 'Unity in diversity.' (2) The State shall strengthen the stability and development of the country by encouraging democratic dialogue and national consensus through participation of all citizens by building strong political, cultural, and moral foundation, and by promoting national unity and social harmony.

(3) The State shall ensure peace and stability by establishing appropriate institutions that encourage people's participation, and by creating the necessary conditions capable of guaranteeing, hastening, and engendering equitable economic and social progress.

Article 7: Democratic Principles

(1) It is a fundamental principle of the State to guarantee its citizens' broad and active participation in all political, economic, social, and cultural life of the country.

(2) Any act that violates the human rights of women, or limits or otherwise thwarts their role and participation is prohibited.

(3) Necessary institutions to encourage and develop people's participation and initiative in the areas where they reside shall be established.

(4) Pursuant to the provisions of this Constitution and laws enacted pursuant thereto, all Eritreans, without distinction, are guaranteed equal opportunity to participate in any positions of leadership in the country.

(5) The organization and operation of all political and public associations and movements shall be guided by the principle of national unity and democracy.

(6) The State shall create the necessary conditions for establishing a democratic, political culture defined by the development of free and critical thinking, tolerance, and national consensus.

Article 8: Competent Justice System

(1) The justice system of Eritrea shall be independent, competent, and accountable, pursuant to the provisions of the constitution and laws.

(2) Courts shall work under a judicial system that can produce fast and equitable judgments that can easily be understood and is accessible to all people.

(3) Judges shall be free from corruption or discrimination and, in rendering their judgment, they shall make no distinctions among persons.

(4) The State shall encourage out-of-court settlement of disputes through conciliation, mediation, or arbitration.

Article 9: Competent Public Administration

(1) Eritrea shall have an efficient, effective, and accountable public service.

(2) All administrative institutions shall be free from corruption, discrimination, and delay in the delivery of services.

Article 10: Economic and Social Development

(1) The State shall endeavor to create opportunities to ensure the fulfillment of citizens' rights to social justice and the economic development and fulfill their material and spiritual needs.

(2) The State shall work to bring about a balanced and sustainable development throughout the country and shall use all available means to

ensure that all citizens improve their livelihood in a sustainable manner, through their development.

(3) The State shall have the responsibility to regulate all land, water, and natural resources, and to ensure their management in a balanced and sustainable manner and in the interest of the present and future generations, and to create the right conditions for securing the participation of the people to safeguard the environment.

Article 11: National Culture

(1)   The State shall have the responsibility of creating and maintaining the necessary conditions for enriching national culture, which is the expression of national identity and unity and progress of the Eritrean people.

(2)   The State shall encourage the values of community solidarity and the love and respect of family.

(3)   The State shall promote the development of arts, sports, and science and technology, and shall create an enabling environment for individuals to work in an atmosphere of freedom and manifest their creativity and innovation.

Article 12: National Defense and Security

(1) Defense and security forces of Eritrea shall owe allegiance to and defend the territorial integrity and sovereignty of the country, the constitution and the government-established pursuant thereto.

(2) Defense and security forces are an integral part of society and shall be productive and respectful of the people.

(3) The defense and security of Eritrea are rooted on the people and on their active participation.

(4) The defense and security forces shall be subject and accountable to the law, shall be competent and pass these requirements for posterity.

Article 13: Foreign Policy

The foreign policy of Eritrea is based on respect for the independence and sovereignty of countries, and on promoting the interest of regional and international peace, cooperation, harmony, and development.

CHAPTER III: FUNDAMENTAL RIGHTS, FREEDOMS, AND DUTIES

Article 14: Equality under the Law

(1) All persons are equal before the law.

(2) No person may be discriminated against on account of race, ethnic origin, language, color, sex, religion, disability, political belief, opinion, social or economic status, or any other factors.

(3) The National Assembly shall, pursuant to the provisions of this Article, enact laws that can assist in eliminating inequalities existing in the Eritrean society.

Article 15: Right to Life and Liberty

(1) No person shall be deprived of their right to life without due process of law.

(2) No person shall be deprived of liberty without due process of law.

Article 16: Right to Human Dignity

(1) The dignity of all persons shall be inviolable.

(2) No person shall be subject to torture, cruelty, or inhumane or degrading treatment or punishment.

(3) No person shall be held in slavery or servitude or required to perform forced labor not authorized by law.

Article 17: Arrest, Detention and Fair Trial

(1) No person may be arrested or detained, save pursuant to due process of law.

(2) No person shall be tried or convicted for any act or omission which did not constitute a criminal offence at the time it was committed.

(3) Every person arrested or detained shall be informed of the grounds for his arrest or detention, and the rights he has in connection with his arrest or detention in a language he understands.

(4) Every person who is arrested and detained in custody shall be brought before the court within forty-eight (48) hours of his arrest, and if this is not reasonably possible, as soon as possible thereafter; no such person shall be detained in custody beyond such period without the authority of the court.

(5) Every person shall have the right to petition the court for a Writ of Habeas Corpus. Where the arresting officer fails to bring him before the court of law and provide the reason for their arrest, the court shall accept the petition and order the release of the prisoner.

(6) Every person charged with an offence shall be entitled to a fair and public hearing by a court of law, provided, however, that such a court may exclude the press and/or the public from all or any part of the trial for reasons of morals, the public order or national security, as is necessary in a just and democratic society.

(7) A person charged with an offence shall be presumed to be innocent, and shall not be punished, unless he is found guilty by a court.

(8) Where an accused is convicted, he shall have the right to appeal. No person shall be liable to be tried again for any criminal offence on which judgement has been rendered.

Article 18: Right to Privacy

(1) Every person shall have the right to privacy.

(2) No person shall be subjected to unlawful search, including his home or other property; there shall be no unlawful entry to his premises and no unlawful seizure of his personal possessions; nor shall the privacy of his correspondence, communication or other property be violated.

No government is or government official is above the law, no person is above the law. Everyone must obey the law

Article 19; Freedom of Conscience, Religion, Expression of Opinion, Movement, Assembly and Organization

(1) Every person shall have the right to freedom of thought, conscience, and belief.
(2) Every person shall have the freedom of speech and expression, which includes freedom of the press and other media.
(3) Every citizen shall have the right of access to information.
(4) Every person shall have the freedom to practice any religion and to manifest such practice.
(5) All persons shall have the right to assemble and to demonstrate together with others peaceably. (6) Every citizen shall have the right to form organizations for political, social, economic, and cultural ends, and to practice any profession or engage in any occupation or trade.
(7) Every citizen shall have the right to move freely throughout Eritrea or reside and settle in any part thereof.
(8) Every citizen shall have the right to leave and return to Eritrea and be provided with passport or any other travel documents.

Article 20: Right to Vote and to be a Candidate to an Elective Office

Every citizen who fulfills the requirements of the electoral law shall have the right to vote or to campaign to be elected to any office of leadership in government.

Article 21: Economic, Social and Cultural Rights and Responsibilities

(1) Every citizen shall have the right of equal access to publicly funded social services. The State shall endeavor, within the limit of its resources, to make available to all citizens health, education, cultural and other social services.
(2) The State shall secure, within available means, the social welfare of all citizens and particularly those disadvantaged.
(3) Every citizen shall have the right to engage freely in any economic activity and to pursue a livelihood.

(4) The State and society shall have the responsibility of identifying, preserving, developing, when necessary, and bequeathing to succeeding generation historical and cultural heritage; this shall lay the necessary groundwork for the development of arts, sport, science, and technology, and shall encourage citizens to participate in such endeavors.

(5) The National Assembly shall enact laws that guarantee and secure the social welfare of citizens and other rights and responsibilities listed in this Article.

Article 22: Family

(1) The family is the natural and fundamental unit of society and is entitled to the protection and special care of the State and society.

(2) Men and women of full legal age shall have the right, upon their consent, to marry and to find a family freely, without any discrimination, and they shall have equal rights and duties as to all family affairs.

(3) Parents have the right and duty to bring up their children with proper care and affection; and, in turn, children have the right and the duty to respect their parents and to sustain them in their old age.

Article 23: Right to Property

(1) Subject to the provisions of Sub-Article 2 of this Article, any citizen shall have the right, anywhere in Eritrea, to acquire, own and dispose of all property individually or in association with others, and to bequeath to his heirs or legatees.

(2) All land, water, and natural resources below and above the surface of the territory of Eritrea belongs to the State. Usufruct rights of citizens shall be determined by law.

(3) The State or any of its organs authorized by law may expropriate property in the national or public interest, subject to the payment of just compensation and in accordance with due process of law.

Article 24: Administrative Justice

(1) Any person with a complaint shall have the right to be heard respectfully by administrative officials, and to receive appropriate and prompt answers from them.

(2) Any person whose rights or interests are interfered with or threatened shall have the right to seek due administrative redress.

Article 25: Duties of Citizens

All citizens shall have the duty to:

1. Owe allegiance to Eritrea, strive for its development, and promote its prosperity.
2. Be ready to defend the country.
3. Complete one's duty in the National Service.
4. Advance national unity and the well-being of the people.
5. Know, respect, and defend the Constitution.
6. Respect the rights and freedoms of others.
7. Respect the rule of law and comply with the requirements of the law.

Article 26: Limitation upon Fundamental Rights and Freedoms

(1) The fundamental rights and freedoms guaranteed under this Constitution may be limited only as far as is necessary in a just and democratic society in the interests of national security, public safety or the economic well-being of the country, health, or morals, for the prevention of public disorder or crime, or for the protection of the rights and freedoms of others.

(2) Any law providing for the limitation of the fundamental rights and freedoms guaranteed in this Constitution must:

a) Be consistent with the principles of a just and democratic society.

b) Be of typical application and not negate the essential content of the right or freedom in question.

c) Specify the ascertainable extent of such limitation and identify the Article or Articles hereof on which authority to enact such limitation is claimed to rest.

(3) Notwithstanding the provisions of Sub-Article 1 of this Article and other Articles of this Constitution to the contrary, the fundamental rights and

freedoms guaranteed under Articles <u>14 (1) and (2)</u>, <u>17 (2)</u>, <u>19 (4)</u> of this Constitution shall not be limited.

Article 27: State of Emergency

(1) At a time when public safety or the security or stability of the State is threatened by external invasion, by civil disorder or by natural disaster, the President may, by a proclamation published in the Gazette of Eritrean Laws declare that a state of emergency exists in Eritrea or any part thereof.

(2) A declaration under Sub-Article 1 hereof shall not become effective unless approved by a resolution passed by a two-third majority votes of all members of the National Assembly. In the case of a declaration made when the National Assembly is session, the declaration shall be presented within two days after its publication, or otherwise, the National Assembly shall be summoned to meet and approve the publication within thirty days of its declaration.

(3) A declaration approved by the National Assembly pursuant to Sub-Article 2 hereof shall continue to be in force until the expiration of a period of six months after such approval. The National Assembly may, by a resolution of two-third majority votes of all its members, extend its approval of the declaration for periods of three months at a time.

(4) The National Assembly may by resolution at any time revoke a declaration approved by it pursuant to the provisions of this Article.

(5) Any measures undertaken, or laws enacted pursuant to a declaration of a state of emergency shall not:

a) Suspend Article 26 (3) of the Constitution.

b) Grant pardon or amnesty to any person or persons who, acting under the authority of the State, have committed illegal acts; or

c) Introduce martial law when no external invasion exists, or civil disorder prevails.

Article 28: Enforcement of Fundamental Rights and Freedoms

(1) Save as far as it may be authorized to do so by this Constitution, the National Assembly or any subordinate legislative authority shall not make any law, and the Executive and the agencies of government shall not take

any action which abolishes or abridges the fundamental rights and freedoms conferred by this Constitution. Any law or action in violation thereof shall be invalid.

(2) Aggrieved persons who claim that a fundamental right or freedom guaranteed by this Constitution has been denied or violated shall be entitled to approach a competent court to enforce or protect such a right or freedom. Where the court ascertains that such fundamental right or freedom has been denied or violated, the court shall have the power to make all such orders as shall be necessary, to secure such applicants the enjoyment of such fundamental right or freedom, and where such applicants suffer damage, to include an award of monetary compensation.

Article 29: Residual Rights

The rights enumerated in this Chapter shall not preclude other rights which ensue from the spirit of this Constitution and the principles of a society based on social justice, democracy, and the rule of law.

CHAPTER IV THE NATIONAL ASSEMBLY

Article 30: Representation of the People

(1) Any Eritrean citizen, of eighteen years of age or more, shall have the right to vote.
(2) The National Assembly shall enact an electoral law, which shall prescribe for and ensure the representation and participation of the Eritrean people.

Article 31: Establishment and Duration of the National Assembly

(1) There shall be a National Assembly which shall be a supreme representative and legislative body.

(2) The National Assembly shall be composed of representatives elected by the people.

(3) Members of the National Assembly shall be elected by direct and secret ballot by all citizens who are qualified to vote.

(4) Members of the National Assembly are representatives of the Eritrean people. In discharging their duties, they are governed by the objectives and principles of the Constitution, the interest of the people and the country and their conscience.

(5) The first session of the National Assembly shall be held within one month after a general election, and its term shall be five years from the date of such first session. Where there exists a state of emergency which would prevent a normal general election from being held, the National Assembly may, by resolution supported by not less than two- thirds vote of all its members, extend the life of the National Assembly for a period not exceeding six months.

(6) The qualifications and election of the members of the National Assembly and the conditions for vacating their seats shall be determined by law.

Article 32: Powers and Duties of the National Assembly

(1) Pursuant to the provisions of this Constitution:

a) The National Assembly shall have the power to enact laws and pass resolutions for the peace, stability, development, and good governance of Eritrea.

b) Unless, pursuant to the provisions of this Constitution or authorized by law enacted by the National Assembly, no person or organization shall have the power to make having the force of law.

(2) The National Assembly shall be bound by the objectives and principles of the Constitution and shall strive to realize the objectives stated therein.

(3) The National Assembly shall approve the national budget and enact tax law.

(4) The National Assembly shall ratify international agreements by law.

(5) The National Assembly shall authorize government to borrow money pursuant to law.

(6) The National Assembly shall approve a state of peace, war, or national emergency.

(7) The National Assembly shall have the power to oversee the execution of laws.

(8) The National Assembly shall have the power to elect, from among its members, by absolute majority vote of all its members, the President who shall serve for five years.

(9) Pursuant to the provisions of Sub-Article 6(a) and (b) of Article 41 hereof, the National Assembly, by a vote of two-third majority of all its members, shall have the power to impeach and charge the President before the end of his term of office.

(10) The National Assembly may approve the appointment of any person or persons pursuant to this Constitution.

(11) The National Assembly may pass such resolutions and undertake such measures as are necessary and establish such standing or ad hoc committees as it deems appropriate for discharging its constitutional responsibilities.

Article 33 Approval of Draft Legislation

Any draft law approved by the National Assembly shall be transmitted to the President who, within thirty days, shall sign and have it published in the Gazette of Eritrean Laws.

Article 34 Chairman of the National Assembly

(1) In its first meeting, the National Assembly shall elect, by an absolute majority vote of all its members, a Chairman for five years. (2) The Chairman of the National Assembly shall convene session of the National Assembly and preside at its meetings, and shall, during the recess, coordinate and supervise the operations of standing and ad hoc committees of the National Assembly. (3) The Chairman of the National Assembly may be replaced by an absolute majority vote of all the members of the National Assembly.

Article 35 Oath

Every member of the National Assembly shall take the following oath: "I, ..., swear in the name of the Eritrean martyrs that I will be faithful and worthy of the trust the Eritrean people placed on me; that I will uphold and defend the Constitution of Eritrea; and that I will endeavor to the best of my ability and conscience for the unity and development of my country without seeking or being enticed by private gain."

Article 36 Rules of Procedure in the National Assembly

(1) The National Assembly shall have regular session and shall determine the timing and duration of its regular session. (2) At the request of the President, its Chairman or one-third of all its members, the National Assembly shall have emergency meeting.
(3) The quorum of the National Assembly shall be fifty percent of all the members of the National Assembly. (4) Except as otherwise prescribed by this Constitution or other laws, any question proposed for decision of the National Assembly shall be determined by a majority vote of those present

and voting, and in case of a tie of votes, the Chairman may exercise a casting vote. (5) The National Assembly shall issue rules and regulations concerning its organization, tasks, operations, and internal processes and those of the standing and ad hoc committees, including the rules governing the code of ethics of its members and transparency of its operations.

Article 37: Office and Committees of the National Assembly

(1) The National Assembly shall have a secretariat under the direction of its chairman and committees for various fields of interest, as circumstance may dictate.

(2) The various committees established pursuant to the provisions of Sub-Article 1 of this Article shall have the power to call any person to appear before them to give evidence or to submit documents.

Article 38: Duties, Immunities and Privileges of Members of the National Assembly

(1) All members of the National Assembly shall maintain the high image of the National Assembly. They shall regard themselves as humble servants of the people and maintain close contact with them.

(2) No member of the National Assembly nor member of its committees may be arrested or charged for any crimes he commits during the session of the National Assembly, unless he be apprehended in flagrante delicto. Nevertheless, where the National Assembly, by a majority vote of those present and voting, revokes his immunity, the member may be charged.

(3) No member of the National Assembly may be arrested or charged for words uttered, or written statements submitted by him at any meeting of the National Assembly or any meeting of its committees or any utterance or statement made outside the National Assembly in connection with his duty as member thereof.

(4) The duties, responsibilities, immunities, and compensation of the members of the National Assembly shall be determined by law, and all members shall be entitled to the protection of such immunities and shall perform the duties enumerated therein.

No government is or government official is above the law, no person is above the law. Everyone must obey the law

CHAPTER V: THE EXECUTIVE

Article 39: The President - Head of State and Government

(1) The President of Eritrea is Head of State and Government and Commander-in- Chief of the Armed Forces of Eritrea.

(2) The executive authority is vested in the President, and shall be exercised, in consultation with the Cabinet, pursuant to the provisions of this Constitution.

(3) The President shall ensure the respect of the Constitution; the integrity of the State; the efficiency and effectiveness of the public service; the interests and safety of all citizens, including the enjoyment of their fundamental rights and freedoms recognized under this Constitution.

Article 40: Qualifications to be a Candidate to the Office of the President

Any member of the National Assembly to be elected President of Eritrea shall be a citizen of Eritrea by birth.

Article 4:1 Election and Term of Office of the President

(1)   The President shall be elected from amongst the members of the National Assembly by a vote of the majority of its members. A candidate for the office of the President must be nominated by at least a 20-percent vote of all the members of the National Assembly.

(2)   The term of office of the President shall be five years, equal to the term of office of the National Assembly that elects him.

(3)   No person shall be elected to hold office of the President for more than two terms.

(4)   When the office of the President becomes vacant due to death or resignation of the incumbent, or due to the reasons enumerated in Sub-Article 6 of this Article, the Chairman of the National Assembly shall

assume the office of the President. The Chairman shall serve as acting President for not more than thirty days, during which time, the National Assembly shall elect another President to serve the remaining term of his predecessor.

(5)   The term of office of the person elected to serve as President under Sub-Article 4 of this Article shall not be considered as a full term for purposes of Sub-Article 3 of this Article.

(6) The President may be removed from office by a two-third majority vote of all members of   the National Assembly for the following reasons:

a) Violation of the Constitution or grave violation of the law.

b) Conducting himself in a manner which brings the authority or honor of the office of President into ridicule, contempt, and disrepute.

c) Being incapable of performing the functions of his office by reason of physical or mental incapacity.

(7) The procedures for the election and removal of the President from office shall be determined by law.

Article 42: Powers and Duties of the President

The President shall have the following powers and duties:

1. Once every year, deliver a speech in the National Assembly on the state of the country and the policies of his government.

2. Subject to the provisions of Article 27 hereof, declare state of emergency, and when the defense of the country requires, state of war.

3. Summon the National Assembly to an emergency meeting and present his views to it.

4. Sign and publish in the Gazette of Eritrean Laws draft laws approved by the National Assembly.

5. Ensure the execution of laws and resolutions of the National Assembly.

6. Negotiate and sign international agreements and delegate such power.

7. Appoint with the approval of the National Assembly, ministers, commissioners, the Auditor-General, head of the National Bank, the Chief Justice of the Supreme Court and any other person or persons who are required by any other provisions of this Constitution or other laws to be appointed by the President.

8. Appoint justices of the Supreme Court upon proposal of the Judicial Service Commission and approval of the National Assembly.

9. Appoint judges of the lower courts upon proposal of the Judicial Service Commission.

10. Appoint and receive ambassadors and diplomatic representatives. Appoint high-ranking members of the Armed and the Security Forces.

11. Pardon, grant amnesty or reprieve offenders.

12. Establish and dissolve such government ministries and departments necessary or expedient for the good governance of Eritrea, in consultation with the Public Service Administration.

13. Preside over meetings of the Cabinet and coordinate its activities.

15. Present legislative proposals to the National Assembly.

16. Confer medals or other honors on citizens, residents, and friends of Eritrea in consultation with relevant persons and institutions.

17. Pursuant to the provisions of this Constitution, remove any person appointed by him.

Article 43: Immunity from Civil and Criminal Proceedings

Any person holding the office of the President may not be sued in any civil proceedings or charged for a crime, save where such proceedings concern an act done in his official capacity as President or proceedings involving Sub-Article 6(a) and (b) of Article 41 hereof.

Article 44: Privileges to be given to Former Presidents

Provisions shall be made by law for the privileges that shall be granted to former Presidents.

Article 45: Oath

Upon his election, the President shall take the following oath: "I swear in the name of the Eritrean martyrs that I will uphold and defend the Constitution of Eritrea, and that I will strive with the best of my ability and conscience to serve the people of Eritrea."

No government is or government official is above the law, no person is above the law. Everyone must obey the law

Article 46: The Cabinet

(1) There shall be a ministerial Cabinet, which shall be presided by the President.

(2) The President may select ministers from among members of the National Assembly or from among persons who are not members of the National Assembly.

(3) The Cabinet shall assist the President in:

a) Directing, supervising, and coordinating the affairs of government.

b) Conducting study on and preparing the annual budget.

c) Conducting study and preparing draft laws to be presented to the National Assembly.

d) Conducting study on and preparing policies and plans of government.

(4) The President may issue rules and regulations for the organization, functions, and operation of his office, the Cabinet or other government institutions, and for the code of ethics involving officials of the executive branch of government.

Article 47: Ministerial Accountability

(1) All ministers shall be accountable:

a) Individually to the President for the administration of their own ministries; and

b) Collectively to the National Assembly, through the President, for the administration of the work of the Cabinet.

(2) The National Assembly or its committees may, through the Office of the President, summon any minister to appear before them to question him concerning the policies or operation of his ministry.

CHAPTER VI: THE ADMINISTRATION OF JUSTICE

No government is or government official is above the law, no person is above the law. Everyone must obey the law

Article 48: The Judiciary

(1) The judicial power shall be vested in a Supreme Court, and in such other lower courts as shall be established by law and shall be exercised in the name of the people pursuant to this Constitution and laws issued thereunder.
(2) In exercising their judicial power, courts shall be free from direction, control and supervision of any person or authority. Judges shall be subject only to the law, to a judicial code of ethics determined by law and to their conscience.
(3) A person exercising judicial power shall not be liable to any suit for any act or omission in the course of exercising that judicial power.
(4) All organs of the State shall accord to the courts such assistance, as they may require protecting their independence and dignity so that they may exercise their judicial power appropriately and effectively, pursuant to the provisions of this Constitution and laws issued thereunder.

Article 49: The Supreme Court

(1) The Supreme Court shall be the court of last resort and shall be presided by the Chief Justice. (2) The Supreme Court shall have the power of:
a) Sole jurisdiction of interpreting this Constitution and the constitutionality of any law enacted or any measure undertaken by government.
b) Sole jurisdiction of hearing and adjudicating upon charges against a President who has been impeached by the National Assembly, pursuant to the provisions of Sub-Article 6 (a) and (b) of Article 41 hereof; and
c) Hearing and adjudicating cases appealed from lower courts pursuant to law.

(3) The organization and operation of the Supreme Court shall be determined by law.
(4) The tenure of justices of the Supreme Court shall be determined by law.

Article: 50 Lower Courts

The organization, jurisdiction and the procedures of lower courts and the tenure of their judges shall be determined by law.

Article 51: Oath

Every judge shall take the following oath: "I, ... swear in the name of the Eritrean martyrs that I will adjudicate in accordance with the provisions of the Constitution and laws enacted thereunder, and I will exercise the judicial authority vested in me, subject only to the law and my conscience, without seeking or being enticed by any private gain."

Article 52: Removal of Judges from Office

(1) A judge may be removed from office before the expiry of his tenure of office by the President only, acting on the recommendation of the Judicial Service Commission, pursuant to the provisions of Sub-Article 2 of this Article for physical or mental incapacity, violation of the law or judicial code of ethics.

(2) The Judicial Service Commission shall investigate whether or not a judge should be removed from office on grounds of those enumerated in Sub-Article 1 of this Article. In case the Judicial Service Commission decides that a judge should be removed from office, it shall present its recommendation to the President.

(3) The President may, on the recommendation of the Judicial Service Commission, suspend from office a judge who is under investigation.

Article 53: The Judicial Service Commission

(1) There shall be established a Judicial Service Commission, which shall be responsible for submitting recommendations for the recruitment of judges and the terms and conditions of their services.

(2) The powers, organization and duties of the Judicial Service Commission shall be determined by law.

CHAPTER VII: MISCELLANEOUS PROVISIONS

Article 54: Auditor General

(1) There shall be an Auditor General who audits the revenues, expenditures, and other financial operations of government, and who reports annually, his findings to the National Assembly.

(2) The Auditor General shall be appointed for five years by the President with the approval of the National Assembly. He shall be accountable to the National Assembly.

(3) The detailed powers, duties and organization of the Auditor General shall be determined by law.

Article 55: National Bank

(1) There shall be a National Bank, which performs the functions of a central bank, controls the financial institutions, and manages the national currency.

(2) The National Bank shall have a Governor appointed by the President with the approval of the National Assembly. There shall be a Board of Directors presided by the Governor, and whose members shall be appointed by the President.

(3) The detailed powers, duties and organization of the National Bank shall be determined by law.

Article 56: Public Service Administration

(1) A Public Service Administration, which shall be responsible for recruitment and selection of civil servants, as well as for determining the terms and conditions of their employment, including their rights and duties shall be established.

(2) The detailed powers, duties and organization of the Public Service Administration shall be determined by law.

Article 57: Electoral Commission

(1) There shall be established an Electoral Commission, operating independently, without interference, which shall, on the basis of the electoral law, ensure that free and fair elections are held, and manage their implementation. It shall also decide on issues raised in the course of the electoral process and formulate and implement civic educational programmers relating to elections and other democratic procedures.

(2) An Electoral Commissioner shall be appointed by the President with the approval of the National Assembly.

(3) The detailed powers, duties and organization of the Electoral Commission shall be determined by law.

Article 58: Amendment of the Constitution

(1) A proposal for the amendment of any provision of this Constitution may be initiated and tabled by the President or 50 percent of all the members of the National Assembly.

(2) Any provision of this Constitution may be amended as follows:

a) Where the National Assembly by a three-quarters majority vote of all its members proposes an amendment with reference to a specific Article of the Constitution tabled to be amended; and

b) Where, one year after it has proposed such an amendment, the National Assembly, after deliberation, again approves the same amendment by four-fifths majority vote of all its members.

The State of Eritrea's Unimplemented 1997 Constitution based on Autonomy and Independence

Chapter 20

Constitution of the State of Eritrea in Tigrigna language.

ቅዋም ኤርትራ

ብቅዋማዊ ባይቶ ብ23 ግንቦት 1997 ዝጸደቐ

ትሕዝቶ

2

መቕድም

ንሕና፡ እዞም ብናይ ሓባር ቃልሲ ንመሰልናን ሓደ መጻኢናን ስሙር ሃገር ዝኾንና ህዝቢ ኤርትራ፡ ኣብቲ ንነዊሕ ዝናዊ ታሪኽ ዝተሰርሓሉን ሓርነታዊ ሰውራ፡ ምእንቲ ናጽነትናን መሰልናን ህይወትም ንዘበጀው ዓሰርተታት-ኣሸሓት ጀጋኑ ሰማእታትናን፡ ንጽንዓት ኩሎም ሓርበኛታት ኤርትራውያንን እናመስገንና፡ ኣብቲ ዘውረሱና ናይ ሓድነትን ፍትሕን ተረር ምድሪ ረጊጽናን፦

- ነዚ ብብቱዕ ገድሊ ዝተረኽበ ናጽነትን ሓድነትን፡ ሰላምን ርግኣትን ምክልኻልን፡ ድልድልትን ስልጡንትን ሃገር ብምህናጽ ምዕቃቡን ምምዕባሉን፡ ቅዱስ ግቡእ ዜጋታት ምዃኑ ብምግንዛብ፣

- ምዕብልቲ ሃገር ንምህናጽ፡ እቲ ኣብ ሓርነታዊ ሰውራና ዘማዕበልናዮን ዘወተናን፡ ናይ ሓድነትን ማዕርነትን፡ ፍቕሪ ሓቅን ፍትሕን፡ ርእሰ-ምርኮሳን ፍቕሪ ስራሕን... ክብርታት ሓመረት ሃገራዊ ክብርታትና ክኸውን ከም ዘለዎም ብምርዳእ፣

- ናይ ሕብረተሰብና ጽቡቕ ናይ ኮማዊ ምትሕግጋዝ፡ ፍቕሪ ስድራቤት፡ ኣኽብሮት ንሽማግለታት፡ ሓድሕዳዊ ሓልዮትን ምክብባርን ያታዊ ክብርታት ምውራሱን ምስናኑን፡ ንምዕባለን ጥዕየትን ሕብረተሰብና ኣድላዪ ምዃኑ ብምምልካት፣

- መሰል ዜጋታት፡ ሰብአዊ ክብረት፡ ማዕርነትን ምዕሩይ ምዕባለን ዘውሕስ፡ ናይ ዜጋታት ነገራውን መንፈሳውን ድልየት ዘረውየሉ ኩነታት ዘጣየሕ፡ አብ ድልየት ህዝብን ረብሕኡን ተሳትፎኡን እተመስረተ ደሞክራሲያዊ ስርዓት ምትካል፡ ንጀጠባዊ ምዕባለ፡ ንማሕበራዊ ስኒትን ግስጋሰን መሰረት ምዃኑ ብምርግጋጽ፡

- ቅያ ዝመልአ ተሳትፎ ኤርትራውያን ደቀንስትዮ አብ ቃልሲ ንሓርነትን መሰልን፡ ከምኡውን አብዚ ቃልሲ እዚ አብ መንን ደቀንስትዮን ደቂተባዕትዮን ዝማዕበለ አብ ማዕርነትን ምክብባርን እተመስረተ ጽኑዕ ምሕዝነትን፡ መሰረት ዘይንቅነቅ መብጽዓና ቃልስናን ንማዕርነትን ምሕዝነትን ደቀንስትዮን ደቂተባዕትዮን ምዃኑ ብምግንዛብ፡

- ንህይወትናን ህይወት መጻኢ ወሎዶታትናን ዝሰዕብን ዝጥዕን ፍትሕን ሰላምን ዘስፍን፡ አብ ደሞክራስን ሃገራዊ ሓድነትን እተሰረተ፡ ግዙአት ሕጊ ዘንግስ ቅዋም ከም ኪዳን አብ መንጎናን አብ መንን እቲ ብፍታውና እነቖሞ መንግስትናን ክኸውን ብምድላይ፡

- ሎሚ 23 ግንቦት 1997፡ አብዚ ታሪኻዊ ዕለት እዚ፡ ድሕሪ ሰፊሕ ህዝባዊ ክትዕ፡ ብመገዲ ቅዋማዊ ባይቶ፡ ከም ዝለዓለ ሕጊ ናጽን ልኡላዊትን ሃገርና ኤርትራ፡ እዚ ሃገራዊ ቅዋም እዚ ብወግዒ ንቕበሎን ነጽድቖን አለና።

4

ምዕራፍ ሓደ - ሓፈሻዊ ድንጋጌታት

ዓንቀጽ 1 - ሃገረ-ኤርትራን ክሊ ግዝኣታን

1. ኤርትራ፡ ደሞክራስን ማሕበራዊ ፍትሕን ዝመሰረታ ብግዝኣተ-ሕጊ እትመሓደር ናጻን ልኡላዊትን ሃገር እያ።

2. ሃገራዊ ግዝኣት ኤርትራ፡ ነቲ ፍሉጥ ዝዶባቱ መሬት፡ እንተላይ ማያዊ ክሉን ደሴታቱን ክሊ ኣየሩን የጠቓልል።

3. ኣብ ሃገረ-ኤርትራ ልኡላዊ ስልጣን ናይ ህዝቢ እዩ። እዚ ቅዋም እዚ ብዝእዝዞ ስርዓት ኣቢሉ ኸኣ ኣብ ግብሪ ይውዕል።

4. እቲ ንልኡላዊ ስልጣን ህዝቢ ወኪሉ ብደሞክራሲያዊ ኣገባብ ዝምስረት መንግስቲ ኤርትራ፡ ኣሳታፍን ድልዱልን ትካላት ብምህናጽ፡ ንብቑዕ ደሞክራሲያዊ ፖለቲካዊ ስርዓት መሰረት ይኸውን።

5. ኤርትራ ብኣሃዱኣዊ መንግስቲ ናብ ዞባዊ ምምሕዳራት ተኸፋፊላ ትመሓደር። እቲ ዞባዊ ምምሕዳራት ዝህልዎ ኣቃውማን ስልጣንን ከኣ ብሕጊ ይውሰን።

5

ዓንቀጽ 3 - ዜግነት

1. ካብ ኤርትራዊ ኣቦ ወይ ኤርትራዊት ኣደ እተወልደ፡ ኤርትራዊ ዜጋ ብትውልዲ እዩ።

2. ናይ ካልኦት ሃገራት ዜጋ፡ ሕጊ ብዝውስኖ መሰረት ኤርትራዊ ዜግነት ክወስድ ይኽእል።

3. ንዜግነት ዝምልከት ዝርዝር ሕግታትን ቅጥዕታትን ብሕጊ ይውሰን።

ዓንቀጽ 4 - ሃገራዊ ትእምርትታትን ቋንቋታትን

1. ሃገራዊት ባንዴራ ኤርትራ ወርቃዊ ኣቐጽልቲ ኣውሊዕ ዘለዋ፡ ቀጠልያን ቀይሕን ሰማያውን ዝምድራ እያ። ዝርዝራ ብሕጊ ይውሰን።

2. ኤርትራ፡ ንታሪኽን ሃንቀውታን ህዝባ ዘንጸባርቕ፡ ብሕጊ ዝውሰን ሃገራዊ መዝሙርን ኣርማን ይህልዋ።

3. ኣብ ኤርትራ፡ ማዕርነት ኩሉ ኤርትራዊ ቋንቋታት እተሓለወ እዩ።

ዓንቀጽ 5 - ንጾታ ዝምልከት ኣጸሓሕፋ

እዚ ቅዋም እዚ፡ ጾታዊ ኣጸሓሕፋኡ ብዘየገድስ፡ ኩሉ ዓንቀጻት ንኽልቲኡ ጾታታት ብማዕረ ይምልከት።

7

ዓንቀጽ 2 - ልዕልና ቅዋም

1. እዚ ቅዋም እዚ ሕጋዊ መግለጺ ልኡላውነት ህዝቢ
   ኤርትራ እዩ።

2. እዚ ቅዋም እዚ፡ መንግስቲ ዝምስረተሉን ዝምረሓሉን
   መሰረታዊ መትከላት የነጽርን፡ ኣቃውማኡን ኣካይዳኡን
   ይውስንን። በዚ ከኣ ምንጪ ሕጋውነት መንግስትን፡
   መሰረት ንምሕላው መሰልን ክብረትን ዜጋታትን፡
   ከምኡ'ውን መሰረት ንፍትሓዊ ኣመሓዳድራ ይኸውን።

3. እዚ ቅዋም እዚ፡ እቲ ዝለዓለ ሕግን ምንጪ ናይ ኩሉ
   ሕግታትን ሃገረ-ኤርትራ ስለዝኾነ፡ ኣንጻር ፈደሉን
   መንፈሱን ዝኾነ ዝኾነ ዝኾነ ሕጊ፡ ትእዛዝ ወይ
   ተግባር ፍሩስ እዩ።

4. ኩሎም ኣካላት መንግስትን፡ ከምኡ'ውን ኩሎም
   ማሕበራትን ትካላትን ዜጋታትን፡ ነዚ ቅዋም እዚ
   እሙናት ክኾኑ ክምእዙዙ፡ ኣብ ግብሪ ናይ ምውዓሉ
   ሓላፍነት ክስከሙን ኣለዎም።

5. እዚ ቅዋም እዚ፡ ኣብ ህዝብን ኣካላት መንግስትን
   ቅዋማዊ ባህሊ ንምምዕባልን፡ መሰልን ግቡእን ዜጋታት
   ንምኽባርን መሰረት ይኸውን።

6

174

ምዕራፍ ክልተ - ሃገራዊ ዕላማታትን መሪሒ መትከላትን

ዓንቀጽ 6 - ሃገራዊ ሓድነትን ርግኣትን

1. ህዝብን መንግስትን ኤርትራ፡ ስምርትን ስልጥንትን ሃገር ንምህናጽ ኣብ ዝገብርዎ ጾዕሪ፡ ንብዙሕነት ሕብረተሰብ ኤርትራ ኣብ ግምት ብምእታው፡ ሓድነት ኣብ ብዙሕነት ንዝብል መትከል ከም መሪሒ መትከል ይወስድዎ።

2. መንግስቲ፡ ብተሳትፎ ኩሉ ዜጋ፡ ብደሞክራሲያዊ ልዝብን ሃገራዊ ሓባራዊ መረዳእታን ብምምዕባልን፡ ናይ ሓድነትን ማሕበራዊ ስኒትን ድልዱል ፖለቲካውን ባህላውን ሰረት ብምህናጽ፡ መሰረት ሃገራዊ ርግኣትን ምዕባለን የደልድል።

3. መንግስቲ፡ ብቛንቋትን ኣሰተፍትን ትካላት ብምፍጣር፡ ንእተመጣጠነ ቁጠባውን ማሕበራውን ምዕባለ ዘውሕስን ዘቃላጥፍን ምቹእ ሰላማውን ርጉእን ኩነታት የረጋግጽ።

ዓንቀጽ 7 - ደሞክራሲያዊ መትከላት

1. ምርግጋጽ ሰፊሕን ንጡፍን ተሳታፎ ዜጋታት ኣብ ፖለቲካዊ፡ ቁጠባዊ፡ ማሕበራዊ፡ ከምኡ'ውን ኣብ ባህላዊ ህይወት፡ መሰረታዊ መትከል ሃገረ-ኤርትራ እዩ።

8

2. ሓይልታት ምክልኻልን ጸጥታን ካብ ሕብረተሰብ
   ዘይተነጻሉ፡ ኣፍረይትን ኣኸበርቲ ህዝብን ክኾኑ
   ኣለዎም።

3. ሓይልታት ምክልኻልን ጸጥታን ብሕጊ ዝግዝኡ፡
   ተሓታትን ብቑዓትን ክኾኑ ኣለዎም።

4. ምክልኻልን ጸጥታን ኤርትራ ኣብ ህዝብን ተሳትፎኡን
   እተመስረተ እዩ።

ዓንቀጽ 13 - ፖሊሲ ወጻኢ።

ናይ ኤርትራ ናይ ወጻኢ ፖሊሲ፡ ኣብ ናጽነትን ልኡላውነትን
ሃገር፡ ከምኡ'ውን ኣብ ረብሓ ዞባውን ኣህጉራውን ሰላም፡
ምትሕግጋዝ፡ ምርግጋእን ምዕባለን እተመስረተ እዩ።

ምዕራፍ ሰለስተ - መሰረታዊ መሰላትን ሓርነታትን ግቡኣትን

ዓንቀጽ 14 - ማዕርነት ኣብ ቅድሚ ሕጊ

1. ኩሉ ሰብ ኣብ ቅድሚ ሕጊ ማዕረ እዩ።

2. ኣንጻር ዝኾነ ይኹን ሰብ፡ ኣብ ዓሌት፡ ኣብ ኤትኒካዊ
   መበቆል፡ ኣብ ሕብሪ፡ ኣብ ጾታ፡ ኣብ ቋንቋ፡ ኣብ
   ሃይማኖት፡ ኣብ ስንክልና፡ ኣብ ዕድመ፡ ኣብ ሃይማኖት፡

ኣብ ስንክልና፡ ኣብ ዕድመ፡ ኣብ ፖለቲካዊ ኣረኣእያ ወይ ኣብ ማሕበራውን ቁጠባውን ደረጃን ካልእ ዘይግቡእ ረቛሒታትን እተመስረተ ኣድልዎ ኣይግበርን።

3. ሃገራዊ ባይቶ፡ ኣብ ሕብረተሰብ ንዘሎ ዘይማዕርነት ንምውጋድ ዝሕግዝ ሕግታት የውጽእ።

ዓንቀጽ 15 - **መሰል ህይወትን ናጽነትን**

1. ዝኾነ ሰብ፡ ብዘይ ግቡእ ሕጋዊ መስርሕ ህይወቱ ኣይስእንን።

2. ዝኾነ ሰብ፡ ብዘይ ግቡእ ሕጋዊ መስርሕ ናጽነቱ ኣይንፈግን።

ዓንቀጽ 16 - **መሰል ሰብኣዊ ክብረት**

1. ናይ ዝኾነ ሰብ ሰብኣዊ ክብረት ኣይድፈርን።

2. ንዝኾነ ሰብ፡ ምስቓይ፡ ብጭካነን ውርደትን ዘይሰብኣዊ መገድን ምሓዝን ምቕጻዕን ክልኩል እዩ።

3. ዝኾነ ሰብ፡ ብግልያነት ወይ ብግዲ ብምዕሳብ ክቑረን፡ ወይ'ውን ሕጊ ብዘይፈቕዶ ብሓይሊ ክዓዩ ኣይፍቀድን።

ዓንቀጽ 17 - ማእሰርትን ቀይድን ፍትሓዊ ፍርድን

1. ንዝኾነ ሰብ፡ ብዘይ ግቡእ ሕጋዊ መስርሕ ምእሳር ወይ ምቅያድ አይፍቀድን።

2. ዝኾነ ሰብ፡ ገበን ፈጺሙ አብ እተባህለሉ እዋን አብ ግብሪ ብዘይወዓለ ሓድሽ ሕጊ አይክሰስን፡ አይቅጻዕን።

3. ዝኾነ ሰብ፡ ምኽንያት መእሰሪኡን ምስተኣሰረ ዘለዎ መሰልን ብዝርድኦ ቋንቋ ክግለጸሉ ይግባእ።

4. እተኣሰረ ሰብ፡ አብ ውሽጢ 48 ሰዓት፡ ወይ ከም'ኡ ንምግባር ዘይክኣለሉ ቅቡል ምኽንያት ምስ ዝህሉ ድማ፡ አብ ዝሓጸረ ግዜ፡ አብ ቅድሚ ቤት ፍርዲ ክቐርብ አለዎ። ብዘይ ትእዛዝ ቤት ፍርዲ ኸአ ካብኡ ንላዕሊ ከተሓዝ አይክእልን።

5. ኩሉ ሰብ ናብ ቤት ፍርዲ ብኣካል ንም'ቅራብ መሰል ጥርዓን አለዎ። እቲ ዝእሰረ በዓል ስልጣን፡ ንእሱር ናብ ቤት ፍርዲ ምስ ዘየቅርብን ምኽንያት መእሰሪኡ ምስ ዘየቅርብን፡ ቤት ፍርዲ ነቲ ጥርዓን ተቐቢሉ እሱር ክልቀቅ ይእዝዝ።

6. ዝኾነ ሰብ፡ ጉዳዩ አብ ቤት ፍርዲ ብፍትሓውን ብቅልጡፍን ግሉጽን መገድን ክስማዕ መሰል አለዎ። ቤት ፍርዲ፡ ሓደ ጉዳይ፡ አብ ሓደ ፍትሓውን ደሞክራሲያውን ሕብረተሰብ፡ ብምኽንያት ስነ-ምግባር

14

ወይ ብምኽንያት ሃገራዊ ጸጥታ ብግህዶ ክስማዕ ዘየብሉ ምስ ዝኾውን፡ ንማዕከናት ዜናን ንህዝብን ካብ ምሉእ ወይ ክፋል ናይቲ ጉዳይ ከእግዶም ይኽእል።

7. ክሱስ ብቤት ፍርዲ ገበነኛ ምዃኑ ክሳዕ ዝረጋገጽ ከም ንጹህ ይውሰድ፡ ከቕጽዕ ከላ አይክእልን።

8. ክሱስ ብዝተፈርደ መሰል ይግባይ ይህልዎ። በቲ እተፈረደሉ ጉዳይ ከላ ከም ብሓድሽ አይክሰስን።

ዓንቀጽ 18 - መሰል ብሕትና

1. ኩሉ ሰብ መሰል ብሕትና አለዎ።

2.

   ሀ. ዝኾነ ሰብ፡ ብዘይ ግቡእ ምኽንያት አካላቱ ክፍተሽ፡ ቤቱ ወይ ንብረቱ ክጉርጎር ወይ ክእቶ፡ ከምኡ'ውን ርክባቱን ምጽሕፋን ካልእ ንብረቱን ክድፈር አይፍቀድን።

   ለ. ምፍታሽ ዘፍቅድ ትእዛዝ ቤት ፍርዲ ነቲ ዝፍተሽ ቦታን ዝተሓዝ ሰብን ንብረትን ዝገልጽ ብማሕላ እተደገፈ ምኽኑይ ጥርጠራ ምስ ዝህሉ ጥራይ ይወሃብ።

ዓንቀጽ 19 - ሓርነት ሕልና፡ እምነት፡ ምግላጽ ርእይቶ፡ ምንቅስቓስ፡ ምእካብን ምውዳብን፡

1. ኩሉ ሰብ፡ ናይ ሓሳብ፡ ናይ ሕልናን እምነትን ሓርነት አለዎ።

15

መንባብሮኡ ብቾጸሊ ንኸመሓይሽ ከአ መንግስቲ ብዝከአሎ
ዘበለ ይጽዕር።

3. መንግስቲ፡ ሃብቲ መሬትን ባሕርን፡ አየርን፡ ማይን፡
ብውዱንን ቀጻልነት ብዘለዎን ንረብሓ ህሉው መጻእን
ወለዶታት ብዘረጋግጽን መገዲ ንኸመሓደር፡ ህዝቢ ድማ
አብ ምሕላው አከባቢኡ ንኸሳተፍ አድላዩ ኩነታት ከማዮሕ
ሓላፍነት አለዎ።

ዓንቀጽ 9 - ሃገራዊ ባህሊ

1. መንግስቲ፡ መግለጺ መንነትን ሓድነትን ግስጋሰን ህዝቢ
ኤርትራ ዝኾነ ሃገራዊ ባህሊ ንምምዕባል፡ ምቹእ
ኩነታት ክፈጥርን ክድርኸን ሓልነት ይህልዎ።

2. መንግስቲ፡ ናይ ኮማዊ ሓልዮት ፍቅሪ ስድራቤትን
ክብርታት የተባባዕ።

3. መንግስቲ፡ ስነ-ጥበባት፡ ስነ-ፍልጠት፡ ቴክኖሎጂን
ስፖርትን፡ ዝድንፍዑሉ ክኢላታት ብሓርነት ዝንየሉን
መሃዝነቶም ዝገልጹሉን ምቹእ ኩነታት ንምፍጣር
ይጽዕር።

ዓንቀጽ 10 - ብቌዕ ፍርዳዊ ስርዓት

1. ፍርዳዊ ስርዓት ኤርትራ፡ ብቅዋምን ብሕግን ዝምራሕ፡
ናጽን ብቌዕን ተሓታትን ይኸውን።

10

2. ኩሉ ሰብ፡ ናይ ምዝራብን ሓሳብ ምግላጽን፡ ናይ ፕረስን ካልእት ማዕከናትን ሓርነት አለዎ።

3. ኩሉ ዜጋ፡ ሓበሬታ ናይ ምርካብ መሰል አለዎ።

4. ኩሉ ሰብ፡ ዝኾነ ሃይማኖት ናይ ምኽታልን ምዘውታርን መሰል አለዎ።

5. ኩሉ ሰብ፡ ብሰላማዊ መንገዲ ናይ ምእካብን ሰላማዊ ሰልፊ ናይ ምግባርን መሰል አለዎ።

6. ኩሉ ዜጋ፡ ንፖለቲካዊ፡ ማሕበራዊ፡ ቁጠባውን ባህላውን ዕላማታት ውድባት ከቕውም መሰል አለዎ።

7. ኩሉ ዜጋ፡ ዝኾነ ዜጋ ሕጋዊ ጥያን ጥበብን ከካይድን ከዘውትርን መሰል አለዎ።

8. ኩሉ ዜጋ፡ አብ መላእ ኤርትራ ብሓነት ናይ ምንቅስቓስን አብ ዝኾነ ክፍሊ ኤርትራ ናይ ምንባርን መሰል አለዎ።

9. ኩሉ ዜጋ፡ ካብ ኤርትራ ናይ ምውጻእን ናብ ኤርትራ ናይ ምምላስን፡ ፓስፖርት ወይ ካልእ ሰነዳት መገሻ ናይ ምርካብን መሰል አለዎ።

ዓንቀጽ 20 - መሰል ምድማጽን ኣብ ምርጫ ምውድዳርን

ኩሉ ዜጋ፡ ሕጊ ምርጫ ብዘፍቅዶ መሰረት ክመርጽን ኣብ ምርጫ ክወዳደርን መሰል ኣለዎ።

ዓንቀጽ 21 - ቁጠባዊ፡ ማሕበራዊ፡ ባህላዊ መሰላትን ሓልፍነታትን

1. ኩሉ ዜጋ፡ ብመንግስቲ ብዝወሃብ ማሕበራዊ ኣገልግሎት ናይ ምጥቃም ማዕረ መሰል ኣለዎ። መንግስቲ ሸአ፡ ናይ ጥዕና፡ ናይ ትምህርቲ፡ ናይ ባህልን ካልእን ኣገልግሎትን ናብ ኩሉ ምእንቲ ኽባጽሕ ብዘለዎ ዓቕሚ ይጽዕር።

2. መንግስቲ፡ ዓቕሙ ክሳዕ ዘፍቀደሉ፡ ናይ ዜጋታት፡ ብፍላይ ከአ ጽጉማት ዜጋታት፡ ማሕበራዊ ድሕነት የረጋግጽ።

3. ኩሉ ዜጋ፡ ኣብ ቁጠባዊ ንጥፈታት ብሓርነት ክሳተፍን ዝመረጸ ሕጋዊ ስራሕ ወይ ዋኒን ክኻይድን መሰል ኣለዎ።

4. መንግስትን ሕብረተሰብን ታሪኽውን ባህላውን ወርሻታትን ቅርስታትን ንምልላይን ምዕቃብን፡ ከከም ኣድላይነቱ ድማ ንምምዕባሉን፡ ከምኡ'ውን ንምትሕልላፉ ሓልፍነት ኣለዎ። ንምዕባለ ስነ-ጥበብ

ሰነ-ፍልጠት፡ ሰነ-ኪነትን ስፖርትን፡ ምቹእ ኩነታት
ብምፍጣር ከአ ተሳታፍነት ዜጋታት የተባብዕ።

5. ሃገራዊ ባይቶ፡ ማሕበራዊ ድሕነት ዜጋታት፡ መሰላትን
ኩነታትን ዕየን ካልአ ኣብዚ ዓንቀጽ እዚ እተጠቕሰ
መሰላትን ንምርግጋጽን ንምትግባርን ሕጋታት
የውጽእ።

ዓንቀጽ 22 - ስድራቤት

1. ስድራቤት ናይ ሕብረተሰብ ባህርያዊትን መሰረታዊትን
እህዱ እያ። ብሕብረተሰብን ብመንግስትን ከአ
ክትሕሎን ክትሕብሓብን ይግባእ።

2. ብሕጊ ዝኣክሉ ሰብኣይን ሰበይትን፡ ብናጻን ብምሉእ
ፍቓዶምን ብዘይ ዝኾነ ይኹን ኣድልዎን ከምርዓውን
ስድራቤት ክምስርቱን መሰል ኣለዎም። ኣብ ኩሉ
ጉዳይ ስድራ ቤት ከአ ማዕረ መሰልን ግቡእን ኣለዎም።

3. ወለዲ ንደቆም ብግቡእ እናኬስኩሱን እናተኾናኾኑን
ክዕብዩዎም መሰልን ግዴታን ኣለዎም። ውሉዳት ከአ
ብግዲኦም ንወለዶም ክኸብሩን ምስ ዝሽምግሉ
ክሕግዙዎምን መሰሎምን ግዴትኦምን እዩ።

ዓንቀጽ 23 - መሰል ንብረት

1. ኣብ ናይዚ ዓንቀጽ እዚ ንኡስ-ዓንቀጽ (2) እተደንገገ
ከም ዘሎዎ ኾይኑ፡ ዝኾነ ዜጋ፡ ኣብ ዝኾነ ክፍሊ

18

ኤርትራ፡ ብውልቂ ወይ ብሓባር ምስ ካልኦት፡ ንብረት
ንምጥራይን ንወረስቲ፡ ንምትሕልላፍን መሰል እለዎ።

2. መሬትን ኩሉ ባህርያዊ ሃብትን ንብረት መንግስቲ
ኮይኑ፡ ዜጋታት አብ መሬት ዝህልዎም ናይ
ተጠቃምነት መሰል ብሕጊ ይውሰን።

3. መንግስቲ፡ ምእንቲ ሃገራዊ ረብሓን ጥቕሚ ህዝብን፡
ብግቡእ ሕጋዊ መስርሕ፡ ዝግባእ ካሕሳ ብምኽፋል
ንብረት ክወስድ ይኽእል።

ዓንቀጽ 24 - ምምሕዳራዊ ፍትሒ

1. ዝኾነ ምምሕዳራዊ ጉዳይ ዘለዎ ሰብ፡ በቲ ዝምልከቶ
ምምሕዳራዊ በዓል ስልጣን ብእኽብሮት ክስማዕን፡
ቅልጡፍን ርትዓውን መልሲ ክረክብን መሰል አለዎ።

2. ዝኾነ ምምሕዳራዊ ጉዳይ ዘለዎ ሰብ፡ መሰላቱ ወይ
ረብሓታቱ ምስ ዝትንከፍ ወይ ምስ ዝሕደግ ግቡእ
ምምሕዳራዊ መኣረምታ ክግበረሉ መሰል አለዎ።

ዓንቀጽ 25 - ግቡእ ዜጋታት

ኩሉ ዜጋ እዚ ዝስዕብ ግቡኣት አለዎ፡-

1. ንኤርትራ እሙን ምዃን። ንምዕባሌኣን ንራህዋን ከኣ
ምስራሕ፣

19

2. ንምክልኻል ሃገር ድልዉ ምኻን፣

3. ሃገራዊ ኣገልግሎት ምፍጻም፣

4. ሃገራዊ ሓድነት ምድንፋዕ፣

5. ንቅዋም ምኽባርን ምክልኻልን፣

6. ናይ ካልኦት መሰል ምኽባርን፣

7. ብሕጊ ዝእዘዙ ግቡእት ምፍጻምን።

ዓንቀጽ 26 - ደረት መሰረታዊ መሰላትን ሓርነታትን

1. በዚ ቅዋም እዚ ዝተዋሕሰ መሰረታዊ መሰላትን ሓርነታትን፣ ንረብሓ ሃገራዊ ጸጥታ፣ ንህዝባዊ ድሕነት ወይ ንቛጠባዊ ድሕነት ሃገር፣ ንምሕላው ስነ-ምግባርን ጥዕናን፣ ንምክልኻል ዕግርግር ወይ ገበን፣ ንምዕቃብ መሰልን ሓርነታትን ካልኦት ተባሂሉ ክድረት ይከኣል።

2. በዚ ቅዋም እዚ ንእተዋሕሰ መሰረታዊ መሰላትን ሓርነታትን ዝድረት ዝኾነ ሕጊ፡-

ሀ. ምስ መትከላት ደሞክራስን ፍትሕን ዝሳነ፣

20

ለ.	ሓፈሻዊ ተፈጻምነት ዝህልዎን ንቻንዲ ትሕዝቶ
	ናይቲ ኣብ ሕቶ ዘሎ መሰል ዘየወግድን፣

ሐ.	ናይቲ ምድራት ትሕዝቶ ብንጹር ዝገልጽን፣
	እቲ ናይ ምድራት መዝነት እተመስረተሉ
	ናይዚ ቅዋምዚ ዓንቀጽ ዝረቍሕን ክኸውን
	ኣለዎ።

3. ናይዚ ዓንቀጽ እዚ ንኡስ-ዓንቀጽ(1)፣ ኣብ ናይዚ ቅዋም
እዚ ዓንቀጻት 14(1) (2)፣ 15፣ 16፣ 17(2) (5) (7) (8)፣
19(1) ንእተደነገ መሰላትን ሓርነትን ክድርት
ኣይፍቀድን።

ዓንቀጽ 27 - ህጹጽ ኩነታት

1. ድሕነት ሃገር፣ ጸጥታን ርግኣትን መንግስቲ፣ ብኩናት፣
ብወራርን ብሓፈሻዊ ህውከትን ኣብ ሓደጋ ምስዝኣቱ፣ ወይ
ኣብ እዋን ባህርያዊ ሓደጋ፣ ፕረዚደንት ኣብ ወገናዊ
ጋዜጣ፣ ኣብ መላእ ኤርትራ ወይ ኣብ ገለ ክፋል ህጹጽ
ኩነታት ከም ዘሎ ክእውጅ ይኸእል።

2. እቲ ኣብ ትሕቲ ናይዚ ዓንቀጽ እዚ ንኡስ - ዓንቀጽ (1)
ዝወጽእ ኣዋጅ፣ ብሃገራዊ ባይቶ ብኽለተ-ሲሶ ድምጺ ናይ
ኩሎም ኣባላቱ ከይጸደቐ ኣይረግእን። ስለዚ ፣ ሃገራዊ ባይቶ
ኣብ እኼባ ምስ ዝህሉ ኣብ ውሽጢ ኽልተ መዓልቲ፣ እንተ
ዘይኮነ ድማ ኣብ ውሽጢ ሰላሳ መዓልቲ ንህጹጽ እኼባ
ተጸዊዑ ከጽድቖ ኣለዎ።

21

3. ብመሰረት ንኡስ ዓንቀጽ (2) ብሃገራዊ ባይቶ ዝጸደቐ
   ኣዋጅ ህጹጽ ኩነታት፡ ክሳብ ሾዱሽተ ወርሒ ክጸንዕ
   ይኽእል። ሃገራዊ ባይቶ ከኣ ብኽልተ-ሲሶ ድምጺ
   ኩሉም ኣባላቱ ነቲ ኣዋጅ ኣብ ሓደ እዋን ንሰለስተ
   ወርሒ ከናውሓ ይኽእል።

4. ሃገራዊ ባይቶ ብመሰረት እዚ ዓንቀጽ እዚ ንዘጸደቐ
   ኣዋጅ ብውሳነ ክስዕሮ ይኽእል።

5. ኣዋጅ ህጹጽ ኩነታትን ብእኡ መሰረት ዝውሰድ ዝኾነ
   ይኹን ስጉምትን ዝውሰን ሕጋጋትን፡ ነዚ ዝስዕብ
   ከፍቅድ ወይ ክመዝዝ ኣይክእልን፦

   ሀ. ዓንቀጻት 14 (1) (2)፣ 16፣ 17 (2)፣ 19 (1)
      ምድስካል።

   ለ. ኣብ እዋን ህጹጽ ኩነታት፡ መንግስቲ ወይ
      ኣብ ትሕቲ መዝነቱ ብዝሰርሑ ሰባት
      ንዝተፈጸመ ዘይሕጋዊ ተግባራት ምምሓር።

   ሐ. ወራርን ሓፈሻዊ ህውከትን ኣብ ዘይብሉ እዋን
      ውተሃደራዊ ሕጊ ምእዋጅ።

ዓንቀጽ 28 - እተገብአ መሰረታዊ መሰላትን ሓርነታትን

1. በዚ ቅዋም'ዚ እተፈቕደ እንተ ዘይኮይኑ፡ ብሃገራዊ ባይቶ
   ወይ ብኻልእ ለጠቕ ዝበለ ሕጋጊ ኣካል ነቲ ኣብዚ ምዕራፍ
   እዚ ተዋሂቡ ዘሎ መሰረታዊ መሰላትን ሓርነታትን ዝግህስ
   ወይ ዝድርት ዝኾነ ይኹን ሕጊ ክሕገግ፡ ብፈጻሚ ኣካልን

22

ክፍልታት መንግስትን ከአ ዝኾነ ይኹን ስጉምቲ ክወስድ
ኣይፍቀድን። ዝኾነ ይኹን ነዚ መሰረታዊ መሰላትን
ሓርነታትን ዝግህስ ሕጊ ወይ ተግባር ከአ ፍሩስ እዩ።

2. በዚ ቅዋም እዚ ዝተዋሕሰ መሰረታዊ መሰላትን ሓርነታትን
ተነፊጉና ዝብል ሰብ፡ ንዝምልከቶ ቤት ፍርዲ ክመርዕ
መሰል አለዎ። ቤት ፍርዲ ኸአ መሰላትን ሓርነታትን
ኣመልካቲ ብዘይ ሕጋዊ መገዲ ምንፋት ወይ ምጥሓሱ
እንተደአ እረጋጊጹ፡ ነቲ መሰላትን ሓርነታትን ንምሕላውን
ንምርግጋጽን፡ ከምኡ'ውን ዘወረዶ ጉድኣት ንምእራምን
ትእዛዛትን ውሳኔታትን ከሕልፍ ካሕሳ'ውን ከውህብ ስልጣን
አለዎ።

ዓንቀጽ 29 - ካልኦት መሰላት

ኣብዚ ምዕራፍ እዚ እተዘርዘረ መሰላት፡ ካብ ናይዚ ቅዋም
እዚ መንፈስን ካብ መትከላት ማሕበራዊ ፍትሕን ደሞክራሲን
ግዝኣተ ሕግን ንዚፍልፍል ካልእ መሰላት ኣይክልክልን።

ምዕራፍ ኣርባዕተ - ሃገራዊ ባይቶ

ዓንቀጽ 30 - ውክልና ሀዝቢ

1. ካብ 18 ዓመት ንላዕሊ ዝዕድሚኡ ኤርትራዊ ዜጋ ከድምጽ
መሰል አለዎ።

2. ሃገራዊ ባይቶ፡ ወከልን ኣሳታፍን ዝኾነ ሕጊ ምርጫ
የውጽእ።

23

ዓንቀጽ 32 - ስልጣንን ዕማማትን ሃገራዊ ባይቶ

1. ብመሰረት ናይዚ ቅዋም እዚ ድንጋጌታት፦

    ሀ. ሃገራዊ ባይቶ፡ ንስላምን ርግኣትን ምዕባለን
        ፍትሓዊ አመሓዳድራን ኤርትራ ዘገልግሉ
        ሕግታትን ውሳኔታትን የውጽእ፣

    ለ. ብመሰረት እዚ ቅዋም እዝን ሃገራዊ ባይቶ
        ዘውጽኦ ሕጊ ብዘፍቅዶ መሰረትን እንተ
        ዘይኮይኑ፡ አብ ኤርትራ ዝኾነ ሰብ ወይ አካል
        ሓይሊ ሕጊ ዘሎም ውሳኔ ክወስድ
        አይክእልን።

2. ሃገራዊ ባይቶ፡ ብዕላማታትን መትከላትን ቅዋም ክቕየድን
   ንምዕዋቱ ክስርሕን ግዴታ አሎዎ።

3. ሃገራዊ ባዬት ምጽዳቕን ናይ ግብሪ ሕጊ ምውጽእን ስልጣን
   ሃገራዊ ባይቶ ይኸውን።

4. ሃገራዊ ባይቶ፡ አህጉራዊ ስምምዓት የጽድቕ።

5. ሃገራዊ ባይቶ፡ ሊቓሕ መንግስቲ የጽድቕ።

6. ሃገራዊ ባይቶ፡ ኩነተ ሰላምን ኩናትን፡ ከምኡውን አዋጅ
   ህጹጽ ኩነታት የርግእ።

25

7. ሃገራዊ ባይቶ፡ ኣፈጻጽማ ሕግታት ናይ ምቁጽጻር ስልጣን አሎም።

8. ሃገራዊ ባይቶ፡ ብፍጹም ብዝሒ ድምጺ ካብ ኣባላቱ ንሓሙሽተ ዓመት ፕረዚደንት ይመርጽ።

9. ሃገራዊ ባይቶ፡ ብመሰረት ዓንቀጽ 41 (6) (ሀ)ን (ለ)ን (ሐ)ን ብኽልተ ሲሶ ድምጺ ንፕረዚደንት ቅድሚ ናይ ስልጣን ዕድሚኡ ምእካሉ ካብ ስልጣን ከውርዶ ወይ ከውርዶን ክኽሰን ይኽእል።

10. ሃገራዊ ባይቶ፡ ብመሰረት እዚ ቅጥዋ እዚ ሸመት የጽድቅ።

11. ሃገራዊ ባይቶ፡ ጥርኑን ህዝቢ ዝምርምር ቀዋሚ ኮሚቴ ይምዝዝ።

12. ሃገራዊ ባይቶ፡ ቅዋማዊ መዝነቱ ኣብ ግብሪ ንምውዓል ኩሉ ዘድሊ ዘበለ ውሳኔታት ክሕልፍን ስጉምቲ ክወስድን፡ ቀዋምን ግዝያውን ኮሚቴታት ክመዝዝን ይኽእል።

ዓንቀጽ 33 - ምጽዳቕ ንድፈ ሕጊ

ንድፈ ሕጊ ብሃገራዊ ባይቶ ምስ ጸደቐ ናብ ፕረሲደንት ይመሓላለፍ። ፕረሲደንት ከኣ ኣብ ውሽጢ ሰላሳ መዓልቲ ፈሪሙ ኣብ ወግዓዊ ጋዜጣ ከም ዝሕተም ይገብር።

26

190

ዓንቀጽ 31 - ኣቃውማን ዕድመን ሃገራዊ ባይቶ

1. ኣብ ኤርትራ፡ እቲ ዝለዓለ ወካልን ሒጋግን ኣካል ዝኾነ ሃገራዊ ባይቶ ይህሉ።

2. ሃገራዊ ባይቶ ብህዝቢ፡ ብእተመርጹ ወከልቲ ይቐውም።

3. ኣመራርጻ ኣባላት ሃገራዊ ባይቶ ብምስጢራዊ ድምጺ ዜጋታት ይፍጸም።

4. ኣባላት ሃገራዊ ባይቶ ወከልቲ መላእ ህዝቢ ኤርትራ እዮም። ኣብ ምፍጻም መዝነቶም ከኣ፡ ብዕላማታትን መትከላትን ቅዋም፡ ብረብሓ ህዝብን ሃገርን ብሕልናኣምን ይምርሑ።

5. ዕድመ ሃገራዊ ባይቶ፡ ድሕሪ ሓፈሻዊ ምርጫ ኣብ ሓደ ወርሒ ካብ ዝኽየድ ቀዳማይ ኣኼባኡ፡ ጀሚሩ ንሓሙሽተ ዓመታት ይኸውን። ኣብ እዋን ህጹጽ ኩነታት፡ ሓፈሻዊ ምርጫ ንምክያድ ዝኽልክል ኣጋዳዲ ኹነታት ምስ ዘጋጥም፡ ዕድመ ሃገራዊ ባይቶ፡ ብኽልተ - ሲሶ ድምጺ ኩለም ኣባላቱ ንሽዱሽተ ወርሒ ክናዋሕ ይከኣል።

6. ሓደ ዜጋ ኣባል ሃገራዊ ባይቶ ኮይኑ ንኽምረጽ ዘብቅዓ ቅድመ ኩነትን ኣባልነቱ ዝስረዘሉ ኩነታትን ካልእት ተዛመድቲ ጉዳያትን ዝውስን ሕጊ ይወጽእ።

24

ዓንቀጽ 34 - ኣቦ መንበር ሃገራዊ ባይቶ

1. ሃገራዊ ባይቶ፡ ኣብ ቀዳማይ ኣኼባኡ ብፍጹም ብዝሒ ድምጺ ካብ ኣባላቱ ኣቦ መንበሩ ንሓሙሽተ ዓመት ይመርጽ።

2. ኣቦመንበር ሃገራዊ ባይቶ፡ ኣኼባታት ሃገራዊ ባይቶ ይጽውዕን ይመርሕን፣ ኣብ መንጎ ኣኼባታት ከኣ፡ ናይ ቀዋምን ግዝያውን ኮሚተታትን ቤት ጽሕፈትን ባይቶ ስርሓት፡ የወሃህድን ይመርሕን።

ዓንቀጽ 35 - ማሕላ

ነፍሲ ወከፍ ኣባል ሃገራዊ ባይቶ ነዚ ዝስዕብ ማሕላ ይፍጽም።

"ኣነ ----------------፡ ነቲ ኣባል ሃገራዊ ባይቶ ኤርትራ ከኸውን ዝመረጸኒ ህዝቢ ዘሰከመኒ ሓደራ እሙንን ብቑዕን ብምዃን፡ ንሃገራዊ ቅዋም ኤርትራ ክምእዘዝን ክከላኸለሉን፡ ንሓድነትን ምዕባለን ሃገረይ ብምሉእ ዓቕመይን ሕልናይን ክጽዕትን ብ---------- እምሕል ኣሎኹ።"

ዓንቀጽ 36 - ኣኼባታት፡ ውሽጣዊ ሕግታትን መምርሒታትን ሃገራዊ ባይቶ

1. ሃገራዊ ባይቶ ምዱብ ኣኼባታት ይገብር፡ ግዜን ንውሓትን ኣኼባታቱ ንሱ ይውስን።

2. ሃገራዊ ባይቶ ብጻውዒት ፕረዚደንት፡ ወይ ብኣቦመንበር ሃገራዊ ባይቶ፡ ወይ ከኣ ብሓደ ሲሶ ኣባላት ሃገራዊ ባይቶ ህጹጽ ኣኼባ ክግበር ይኽእል።

3. ምልኣተ-ጉባኤ ሃገራዊ ባይቶ ብፍርቂ ኣባላቱ ይቖውም።

4. ኣብዚ ቅዋም እዚ እንተ ዘይተወሲኑ፡ ጉዳያት ብብዝሒ ድምጺ ናይቶም እተረኽቡ ኣባላት ይውሰን። ማዕረ ድምጺ ኣብ ዘጋጥመሉ ግዜ ከኣ ኣቦ መንበር ዝደገፎ ውሳነ ይጸድቕ።

5. ሃገራዊ ባይቶ፡ ንኣሰራርሓኡ፡ ኣወዳድባን ዕማማትን ቀዋምን ግዝያውን ኮሚቴታቱን ቤት ጽሕፈቱን፡ ከምኡ`ውን ንስነ-ምግባር ኣባላቱን ንግልጽነት ኣሰራርሓኡን ዝሰርዕ ወሽጣዊ ሕግታትን መምርሒታትን የውጽእ።

ዓንቀጽ 37 - ቤት ጽሕፈት ሃገራዊ ባይቶን ኮሚቴታትን

1. ሃገራዊ ባይቶ ብኣቦመንበሩ ዝምራሕ ንሃገራዊ ባይቶን ኮሚተታቱን ዘገልግል ቤት ጽሕፈት ይህልዎ።

2. እዘን ብመሰረት ዓንቀጽ 32(12) ዝቖማ ኮሚተታት፡ ዝኾና ይኹን ሰብ ኣብ ቅድሚኣን ቀሪቡ ብምምሓል ሓበሬታ ክም ዝህበንን፡ ከምኡ`ውን ኣድላዪ ሰነዳት ክም ዘቕርበለንን ናይ ምግባር ስልጣን ኣለወን።

28

ዓንቀጽ 38 - ግቡአትን ሓለፋታትን ኣባላት ሃገራዊ ባይቶ

1. ኩሎም ኣባላት ሃገራዊ ባይቶ፡ ከም ኣባላት ሃገራዊ ባይቶ ናይ መዝነቶም ክብሪ ክሕልዉን ተመቐሊሉም ንህዝቢ ከገልግሉን ግቡኦም እዩ።

2. ሓደ ኣባል ሃገራዊ ባይቶ፡ ግበን እንዳፈጸመ እንተ ዘይተታሒዙ፡ ብግበን ኣይክሰስን። ክሲ ምስ ዝቐርበሉ ሃገራዊ ባይቶ ብዝውሁስ ኣገባብ ክኸሰስ ይከኣል።

3. ሓደ ኣባል ሃገራዊ ባይቶ፡ ኣብ ኣኼባ ሃገራዊ ባይቶ ወይ ኣብ ኮሚተታቱ ወይ ካብኡ ወጻኢ ምስ መዝነቱ ኣብ ዝዛመድ ጉዳይ ብዘቐርቦ ሓሳብን ርእይቶን ኣይክሰስን ወይ ኣይሕተትን።

4. ንሓለፋታትን ግቡአትን ኩነታት መዝነትን ደሞዝን ኣባላት ሃገራዊ ባይቶ ዝምልከት ሕግታት ብሃገራዊ ባይቶ ይጸድቕ። ናይ ኹሎም ኣባላት ሃገራዊ ባይቶ ሓለፋታት ድማ እተሓለወ ይኸውን።

ምዕራፍ ሓሙሽተ - ፈጻሚ ኣካል

ዓንቀጽ 39 - ፕረዚደንት፡ መራሒ ሃገርን መንግስትን

1. ፕረዚደንት ኤርትራ፡ መራሕ ሃገርን መንግስትን፡ ላዕለዋይ ኣዛዚ ሓይሊታት ምክልኻልን ኤርትራ እዩ።

2. ፈጸሚ ስልጣን ሃገረ-ኤርትራ ኣብ ኢድ ፕረዚደንት ኢዩ። ፕረዚደንት ድማ ምስ ካቢኔ ሚኒስትራቱ እናተማኸረ ብመሰረት እዚ ቅዋም እዚ ኣብ ግብሪ የውዕሎ።

3. ፕረዚደንት፡ ምእዛዝ ንቅዋም፡ ህላወን ክብረትን መንግስቲ፡ ግቡእ ኣስራርሓ ምምሕዳራዊ ትካላት፡ ረብሓን ድሕነትን ከምኡ`ውን በዚ ቅዋም`ዚ እተፈልጠ ናይ ኩሉ ዜጋ መሰረታዊ መሰላትን ሓርነታትን የረጋግጽ።

ዓንቀጽ 40 - ናይ ዝምረጽ ፕረዚደንት ብቕዓት

ሓደ ኣባል ሃገራዊ ባይቶ፡ ንፕረዚደንትነት ንኽምረጽ፡ ብትውልዲ ኤርትራዊ ዜጋ ክኸውን ኣለዎ።

ዓንቀጽ 41 - ኣመራርጻን ዕድመ ስልጣንን ፕረዚደንት

1. ፕረዚደንት ካብ ኣባላት ሃገራዊ ባይቶ ብፍጹም ብዝሒ ድምጺ ይምረጽ። ሓደ ኣባል ሃገራዊ ባይቶ ንፕረዚደንትነት ንኽሕጸ ናይ 20% ኣባላት ሃገራዊ ባይቶ ደገፍ ክረክብ ኣለዎ።

2. ዕድመ ስልጣን ፕረዚደንት ማዕረ እቲ ዝመርጾ ሃገራዊ ባይቶ ንሓሙሽተ ዓመት ይኸውን።

3. ሓደ ሰብ ካብ ክልተ ግዜ ንላዕሊ ንፕረዚደንትነት ኣይምረጽን።

4. ፕረሲደንት፡ ብሞት፡ ወይ ብፍቓዱ ካብ ስልጣን ብምውራድ፡ ወይ ብመሰረት ንኡስ-ዓንቀጽ (6) ካብ ስልጣን ተኣልዩ ቦታኡ ምስ ዝለቕቕ፡ ብኣቦ መንበር ሃገራዊ ባይቶ ይትካእ። ኣቦመንበር ሃገራዊ ባይቶ ኸኣ፡ ክሳዕ ካልእ ፕረሲደንት ዝምረጽ ካብ ሳላሳ መዓልታት ንዘይነውሕ ግዜ ግዝያዊ ፕረሲደንት ኮይኑ የገልግል።

5. እቲ ብመሰረት ናይዚ ዓንቀጽ እዚ ንኡስ-ዓንቀጽ (4) ፕረሲደንት ዝምረጽ ሰብ፡ ንዕላማታት ንኡስ-ዓንቀጽ (3) ከም ምሉእ ግዜ ኣይቁጸረሉን።

6. ንፕረሲደንት፡ ብኽልተ-ሲሶ ድምጺ ኣባላት ሃገራዊ ባይቶ በዚ ዝስዕብ ምኽንያታት ካብ ስልጣን ምውራዱ ይከኣል፦

   ሀ. ንቅዋም ብምጥሓስ ወይ ንሕጊ ብዕቱብ ብምጥሓስ ገበነኛ ኮይኑ ምስ ዝርከብ።

   ለ. ንስልጣኑ ክብረትን ፕረዚደንት ዘየብቅዕ ዝንብር ድኽመትን ስነ-ምግባራዊ ውድቀትን ምስ ዘርኢ።

   ሐ. ስልጣን ፕረሲደንት ንምፍጻም ዘየኽእሎ ኣካላዊ ወይ ኣእምሮኣዊ ጉድለት ምስ ዘንፀር።

7. ሃገራዊ ባይቶ፡ ፕረዚደንት ዝምረጽሉ፡ ከምኡ'ውን ካብ ስልጣን ዝወርደሉ፡ ቅጥዕታት ብሕጊ ይውስን።

ዓንቀጽ 42 - ስልጣንን ዕማማትን ፕረዚደንት

ፕረዚደንት እዚ ዝስዕብ ስልጣንን ዕማማትን ይህልዎ፦

31

196

1. ኣብ ዓመት ሓንሳእ ብዛዕባ ኩነታት ሃገርን ፖሊሲታት መንግስትን ንህዝባዊ ባይቶ መደረ ምግባር፤

2. ብመሰረት ዓንቀጽ (27) ህጹጽ ኸነታት ምእዋጅ። ንምክልኻል ሃገር ኣብ ዝድለየሉ እዋን ከኣ ኩነተ ኵናት ምእዋጅ፤

3. ኣብ ዘድሊ እዋን ህጹጽ ኣኼባ ሃገራዊ ባይቶ ምጽዋዕን ነቲ ኣኼባ መግለጺ ምቅራብን፤

4. ሃገራዊ ባይቶ ንዘጽደቖ ሕጊ ምኽታምን ኣብ ወግዓዊ ጋዜጣ ከም ዝሕተም ምግባርን፤

5. ብሃገራዊ ባይቶ እተወሰነ ሕግታትን ውሳኔታትን ኣብ ግብሪ ምውዓሉ ምርግጋጽ፤

6. ኣህጉራዊ ስምምዓት ምዝታይን ምኽታምን። ከምኡ'ውን ነዚ ስልጣን እዚ ምውካል፤

7. ብምጽዳቕ ሃገራዊ ባይቶ፡ ሚኒስተራት፡ ኮሚሽነራት፡ ጠቅላሊ ኣዲተር፡ ጠቅላሊ ኣመሓዳሪ ሃገራዊ ባንክ፡ ኣቦመንበር ርእሰ ኣብያተፍርዲ፡ ብኸልእ ነዪዚ ቅዋም እዚ ድንጋጌታት ወይ ካልእ ሕግታት ብፕረዚደንት ክሽየሙ ዘለዎም ካልኦት ሰባትን ምሻም፤

8. ብእማመ ኮሚሽን ፍርዳዊ ኣገልግሎትን ብምጽዳቕ ሃገራዊ ባይቶን ፈራዶ ርእሰ ኣብያተ ፍርዲ ምሻም፤

32

9. ብእማ መኮሚሽን ፍርዳዊ ኣገልግሎት ዳዩ ታሕተዎት እብይተ ፍርዲ ምሻም፣

10. ኣምባሳደራትን ዲፕሎማስያዊ ወኪላትን ምምዛዝን ምቕባልን፣

11. ላዕለዎት ሓለፍቲ ሓይልታት ምክልኻልን ጸዋታን ኤርትራ ምምዛዝ፣

12. ዓንቀጽ 27(5-ለ) እተዓቀበ ኮይኑ፡ ንበደለኛታት ፍርዲ ምንካይን ምሕረት ምሃብን፣

13. ንብቑዕ ምምሕዳር ኣድላዩ ምስ ዝኾውን፡ ምስ ምምሕዳር ሲቪላዊ ኣገልግሎት ብምምኻር፡ ሚኒስትሪታትን ክፍልታትን መንግስቲ ምጇም ወይ ምፍራስ፣

14. እኼባታት ካቢኔ ምምራሕን ንጥፈታቱ ምውህሃድን፣

15. ናብ ሃገራዊ ባይቶ ንምጽዳቕ ዝቐርቡ ንድፈ ሕግታትን ባጀትን ምእማም፣

16. ምስ ዝምልከቶም ትካላትን ሰባትን ብምምኻር፡ ንዜጋታት ኤርትራ፡ ከምኡውን ንኻልኦት ተቐማጦ ኣዕሩኽን ኤርትራ፡ ናይ ክብሪ ንሻናት ምሻላም፣

17. ዓንቀጽ 52 (1) ዝተሓለወ ኮይኑ፡ ብፕረዚደንት ዝተሸመ ሰብ ካብ መዝነቱ ብፕረዚደንት ምውራዱ ይኸእል።

33

ዓንቀጽ 43 - ካብ ጉዳይ ሲቪላውን ገበናውን ክሲ ናጻ ምዃን

1. ስልጣን ፕረዚደንት ዝሓዘ ሰብ፡-

   ሀ. ምስ መንግስታዊ ስርሑ ከም ፕረዚደንት ብተዛማዶ ጉዳይ እንተዘይኮይኑ ብሲቪላዊ ጉዳይ ኣይክሰስን። ኣብ ክንድኡ ግን መንግስቲ ክኽሰስ ይኽእል።

   ለ. ብመሰረት ዓንቀጽ 41 (6) (ሀ)ን (ለ)ን እንተዘይኮይኑ ብገበን ኣይክሰስን።

2. ፕረዚደንት ካብ መዝነቱ ምስ ወረደ ዝኾነ ቤት ፍርዲ ኣብ መንግስታዊ ስርሑ ብዝፈጸሞ ተግባር ኣብ ልዕሊኡ ንዚቐርብ ሲቪላዊ ክሲ ኣይቅበልን።

ዓንቀጽ 44 - ፕረዚደንት ንዝነብረ ሰብ ዝወሃብ ሓለፋ

ፕረዚደንት ንዝነብረ ሰብ ዝወሃብ ሓለፋ ብሕጊ ይውሰን።

ዓንቀጽ 45 - ማሕላ

ፕረዚደንት ዝተመርጸ፡ ነዚ ዝስዕብ ማሕላ ይፍጽም፤

"ኣነ_____፡ ከም ፕረዚደንት ሃገረ-ኤርትራ፡ ንቕዋም ኤርትራ ከምእዘዝን ከከላኸለሉን፡ ንህዝቢ

34

ኤርትራ፡ ብምሉእ ዓቕመይን ሕልናይን ከገልግሎን፡ ብ
_____ እምሕል አለኹ። "

ዓንቀጽ 46 - ካቢኔ

1. ብፕረዚደንት ዝምራሕ ናይ ሚኒስተራት ካቢኔ ይህሉ።

2. ፕረዚደንት ካብ አባላትን ዘይአባላትን ሃገራዊ ባይቶ
   ሚኒስተራት ክሾይም ይኽእል።

3. ካቢኔ ንፕረዚደንት አብዚ ዝስዕብ ይሕግዙ፡

   ሀ.   ስርሓት መንግስቲ አብ ምምራሕን ምውህሃድን
        ምክትታልን፡

   ለ.   ናብ ሃገራዊ ባይቶ ዝቐርብ ሃገራዊ ባጀት
        መንግስቲ አብ ምጽናዕን ምድላውን፡

   ሐ.   ናብ ሃገራዊ ባይቶ ዝቐርብ ንድፊ ሕጋታት አብ
        ምጽናዕን ምድላውን

   መ.   ፖሊስታትን ውጥናትን አብ ምጽናዕን
        ምድላውን።

4. ፕረዚደንት፡ ንኣወዳድባ፡ ንኣሰራርሓ፡ ንዕማማት ስነ-
   ምግባርን ካቢኔን ቤት ጽሕፈት ፕረዚደንትን ዝምልከት
   መምርሒ የውጽእ።

ዓንቀጽ 47 - ተሓታትነት ሚኒስተራት

1. ኩሎም ሚኒስተራት፡

35

4. ኩሉ ኣካላት መንግስቲ፡ ብመሰረት እዚ ቅዋም እዝን ካልእ
ሕጋታትን፡ ኣብያተ ፍርዲ ስርሑ ብግቡእን ብጽፉፍን
መገዲ ምእንቲ ክፍጽም፡ ናጽነቱን ክብረቱን ምእንቲ
ክሕሎን፡ ኣድላዪ ምትሕግጋዝ ክገብር ኣለዎ።

ዓንቀጽ - 49 ርእሰ ኣብያተ ፍርዲ

1. ርእሰ ኣብያተ ፍርዲ እቲ ዝለዓለ ይግባይ ዝበሃሎ ቤት
ፍርዲ ይኸውን። ብኣቦመንበሩ ድማ ይምራሕ።

2. ርእሰ ኣብያተ ፍርዲ

ሀ. ነዚ ቅዋም እዚ ናይ ምትርጓምን ብዛዕባ ቅዋምነት
ናይቶም ብመንግስቲ ዝወጹ ሕጋታት ወይ
ዝወስዱ ስጉምታት ናይ ምውሳንን በይናዊ
ስልጣን ይህልዎ፣

ለ. ብመሰረት ናይዚ ቅዋም እዚ ዓንቀጽ 41(6) (ሀ)ን
(ለ)ን ፕረዚደንት ካብ ስልጣን ወረዱ ምስ ዝኽሰስ፡
ናይ ምፍራዱ በይናዊ ስልጣን ይህልዎ።

ሐ. ካብ ታሕታይ ኣብያተ ፍርዲ ንዝመጽእ ይግባያት
ይስምዕን ይዳንን።

3. ርእሰ ኣብያተ ፍርዲ ውሽጣዊ ኣወዳድብኡን
ኣሰራርሓኡን ይውስን።

37

ሀ. ንኣመሓዳድራን ስራሕን ሚኒስትሪታቶም ብዝምልከት ብውልቁ ንፕረዚደንት፣

ለ. ከም ካቢኔ ብሓባር ብመገዲ ፕረዚደንት ንሃገራዊ ባይቶ ተሓተቲ እዮም።

2. ሃገራዊ ባይቶ ወይ ኮሚተታቱ ንዝኾነ ይኹን ሚኒስተር ብዛዕባ ፖሊሲታትን ስረሓትን ሚንስትሪኡ ንምሕታት ብመገዲ ቤት ጽሕፈት ፕረዚደንት ክጽውዓ ይኽእል።

ምዕራፍ ሽድሽተ - ምምሕዳር ፍትሒ

ዓንቀጽ 48 - ኣብያተ ፍርዲ

1. ፍርዳዊ ስልጣን ኣብ ኢድ ርእሰ ኣብያተፍርድን ካልእ ብሕጊ ዝቖመ ታሕተዋይ ኣብያተ ፍርድን ይኸውን። ብመሰረት እዚ ቅዋም እዝን ካልእ ሕጋታትን ከኣ ብሽም ህዝቢ ኣብ ግብሪ ይውዕል።

2. ኣብያተ ፍርዲ ኣብ ምፍጻም ፍርዳዊ መዙ ካብ ምቑጽጻርን ምምራሕን ዝኾነ ይኹን ሰብ ወይ ስልጣን ናጻ እዩ። ፈራዶ ንሕግን ብሕጊ ንዝውሰን ስነ ምግባርን ንሕልንኦምን ተኣዘዝቲ ይኾኑ።

3. ዳኛ ኣብ ምትግባር ፍርዳዊ ስልጣን ብዝፍጽሞ ተግባራት ኣይክሰስን።

4. ዕድመ ኣገልግሎትን ብዝሕን ደያኑ ርእሰ ኣብያተ ፍርዲ
   ብሕጊ ይውስን።

ዓንቀጽ 50 - ታሕታይ ኣብያተ ፍርዲ

ስልጣንን ኣወዳድባን ኣሰራርሓን ታሕታይ ኣብያተ ፍርድን
ዕድመ ኣገልግሎት ደያንኡን ብሕጊ ይውስን።

ዓንቀጽ 51 - ማሕላ

ኩሉ ፈራዳይ ነዚ ዝስዕብ ማሕላ ይፍጽም፦-

"እነ_____ ብቅዋምን ብኻልእት ሕግታትን
ተማእዚዘ ፍትሒ ከብይን፣ ኣብ ምፍጻም ፍትሒ ንሕግን
ንሕልናይን እሙን ብምኳን መዝነተይ ከፍጽም፣ ብ
_____እምሕል እሎኹ።

ዓንቀጽ 52 - ምልጋስ ፈራዳይ

1. ብምኽንያት ኣእምሮኣዊ ወይ ኣካላዊ ዘይብቅዓት ወይ
   ብምጥሓስ ሕጊ ወይ ስነምግባር፣ ብመሰረት ኣብ ታሕቲ ዘሎ
   ንኡስ-ዓንቀጽ(2)፣ ሓደ ፈራዳይ ቅድሚ ዕድመ ስራሑ
   ምእካሉ፣ ብእማመ ኮሚሽን ፍርዳዊ ኣገልግሎት
   ብፕረዚደንት ጥራይ ካብ ስራሑ ክልገስ ይኽእል።

2. ኣብ ንኡስ ዓንቀጽ (1) ብእተወሰነ መሰረት፣ ኮሚሽን
   ፍርዳዊ ኣገልግሎት ሓደ ፈራዳይ ካብ ስራሑ ኬልግስ ከም
   ዘለዎን ዘይብሉን መርመራ የካይድ። ኮሚሽን ፍርዳዊ

38

አገልግሎት ሐደ ፌራዳይ ካብ ስራሑ ክእለ እንተድኣ ወሲኑ ሽኣ እማመኡ ናብ ፕሬዚደንት የቅርብ።

3. ፕሬዚደንት፡ ኮሚሽን ፍርዳዊ አገልግሎት ብዘቅረበሉ ርእይቶ መሰረት፡ ንሓደ አብ ትሕቲ መርመራ ዘሎ ፌራዳይ ካብ ስራሑ ክግልሎ ይኽእል።

ዓንቀጽ 53 - ኮሚሽን ፍርዳዊ አገልግሎት

1. ብመሰረት እዚ ቅዋም እዚ፡ አተሓራርያን ኩነታት ስራሕን ፌራዶ ዝከታተልን ብዛዕብኡ ሓሳብ ዘቅርብን ሓደ ኮሚሽን ፍርዳዊ አገልግሎት ይህሉ።

2. ዝርዝር ስልጣንን አወዳድባን ዕማማትን ኮሚሽን ፍርዳዊ አገልግሎት ብሕጊ ይውሰን።

ዓንቀጽ 54 - አኽባር ሕጊ

ስልጣኑን ዕማማቱን ብሕጊ ዝውሰን አኽባሪ ሕጊ ይህሉ።

ምዕራፍ ሸውዓተ - እተፈላለየ ድንጋጌታት

ዓንቀጽ 55 - ጠቅላሊ አዲተር

1. ናይ መንግስቲ አታውን ወጻእን ካልእ ፌናንሳዊ ንጥፈታትን ዝምርምርን ዓመታዊ ጸብጻቡ ናብ ሃገራዊ ባይቶ ዘቅርብን ጠቅላል አዲተር ይህሉ።

2. ጠቅላል አዲተር ብምጽዳቕ ሃገራዊ ባይቶ ብፕረዚደንት
ንሓሙሽተ ዓመታት ይሽየም። ንሃገራዊ ባይቶ ኸኣ
ተሓታቲ ይኸውን።

3. ዝርዝር ስልጣን፡ ኣወዳድባ፡ ዕማማት ጠቅላል አዲተርን
ቤት ጽሕፈቱን ብሕጊ ይውሰን።

ዓንቀጽ 56 - ሃገራዊ ባንክ

1. ከም ማእከላይ ባንክ ዘገልግል፡ ፈናንሳዊ ትካላት ዝቆጻጸርን
ሃገራዊ ባጤራ ዘመሓድርን ሓደ ሃገራዊ ባንክ ይህሉ።

2. ሃገራዊ ባንክ ብምጽዳቕ ሃገራዊ ባይቶ ብፕረዚደንት
ዝምዘዝ ጠቅላል አመሓዳሪ ይህልዎ። አባላቱ
ብፕረዚደንት ዝምዘዙ ቦርድ ሃገራዊ ባንክ ከኣ ይህሉ።

3. ዝርዝር ስልጣን፡ ኣወዳድባ፡ ዕማማት፡ ሃገራዊ ባንክ ብሕጊ
ይውሰን።

ዓንቀጽ 57 - ምምሕዳር ሲቪላዊ ኣገልግሎት

1. ሰራሕተኛታት ሲቪላዊ ኣገልግሎት ዝሕረዩሉ አብ ስራሕ
ዝምደብሉን ካብ ስራሕ ዝሰናበትሉን፡ ንስነ-ምግባሮምን
ግቡአቶምን መሰላቶምን ዘነጽር ሕግታትን ዘማሓድር ቤት
ጽሕፈት ሲቪላዊ ኣገልግሎት ይህሉ።

2. ዝርዝር ስልጣኑ፡ አወዳድባ፡ ዕማማት ምምሕዳር ሲቪላዊ
   አገልግሎት ብሕጊ ይውሰን።

ዓንቀጽ 58 - ኮሚሽን ምርጫ

1. ብመሰረት ሕጊ ምርጫ፡ ምርጫታት ናጻን ርትዓውን ምኳኑ
   ዘረጋግጽ፡ ኣካይዳ ምርጫ ዘመሓድርን፡ ንዝለዓለ ጉዳያት
   ዝውስንን፡ ህዝቢ ብዛዕባ ምርጫታትን ካልእ ደሞክራስያዊ
   ኣገባባትን ከምዝፈልጥ ዝገብርን፡ ናጻን ጣልቃ ዘይብሉን
   ኮሚሽን ምርጫ ይህሉ።

2. ኮሚሽነር ምርጫ፡ ብምጽዳቕ ሃገራዊ ባይቶ ብፕረዚደንት
   ይሸየም። ዕድመ ኣገልግሎቱ ኸአ ብሕጊ ይውሰን።

3. ዝርዝር ስልጣኑ፡ አወዳድባ፡ ዕማማት ኮሚሽን ምርጫ
   ብሕጊ ይውሰን።

ዓንቀጽ 59 - ምምሕያሽ ቕዋም

1. ዝኾነ ናይዚ ቕዋም እዚ ድንጋጌ ንኽምሓየሽ ካብ
   ፕረዚደንት ወይ ካብ ፍርቂ ኣባላት ሃገራዊ ባይቶ ሓሳብ
   ክቐርብ ይኽእል።

2. ዝኾነ ናይዚ ቕዋም እዚ ድንጋጌ፡-

ሀ. ሃገራዊ ባይቶ ብሰለስተ ርብዒ ድምጺ ናይ ኩሎም
አባላቱ ክመሓየሽ አለዎ አለዎ ንዚብሎ ዓንቀጽ
አነጺሩ ንኪመሓየሽ ብምውሳኑ፣

ለ. እቲ ምምሕያሽ ድሕሪ ሓደ ዓመት ከም ብሓድሽ
ብሃገራዊ ባይቶ ተዘትዩሉ ብኦርባዕተ ሕምሲት
ድምጺ ኩሎም አባላቱ ምስ ዝድገፍ፣

ክመሓየሽ ይከአል።

Chapter 21

Global Constitution Checks and Balances

One Global Flag, One global Currency, One global international constitution for a better, safe, fair, just, and secure world.

The United Countries of the World of the world's global Flag of Planet Earth will be the map of earth, when and if a proposal is accepted by all the 193 countries in the world.

We the people of the United Countries of world on behalf of our planet's oath is as follows:
"We solemnly swear (or affirm) that we will faithfully execute the Office of Planet Earth of our world, and will to the best of our abilities, preserve, protect and defend the Constitution of the United Countries of the World."

> According to the Supreme Laws of all nation's Constitution, we have rights to hold any branch of government accountable with checks and balances, in order to curb abuse of power, avoid war crimes in the name of defending and protecting. Invading other countries' autonomy is a criminal act.

Top Mission of Global constitution is balancing and checking constitutions of United States and Constitution of the State of Eritrea, and eventually checking and balancing all Constitution of all countries of the world.

To one day be recognized legitimately and legally recognized as a non-political global organization, with supreme global universal laws of lands, and checks and balances to curb excesses.

When and **if implemented,** the future supreme law/Constitution of the United Countries of the World of the world drafted by the author of this book will become utilized by all nations of the world:

No government will be above the Supreme law/Constitution of United Countries of the World.

No government official will be above the Supreme law/Constitution of United Countries of the World.

No person is above the supreme law/Constitution of United Countries of the World.

Every individual, no matter how wealthy or powerful, is equally subject to the supreme law/Constitution of United Countries of the World.

Everyone must equally obey the Supreme law/Constitution of United Countries of the World. No one must abuse it.

Chapter 22

We the United Countries of the World

We are good citizens who have great ideas, laws, and optimistic dreams of one world under one flag, one currency and one constitution that will govern all nations of the world. One Flag. One currency. One Global constitution. This is the highest level of success our world can ever hope to achieve.

We, as caring, compassionate human beings want a world that will one day be rid of wars.

Causes of Crime, Terrorism and Revolution are:

- Injustice.
- Power hunger.
- Greed.
- Retaliation.
- Jealousy.
- Discrimination.
- Racism.
- Glory.
- Poverty.
- Gold.
- Invasion of foreign lands.

- Modern systemic colonization.
- Systemic Neo-colonialism.
- De capto colonialism.
- Sexual Harassment.
- Human Trafficking.
- Prostitution.
- Illegal Drugs.
- Corruption.
- Forced military conscription.
- Forced labor.
- Treason.
- War.
- Criminal of War.
- Injustice.
- Torture.
- Political unlawful solitary imprisonment.
- Murder.
- Raping.
- Abuse of power.
- Conspiracy theories.
- Propaganda.
- Dirty politicians.
- Dictatorship.
- Oppression.
- Kidnapping.
- Stealing.
- Lying.

- Exploitation of other countries' natural resources.
- Competition of power and glory.
- Credit cards.
- Loans.
- Credit scores.
- The rich getting richer while the poor get poorer.
- Pride.
- Anger.
- Revenge.
- Retaliation.
- Politics.
- Religion.
- Unemployment.
- Police brutality.
- Unlawful police arrests.
- Abuse of power by the police.
- Bias.
- Government officials' abuse of power.
- Alcohol.
- Parental neglect.
- Drug abuse.
- Personal crimes.
- Property crimes.
- Inchoate crimes.
- Statutory crimes.
- Poverty.
- Hunger.

- War movies and war documentaries.
- Abnormalities.
- Psychological disorders.
- Social and economic factors.
- Deprivation.
- Unfair judicial system.
- Unlawful deportation of asylum seekers.

11
Mothers of Crime and Terrorism:

1. Killing is the first mother of Crime.
2. Inequality is the second mother of Crime and Terrorism.
3. Racism is the third mother of Crime and Terrorism.

4. Religion is the fourth mother of Crime and Terrorism.
5. Politics is the fifth mother of Crime and Terrorism.
6. Colonization is the sixth mother of Crime and Terrorism.
7. Greed is the seventh mother of Crime and Terrorism.
8. Poverty is the eighth mother of Crime and Terrorism.
9. Domestic interpersonal violence is the ninth mother of crime.
10. Corruption is the tenth mother of Crime and Terrorism.
11. Lying, cheating, and stealing are the eleventh mothers of crime.

Chapter 23

TRAPS

Traps of Poverty are Credit Cards, Credit Score, Colonization and Superpowerism

We as visionary free thinkers and inventors

unanimously Under the Leadership of our Amazoxa Peace University the Home of True Education CEO, Zerit Teklay Sebhatleab decided by majority vote to pay off all the loan and credit card debt we have, and never ever apply for any credit cards or loans for the rest of our lives.

Here are the reasons why you too must immediately pay off all your credit card and loan debts. This is an urgent priority if you want to be financially free for the rest of your life.

In the course of our research as a Global Non-Political affiliated party/group, we found very important, highly classified information, one of which is the fact that credit cards and loans are the main reasons why the rich get richer, and the poor get poorer. More light on this is shed below:

- The rich systematically exploits society by setting up traps of loans and credit cards. They continue to exploit society by creating fear of the credit score system, which is the number one systemic enemy of humankind. The system known as the credit score system and credit cards are an evil system that poor and middle-class people do not understand and will never understand.
- The United Countries of the World Global Non-Political party will save millions of Americans and millions of people in the world from financial ruin and financial misery caused by the trap of Credit Cards and Credit Scores. Why do you keep spending now, to pay later? Because you are brainwashed by credit card and loan companies without your consent. These companies are very creepy and aim to always put you in financial ruin. Our founding father, our non-political party, AKA, The Yes, We Can honest non-politician, who is the author of this book will be the first in the American and world history to stop the tragic phenomena which is "the rich getting richer and the poor and middle class getting poorer.
- In Our Global Non-Political party, we do not use credit cards (we do not spend money we do not have), and we do not have credit score systems or systematic financial ruin systems.
- We hope to live to see the America of No Credit cards, and The United Countries of the World without credit scores designed by rich banks, and filthy and dirty politicians and dirty lobbyists.

- We are so many and everywhere. We have eyes and voices everywhere in the world.

Chapter 24

Charities Systemic Corruption and Fraud

Our demands, proposals, and concerns

regarding charities' systemic corruption

Freedom of speech and Press Experiment 2:

If you decide to give or donate for a worthy cause, give it to whom it may concern in person. We give those in need by getting them what they need directly, not through third parties.

We do not trust so-called non-profit or charity organizations, and we object to all the crimes being committed in the name of non-profit or charity organizations. In our private investigations, we found that most charities and non-profits get richer by diverting the charity money to their personal pockets, buying mansions, luxury cars, and living luxury lives.

Vision and our future provisions: We the members of our non-political party called United Countries of the World are working on ending homelessness and being the only legal nonprofit charity regulated and controlled by the United Countries of the World government.

Committing crimes in the name of non-profit or charities will forever end, and there will no longer be homeless or hungry people anywhere in the world if our organization takes over the audit of all charities.

We highly commend you for taking our ideas seriously and attentively. We will be the only United Countries of the World, ending homelessness with a non-political party, free of corruption.

Where there are so-called charities and non-profits, there will always be a system of corruption, chief amongst which is, misappropriating charity funds for personal interests and gains. We are the only hope - of true and honest acts - left for humanity.

Every penny we raise in our homeless GoFundMe page, will directly be used to cover sheltering, feeding, and counseling of the homeless.

We will send all the receipts spent on sheltering, feeding, and counseling the homeless to the United Countries of the World Government, and all the receipts spent on sheltering, feeding, and counseling homeless people will be explicitly displayed in our websites, for the public to see.

We highly recommend that the United Countries of the World Government audits all the charities and non-profit organization to submit evidence of where and to what purpose their funds were spent. Many charities and non-profit organizations will be revealed eventually if the United Countries of the World Government does an excellent job.

Chapter 25

Just do the right thing!

To have a good night sleep every day, do the right thing every day.

Your conscience will thank you if you do the right thing every day of your life.

It is guaranteed that you will have a good night sleep for the rest of your life by just consistently doing the right thing every day.

Reread this book to stay focused on doing the right thing every day of your life.

Doing the right thing is not easy in this world that is designed and engineered by greed, thirst for glory, thirst for power, popularity contests, and exploitation of poor continents and their resources.

Replace all your greed, thirst for glory, thirst for power, and continuous exploitation of poor continents and their resources by doing the right thing. By so doing, you will have good night's sleep every day of your life.

Chapter 26

The question is not whether going into a war is good or bad. The real question is whether the war is for independence or for the domination of superpowerism and dictatorship.

The real question is who suffers the most from causes of wars and sanctions. The innocent people, the soldiers involved in the war are the only ones who suffer the most during times of wars, sanctions, and confrontations. While the innocent people, and the soldiers involved in wars suffer the excruciating painful traumas of a war, the governments at war continue plan how to defeat the adversary by believing in their military might, nuclear bombs which ultimately kill innocent people who have nothing to do with their deeply seated competition of dirty political power of who becomes the superpower of the world while the economy of the world continue to crash and while inflation sky rockets at the gas pumps and at the food super markets.

While nothing happens for the executive commanders of the wars who watches the war virtually being in highly secure offices watching the war from television and give speech about it as if they actually were in the war zone themselves, innocent civilians who are victims of the war continue to suffer and die. We the people of the world must not side with any government involved in any war. We must side with the people of victims of wars who has nothing to do with the dirty political agendas of Governments involved in wars.

Whose fault is a war? A war is 100% governments faults, not the innocent people. governments power hunger and competition of controlling Strategic seas, and lands and other hidden agendas are why governments open wars they cannot get out so easily. It is to easy start a war than to start for peace for today's Government's arrogance and ego.

Every human being including a five-year-old child understand a war is an awfully bad terrible thing the humanity suffers from ever since the ancient times of the past wars of the First world war, the second world war, and the cold war for the power hunger of who becomes the most superpower of the world.

and now in year 2022, the year this book is published the world is in so much suffering of superpower countries computing on who becomes the superpower of the world, one by sanctioning the other while the other reacts to the sanctions and remembering history of the past of glory and power. We the United Countries of the world does not side with any governments involved in wars. We are on the side of the people suffering on the ongoing wars in various parts of the world such as civil wars in Ethiopia, wars in the lands of Ukraine. We the United countries of the world have one solution for everything to end all the wars in the world once and for good.

And the solution is that:

ALL SOLDIERS OF THE INVOLVED PARTIES AT WAR TO SAY NO TO A WAR!

All soldiers to say no TO BOMBING INNOCENT CIVILIANS.

This solution is the greatest solution our world can ever hope to magically happen where no soldier of any country goes into a war of any kind. NO Soldiers practically means No wars!

No Nuclear powers practically means No Wars!

No Technological Drone bombings practically means no wars

No retaliation practically means No Wars

 Let us give an example: Imagine a share ride company called Uber without Uber drivers. And also imagine a war commander without soldiers. Uber company without a driver does not exist. And also, a War commander with no soldiers cannot go into a war. Governments without soldiers are powerless. The true power is in the hands of the people and all the soldiers of the world.

The main engine of uber company is the uber drivers. And the main engine of all wars are governments who deceive   innocent soldiers by the name of to defend and protect while the Actual truth is something else such that of Superpoerism and domination of the world.

If the uber drivers Stop driving for Uber for one year   protesting Modern Slavery of the cheap price of uber base pay, Uber ride share cannot exist without a driver. If all the Uber Drivers in the World stop driving for uber for 1 year, Uber company will not exist without the main engine of the drivers, The same thing is true with wars. If all the soldiers of Marine, Army, air force refuse   from going into wars, there will not be any wars in the history of the world for many generations to come.

In the year this book is published year 2022, the inflation has plunged than ever before in the history of the world where gas price is close to $5-6 per gallon because of the wars on going in the world. Millions of people are in suffering the rise of price of goods in groceries because of the ongoing wars caused by governments not by the innocent people who are the immediate victims of wars. Superpower countries need to realize the competition of power on who becomes the most superpower in the world will repeat the history of the first and second world can repeat itself if soldiers do not say enough is enough to wars. A war is a vicious cycle that backfire to anyone involved.

Chapter 27

Artificial intelligence versus human intelligence

The question is not whether Intelligence is sub categorized as one of the Intelligence of a human being and the other type of Intelligence as one of the Artificial Intelligence programed with numbers of one and numbers of zeros. The truly undeniable fact is that there is no such a thing called artificial Intelligence without the presence of human Intelligence. Human intelligence is the superior Intelligence of all the artificial and non-artificial Intelligences combined together. Why? just simply because Artificial Intelligence is nothing but a computer-generated programming of numbers of zeros and numbers of one is coded in the laboratory of machine learning lab supervised by human intelligence. The greatest tragedy of Artificial intelligence is that its effectiveness is limited to energy and electric city. Where there is no constant supply of electricity and energy, Artificial Intelligence cannot be powered on to be operated, therefore we the United countries of the world on behalf of the power of human Intelligence over the power of artificial Intelligence notify the world that human Intelligence will always surpass artificial Intelligence of any kind. No electricity No Artificial intelligence. We commend all those who boast on the Ownership of Artificial Intelligence to be humble on realizing Solving the problems in the world with peaceful human Intelligence is more cost effective than artificial intelligence. Which means If there is no Electricity generating the electrical powers that can turn on a computer power in a power on mode, Artificial intelligence cannot function.

Chapter 27

Risk

~ "I Zerit Teklay Sebhatleab the CEO of Amazoxa Peace University the Home of true Education have learned that the question is not whether everything is a risk or not, I Zerit Teklay Sebhatleab the CEO of Amazoxa Peace University the home of true Education has learned that the question instead is what in this life is not a risk. I Zerit Teklay Sebhatleab the CEO of Amazoxa Peace University the home of true education has learned that Everything in this thing we call "life" is a risk. Above all I Zerit Teklay Sebhatleab the CEO of Amazoxa Peace University the home of true Education have learned that the greatest risk of all time in the history of risks is Not taking a Risk and being Complacent. The Greatest risk I Zerit Teklay Sebhatleab am taking right now in the history of my life journey is The Introduction and Establishment of Amazoxa Peace University the home of true Education in the real world of Formal Education. Why is this a risk? It is a big risk because Prestigious University that exist in the world today may do whatever it takes to eliminate me and my IDEA of Amazoxa Peace University. These Universities They may even go above and beyond to make sure they take care of the lobbyist in Government offices by bribing them to Eliminate my Amazoxa Peace University the home of True Education Existence from the faces of the Earth. Yet they will fail because I Zerit Teklay Sebhatleab have already planted the idea of Amazoxa Peace University the home of true Education in the hearts and minds of billions of people of all nations in the world by sending them the pdf file of This book and Amazoxa Peace University ideas and Intellectual properties   for them to be the beneficiaries my IDEA Amazoxa Peace University The home of true Education I Zerit Teklay Sebhatleab. Any one whom I have sent the pdf file of Amazoxa Peace University Intellectual properties will continue the Legacy of I Zerit Teklay Sebhatleab Idea of Amazoxa Peace University the home of true Education to prevail in the real world of formal Educations. The head Quarters of Amazoxa Peace University the home of true Education Will forever be In Asmara Eritrea. The beneficiaries of Amazoxa Peace University the home of True Education are:

- ✓ The Poor People in the Continent of Africa.
- ✓ The poor People in Eritrea
- ✓ The Poor people in the United States of America
- ✓ The Poor people in Canada
- ✓ The Poor people in Australia

- ✓ The poor people in The federation of Russia
- ✓ The poor people in North Korea
- ✓ The poor People in Afghanistan
- ✓ The Poor people in Pakistan
- ✓ The poor people in Iraq
- ✓ The Poor People in East, West, North, Middle and South countries of the World of Africa.
- ✓ The Poor people in European Union Countries
- ✓ The Poor people in United Kingdom
- ✓ The Poor people in Syria
- ✓ The Poor people in Egypt
- ✓ The Poor people in Italy
- ✓ The Poor people in Argentina
- ✓ The Poor People in Mexico
- ✓ The poor people in Venezuela
- ✓ The poor people in India
- ✓ The poor people in Ukraine
- ✓ The Poop people in Cuba
- ✓ The Poor people in Ireland
- ✓ The poor people in Japan
- ✓ The poor people in South Korea
- ✓ The poor people in Bahamas
- ✓ The poor people in Bahrain
- ✓ The poor people in the Indian Ocean Territory
- ✓ The poor people of all countries where there is United States of America Military Bases abroad
- ✓ The poor people in Crimea
- ✓ The poor people in all Invaded Countries

- ✓ The poor people in all Sanctioned countries
- ✓ The poor people in Balkans
- ✓ The poor people in Belarus
- ✓ The poor people in Burma
- ✓ The poor people in Burundi
- ✓ The poor people in Central African Republic
- ✓ The poor people in Democratic Republic of Congo
- ✓ The poor people in Cuba
- ✓ The poor people in Iran
- ✓ The poor people in North Korea
- ✓ The Poor people in Syria
- ✓ The Poor people in the Federation of Russia
- ✓ The poor people in Donetsk and Luhansk
- ✓ The poor people in Eritrea
- ✓ The poor people in Tigray
- ✓ The poor people in Ethiopia, Somalia, Uganda, Kenya, and all African countries poor people
- ✓ The poor people in Lebanon
- ✓ The poor people in South Sudan
- ✓ The Poor people in Sudan
- ✓ The poor people in Yemen
- ✓ The poor people in Zimbabwe
- ✓ The Poor people in Iraq
- ✓ The Poor people in the United States and the Poor people in Canada, the poor people in South America, the poor people in Latin America, The poor people in the Seven continents: the poor people in the Continent of Africa: The poor people in the continent of North America, The Poor people in the Continent of Asia, The poor people in

239

the continent of Australia, the poor people in the Continent of Europe, the Poor people in the Continent of Outer Space, the poor people in the continent of Antarctica.

I Zerit Teklay Sebhatleab the CEO of Amazoxa Peace University the home of true Education do solemnly swear in front of the Amazoxa Peace University Global Court of law that I Zerit Teklay Sebhatleab by my free will and good intention of the greater good of all the poor people in the world, am giving my testimony and transfer of my Will of all the Assets, Intellectual properties, Crypto currencies, stocks I Zerit Teklay Sebhatleab Own have and will have under my name and under the name of My Global Enterprize Amazoxa Peace University the home of true education will be under the Ownership of all the poor people of all poor countries in the world.

I am publishing my Will in my book for all the World Governments, Corporations and all the poor and rich people in the world to see and acknowledge my Legacy of transfer of all Amazoxa peace university and My personal Wealth to be given to the beneficiary of all the poor people mentioned in the above got forbid if unexpectedly die, or if I unexpectedly get eliminated, or assassinated by Competitor Prestigious Universities in the world. These Universities may kill the physical body of I myself Zzerit Teklay Sebhatleab. But these Universities who intend to do any harm because of Conflict of Interest, they forever fail to kill My IDEAS of Amazoxa Peace University the home of true Education whom I myself Zerit Teklay Sebhatleab Invented

Le the entire world in Particular let the United States of America whom I am A naturalized American citizen of Know if out envy something terrible happens to me, let All My Books assets, personal wealth, Intellectual properties I Zerit Teklay Sebhatleab be given to the poor people of all countries of the world as mentioned above. Under my Will No Government or no State will neither have authority nor entitlement of all my assets if I die. The poor people of all countries of the world are the ONLY BENEFICIEARS OF All my financial assets, real estate, Amazoxa Peace University is the Global Enterprise.

Signatory: Zerit Teklay Sebhatleab

Witnesses: Worldwide Amazoxa Peace University   Board Members Committee

Date: 4/10/2022 9:18:03 AM

Chapter 29

why do we get sick?

~"Why do we get sick? We get sick because of the types of food we eat; we get sick because of the types of drinks we drink; we get sick because of the types of News we see and hear; we get sick because of sleeping too much or sleeping too little, we get sick because of malnutrition."~ Zerit Teklay

I Zerit Teklay Sebhatleab have neve ever been sick in the history of my life. The password because I have never been sick in the history of my life is because the majority of types of food, I eat are Plant based. I have never been sick in the history of my life because I do not drink Alcohol. Only Water and home-made milk is what I drink even though it is not easy to home made fresh milked milk.

I have never been sick in the history of my life because I do not it any Junk foods and processed foods.

I have never been sick in the history of my life because I have never taken any pharmaceutical pills or medications.

I have never been sick in the history of my life because I do not do anything that causes Stress.

I have never been sick in the history of my life because I wake up early morning and I go to sleep Early.

I have never been sick in the history of my life because I do not over think about any Subject matter.

I have never been sick in the history of my life because I do not watch Television a Lot. If Watch television I am selective of watching Exclusiively good news and National Geography channel. I do not watch anything that promote Wars, violence, Hatred, and Confusion

IN GENERAL, I HAVE NEVER BEEN SICK IN THE HISTORY OF MY LIFE, Because I have Self Masters how to become my own primary care doctor of my life. With all the Due respect of all the Doctors in the world who are saving lives every single day as best as they can, I Zerit Teklay Sebahtleab Say to myself and to the world that I Zerit Teklay Sebhatleab, am the best DOCTOR of my own life. But I give Kudos to all the Hero doctors in the world who dedicate their work in Hospitals Patient care and Outpatient care.

I Zerit Teklay Sebhatleab Salute you and honor you all the doctors and Nurses of all countries of the world.

I Zerit Teklay Sebhatleab have learned to Practice being my own doctor in taking diligent care of my own mind, my own body, and my own emotions. I Zerit Teklay Sebhatleab Primary Care Doctor of my own life by understanding the virtues and Wisdom of my independently carried out Experiments and Surgeries experiments in the world of Medicine, I wisely and humbly advise you not to take Pills or medications if you want to live long life of minimum 150 years. If no accident happens to me, I expect to live at least 150 years. This will be a record in the world history if I do not get killed by pharmaceutical companies in an indirect way of being assassinated because of conflict of interest. I hope what happen to Doctor Sebi does not happen to me before I fulfill my work of living long life of minimum 150 years. Please know and understand that the more you depend on pills, medications drugs of any types

the more your natural immune system gets weak. The more your immune system gets weak, the more you will get sick.

So, if you ever get sick any kind of sickness in the journey of your life, the first thing you must not do is not to take any pills or medications that you do not know what they are made off. The pills you take without knowing what they are really made of can be designed not to kill you right away, but to keep you in the limbo of being sick for a long time.

Whenever you get sick, the second thing you must not do is to sleep too much. Never take sleeping pills. Do not sleep too much. Sleeping more than 6 or 8 hours weakens the power of your immune system.

The third thing you must not do, do not get in the State of isolation. Get your mind and body in an active state by being socially active. Never allow your mind to sleep away in dull moments.

When you feel like you are getting a flue type disease,

The beginning of Having good health and long life and preventing any diseases such as Corona, flues start with Eating Organic Natural foods.

Whenever you get sick, instead of getting pills and medications which you do not know how they are made, Try the following self-care treatment natural remedies that you know they are Natural remedies.

The remedy below is made from Natural foods that you know of the natural remedy below does not have any side effects unlike pills and medications because the remedies below is natural foods that you know,

it is tested and Experiments upon the Author and his circle during times of sickness such as flues and the like

When you get sick:

Try this Home-Made Immune system booster, Corona, flues, and all diseases prevention

Step 1: Blend 2 jalapeños + 4 pieces of Garlic + 2 pieces of Turmeric + 2 pieces of Ginger Root + 1 banana + handful of heated sesame seed+ 2 spoons of Oatmeal + one cup of Organic whole milk + 1 spoon of salt + Handful of Organic Kayle+ 1 piece of celery

Step 2: Boil Step 1 to a boiling point and add milk, if necessary, the remedy while boiling.

Step 3: Take one cup of the remedies in the morning after you wake up, One cup in the early afternoon. One cup at night before you go to sleep.

Prevention is better than cure.

"EATING Plant based Organic food is the number one mother of Good health and longevity.

"Eating plant based organic foods is the mother of preventing all diseases of any kind"

"EATING Plant based Organic food is the number one best medicine of all time"

- Zerit SEBHATLEAB

Chapter 30

letter to Superpower countries

I Zerit Teklay Sebhatleab the CEO of Amazoxa Peace University the home of true Education, In the name of Universal peace, Universal Justice, and Universal Prosperity, we all the members of the Future Global Constitution advocates cordially request all the Superpower countries to stop on being the superior police officers of the World for the sake of preventing major World wars. Super powerism could lead to a backfire. Dear Commanders of Superpower country: Do you please mind   Leaving foreign lands alone to freely Govern themselves by pulling your Military bases from foreign lands. The Poor people of those foreign lands will thank you and be historically grateful if you pull out your military bases from all foreign lands. Dear

Commanders of Superpower countries: Do you mind being the champions of peace instead of being the Champions of Wars, Invasions, Sanctions, and Killings of Innocent Civilians? Please Dear Supper Power Countries Do you mind teaching our children the power of being humble instead of the power of being Arrogant. I Zerit Teklay Sebhatleab am the humblest human being I know in the history of being humble. Through Amazoxa Peace Global University, I have Designed a subject matter called "Be Humble"
The World will thrive under the Amazoxa peace University like never before in the history of the world.

4/10/2022 9:51:13 AM

Respectfully,
Amazoxa Peace University the home of true Education CEO, Zerit Teklay Sebhatleab

Amazoxa Peace University the home of true education Board Members of United Countries of the World Government Amazoxa Committee

Chapter 31

INSPIRATION

Quotes that Inspired the Author of this book

~ "Success becomes your habit once you become successful on something. Simply said the password to become successful is to just simply to solve a problem of any magnitude. Solving a problem of any Magnitude is what all the success achieved have in common. Focus, avoiding distractions, setting a specific date deadline and the desire to solve a problem are the four passwords of achieving any success of any level. I personally succeeded in publishing this book because I applied the four passwords of success. The level of your success depends on how big of a problem, and how complex of a problem you are trying to solve. If you solve a personal problem, your success is limited to personal achievement. If you solve a global problem such as a World War, your success becomes the biggest success one can ever hope to achieve in the history of the world of success. Using the four passwords of success. any kind of problem of any magnitude can be solved successfully." ~ Zerit Teklay

~ "World War is the biggest problem of our World today. Solving a major big World War is not only the duty of Governments, but it is also every one's duty and responsibility. So let us prevent any major World War from happening before it happens only by peaceful approach and diplomacy instead of by Arms, Nuclear bombs, and Cyber-attacks. Let us guide each TV news or Social Media platforms not to generate and circulate hatred among nations against nations. and let us also guide ourselves not to generate and circulate hatred among ourselves and among nations. Without any discrimination of any people of any country, my heart goes out and aches with any people of any country whose heart is aching during on-Going Wars and Terrors. Let working for peace be the duty and responsibility of each one of us. In my views, even though the race of humankind will not perish to exist by world wars, it is time for super powerful countries to prevent World War three before it happens. The idea of superpower is a very bad idea, and that very idea of Superpower is and will always be the main idea why our world Wars start. The competition for power of who become a superpower will always lead our world to a vicious cycle of World wars now and then. In my views, the only solution that will end World wars from not starting is when all countries become equally super powerful. Together let us succeed on preventing a major World War from happening by our words and by our deeds and our actions. Let us form a new form of supper power which we can call "Global Constitution equalizer of all powers for the sake of everlasting Global eternal peace" ~ Zerit Teklay

~ "Politics Separates Us, Race disconnects us, Religion divides us, News Manipulates us. Global Constitution Unites us" ~ Zerit Teklay

~ "Sanctioning a country is the highest and truest form of global dictatorship our world has ever seen. The greatest tragedy of sanctioning a country is that: it is not the government of the Sanctioning country that suffers of Sanctioning another country, it is the innocent people of the country sanctioned are the ones who suffers because of their country being Sanctioned. The question is not whether sanctioning a country is a problem or not. The question is that who suffers as the consequences of Sanctioning a country. The innocent people of all countries suffer. Sanction is a problem than it is a solution." ~Zerit Teklay

~ "Invading an autonomous country is the highest and truest form of dictatorship. The question is not whether invading an autonomous country is the highest form of dictatorship or not, the real question instead is who suffers when a country invades another autonomous country. The innocent people of the country being invaded suffers. Invading an autonomous country is a problem than it is a solution. ~" Zerit Teklay

~ "Sanctioning a country or invading an autonomous country are part of the problem not part of the solution of keeping peace. Where there is a sanction and invasion of autonomous country, there will never be true peace ever for many generations to come. There will always be an ever-lasting peace when the two problems of sanctioning or invading an autonomous country Stops." ~ Zerit Teklay

~ "Governments sponsored torture of innocent individuals is the highest form of cruelty in the history of humankind. The greatest tragedy of torture occurs when torture happens to an innocent individual who knows nothing about the reasons of his or her torture. Trying to get an information which does not exist by torturing an innocent individual to the highest degree of torture is a sad tragedy in today's world of torture of wrongfully torturing the wrong person. Can you imagine how brutal it can be a human being torturing another human being? Can you imagine as if you were that person being tortured? Governments sponsored acts of Torturing an innocent individual is a problem than it is a Solution." ~ Zerit Teklay

~ "The question is not whether information needs to be categorized as highly classified or unclassified information, the real question is who does classify information harms or benefits? And why do countries hide their highly classified information from their own citizens they are supposed to serve and protect? The real question is whether our world is better off where there is no such information called highly classified information. The idea of highly classified information is part of the problem than it is part of the solution." ~

~ "The justice system has always been, still is protecting the rich who have powerful lawyers. The Greatest tragedy of the Justice System is that it continues to fail protecting the poor who cannot afford power full lawyers to represent them. There is a famous saying which says, "the law protects the rich." The highest level of injustice than can occur is when an innocent poor person gets guilty sentence for the crime he or she did not commit." ~ Zerit Teklay

~ "Balances and checks Among the Legislative, Executive, and Judicial branches of the United States government is the greatest equalizer of power balance among the three branches of U S Government. What makes the United States Constitution the best constitution of all time is its system of balance and check of its three branches of government. The system of balance and check of the United States Constitution states that "No Person, No Government official is above the supreme law of the land, everyone must obey the law of the land. The question in here is not whether the system of balance and check is perfect or not, the real question instead is whether it is thoroughly always followed or not. When followed Balance and check is the solution for power abuse to be in check and in balance. It is every one's duty to check and balance whether power is abused or not." ~ Zerit Teklay Sebhatleab

~ "The highest level of Self-Care is becoming the primary care doctor of your own mind, your own body, and your own emotion." ~ Zerit Teklay

What is your purpose statement? What does your purpose Statement say?

Zerit's purposes statement says: Infinite Solutions: A solution to everything One World. One Flag. One Constitution.

~"The highest level of education is Wisdom. "Zerit Teklay

~"the highest level of success is not when someone becomes a President a country, the highest level of success is when someone one with a team of others solve major global crisis such as wars, famine, crime, and civil unrest in a glo
bal level.
thinking globally and acting globally in solving problems on a global level is the highest level of success any one can hope to achieve. solving problems in a global level for the greater good of all countries is the highest level of success "~ Zerit Teklay

~ "Life's tragedy is that we get old too soon and wise too late." ~ Benjamin Franklin founding father of the United States

~ "There is no passion to be found playing small." ~ Nelson Mandela President of South Africa

~"Being a good person begins with being a wise person. Then when you follow your conscience, will you be headed in the right direction. "Justice Scalia United States Supreme Court Judge

~ "Doing good is my Passion." ~ Zerit Teklay

~ "The main business of a lawyer is to take the romance, the mystery, the ambiguity out of everything thing he touches. "~Justice Scalia United States Supreme Court Judge

~ "I used to say that the Constitution is not a living document. It is dead, dead, dead. But I have gotten better. I no longer say that. The truth is that the Constitution is not the one that morphs. It is an enduring constitution, not a changing constitution. That is what I have meant when I said the Constitution is dead. "~Justice Scalia United States Supreme Court Judge

~" I attack ideas. I do not attack people. Some particularly good people have some unbelievably bad ideas. And if you cannot separate the two, you got to get another day job. You do not want to be a judge. At least not a judge at a multi-member panel. "~Justice Scalia United States Supreme Court

~ "A man who had made no enemies is probably not a very good man. "~Justice Scalia United States Supreme Court Judge

~ "Words have meaning. And their meaning does not change. "~Justice Scalia United States Supreme Court Judge

~ "Originalism is sort of subspecies of textualism. Textualism means you are governed by text. That is the only thing relevant to your decision, not whether the outcome is desirable, not whether legislative history says this or that. But the text of the Statute. "~Justice Scalia United States Supreme Court Judge

~ "Wringing about state's rights, forget it. They are gone. Basically, the federal government can do whatever it wants. Who is going to protect the states? My court? Ha-we're feds! "~Justice Scalia United States Supreme Court Judge

~ "I would not like to be Replaced by someone who immediately sets undoing what I have tried to do for 25-26 years. "~Justice Scalia United States Supreme Court Judge

~ "It always seems impossible until it is done." ~ Nelson Mandela South African President

~ "If you talk a man in a language that he understands, that goes to his head. If you talk to him in his language, that goes to his heart." ~ Nelson Mandela South African President." ~

"Education is the most powerful weapon which you can use to change the world." ~ Nelson Mandela South African President

I Stand here before you not as a prophet, but as a humble servant of you, the people." ~ Nelson Mandela South African President

~ "If you want to make peace with your enemy, you must work with your enemy. Then he becomes your partner." ~ Nelson Mandela South African President

~ "money won't create success, the freedom to make it will." ~ Nelson Mandela South African President

~ "Where globalization means, as it so often does, that the rich and the powerful now have new means to further enrich and empower themselves at the cost of poorer and weaker, we have a responsibility not allow that happen in the name of Universal freedom." ~ Nelson Mandela South African President

~ "As long as poverty, injustice and gross inequalities exist in our world, none of us can truly rest." ~ Nelson Mandela South African President

I learned that courage was not the absence of fear, but the triumph over it. The brave man is not he who does not feel afraid, but who conquers that fear." ~ Nelson Mandela South African President

~"Good afternoon. Today, as we watch freedom and liberty under attack abroad, I am here to fulfill my responsibilities under the Constitution to preserve freedom and liberty here in the United States of America. For too long, our government, our courts, have not looked like America. It is time that we have a court that reflects the full talents and greatness of our nation with a nominee of extraordinary qualifications, and that we inspire all young people to believe that they can one day serve their country at the highest level. "~ Joe Biden 46th President of the United States

~" Justice Brayer not only gave me the greatest job that any young lawyer could ever hope to have, but he also exemplified every day in every way that

257

a supreme court justice can perform at the highest level of skill and integrity while also being guided by civility, grace, pragmatism, and generosity of spirit. Justice Brayer the members of the Senate will decide if I fill your seat, but please know I can never fill your shoes."~ Ketanji Brown Jackson United States Supreme Court Judge

~"Stated simply, the primary takeaway from the past 250 years of recorded American history is that Presidents are not kings. This means that they do not have subjects, bound by loyalty or blood, whose destiny they are entitled to control. Rather, in this land of liberty, it is indisputable that current and former employees of the White Housework for the People of the United States, and that they take an oath to protect and defend the Constitution of the United States. Moreover, as citizens of the United States, current and former senior-level presidential aides have constitutional rights, including the right to free speech, and they retain these rights even after they have transitioned back into private life."~ "~ Ketanji Brown Jackson United States Supreme Court Judge

~"Independence does not mean you decide the way you want."~ Stephen Breyer United States Supreme Court Judge

~"It doesn't help to fight crime to put people in prison who are innocent."~ Stephen Breyer United States Supreme Court Judge

~"There are loads of Countries that have nice written constitutions like ours. But there are not loads of Countries where they are followed. "~ Stephen Breyer United States Supreme Court Judge

~"Every citizen should figure out what kind of government he or she wants."~ Stephen Breyer United States Supreme Court Judge

~"It is important to every American the law protects his or her basic liberty."~

~"The Strength of self-reliance and is that of science and technology, the short cut to implementing the five-year strategy to give the importance and precedence to science and Technology."~ Kim Jong-un President of North Korea

~ "The days are gone forever when our enemies could blackmail us with nuclear bombs." ~ Kim Jong-un President of North Korea

~"The North and the South were one people sharing one language and one culture for about 5000 years. Ultimately, we should reunite."~ Moon Jae-in President of South Korea

~"A robust economy is a source of National strength for Japan." Shinzo Abe President of Japan

~" Desire plus stability is equal to resolution, Resolution plus hard work is equal to success. To succeed your desire for success should be greater that your fear of failure. "~ Narendra Modi Former president of India

~ "The danger is, because we have always been a harmonious society, we can become complacent, we do not understand that there is a lot of work that we need to do in order to generate that understanding. We do need to have deeper conversations about what it really means for us as a society, and as a people, to promote further multiracialism." ~ Halima Yacob President of Singapore

~Without passion you do not have energy, without energy you have nothing. "~ Donald Trump 45th President of the United States of America

~"If you are interested in 'balancing' work and pleasure, stop trying to balance them. Instead make your work more pleasurable."~ Donald Trump 45th President of the United States of America

~"My mother had a saying: Kamala, you may be the first to do many things, but make sure you are not the last."~ Kamala Harris 46th Vice president of the United States of America

~"Failure at some point in your life is inevitable but giving up is unforgivable."~ Joe Biden 46th President of the United States of America

~"Corruption is a cancer, a cancer that eats away at a citizen's faith in democracy, diminishes the instinct for innovation and creativity; already-tight National budget, crowding out important National investments. It wastes the talent of entire generations. It scares away investments and jobs."~ Joe Biden 46th President of the United States of America

~"Fighting corruption is not just good governance. It is self-defense. It is patriotism. "~ Joe Biden 46th President of the United States of America

~"Corruption is another form of tyranny."~ Joe Biden 46th President of the United States of America

~"No one ever doubts that I mean what I say, the problem is I sometimes say all that I mean."~ Joe Biden 46th President of the United States of America

~"As long as you are going to be thinking anyway, think big." ~Donald Trump 45th President of the United States of America

~"I try to learn from the past, but I plan by focusing exclusively on the present. That is where the fun is."~ Donald Trump 45th President of the United States of America

~"I was not satisfied just to earn a good living; I was looking to make a statement. "~ Donald Trump 45th President of the United States of America

~"one of the key problems today is that politics is such a disgrace, good people don't go into government."~ Donald Trump 45th President of the United States of America

~"The greatest gift is the ability to forget- to forget the bad things and focus on the good."~ Joe Biden 46th President of the United States of America

~"Our future cannot depend on government alone. The ultimate solutions lie in the attitudes and actions of the American people."~" Joe Biden 46th President of the United States of America

~My dad always used to say, champ the measure of a man is not how often he is knocked down, but how quickly he gets up."~ Joe Biden 46th President of the United States of America

~"My dad used to have an expression- It is the lucky person who gets up in the morning, puts both feet on the floor, knows what they are about to do, and thinks it still matters."~ Joe Biden 46th President of the United States of America

~"What I believe Unites the people of this nation, regardless of race or religion or party, young or old, rich or poor, is the simple, profound belief on opportunity for all-the notion that if you work hard and take responsibility, you can get ahead." ~ 44th President of United States President Barack Obama"~

"No matter how intelligent Artificial intelligence gets, Artificial intelligence has always been, is still and will always be dependent of human intelligence to function. Artificial Intelligence without human intelligence is like a car without an engine. The main engine, the main source of Artificial intelligence is human intelligence. That is why Human Intelligence will always surpass Artificial Intelligence. Human intelligence is the most asset of all time in the history of humankind. Let us cultivate Human intelligence over Artificial intelligence for the greater good of all society of all countries of the world." ~ Zerit Teklay

"They who can give up essential liberty for little temporary safety deserve neither Liberty nor safety" - Benjamin Franklin.

~ "when you see something that is not right, not fair, not just, you must speak up. You have to say something; you must do something." ~ John Lewis Former United States Representative

~ "Rosa parks inspired me to find a way to get in the way, to get in trouble…good trouble, necessary trouble." ~ John Lewis Former United States Representative

MLK, Jr. Thought me how to say no to segregation and I can hear me saying now when you straighten up your back, no man can ride you. He said stand up straight and say no to racial discrimination." ~ John Lewis Former United States Representative

~ "Diversity is the engine of invention; it creates creativity that enriches the world." ~ Justin Trudeau Prime Minster of Canada

263

~ "Leadership should be focused on extending the ladder of opportunity for everyone." ~ Justin Trudeau Prime Minster of Canada

~ "Fear is a dangerous thing. Once it sanctioned by the state there is no telling where it might lead. It is always a short path to walk from being suspicious of our fellow citizens to restrict their liberty." ~ Justin Trudeau Prime Minster of Canada

~ "Not ready for the big stage." ~ Justin Trudeau Prime Minster of Canada

~ "We define a Canadian not by skin color, or a language or a background, but by a share set of values and aspirations, hopes and dreams."." ~ Justin Trudeau Prime Minster of Canada

"Eritrea is not for sale! Eritrea is not for sale "~ President of Eritrea President Isaias Afwerki~

~ "It takes a few to make war, but it takes a village and a nation to build peace." ~ Dr. Abby Ahmed Prime Minister of Ethiopia

~ 'I don't have any clue about the criteria, how the Nobel committee selects an individual for the prize." ~ Dr. Abby Ahmed Prime Minister of Ethiopia

~ "Many Ethiopians see yesterday. I see tomorrow." ~ Dr. Abby Ahmed Prime Minister of Ethiopia

~ "War is the epitome of hell for all involved. I know because I have been there and back." ~ Dr. Abby Ahmed Prime Minister of Ethiopia

Working hard on peace process is an exceptionally good thing for yourself, for your region, for your country." ~ Dr. Abby Ahmed Prime Minister of Ethiopia

"Aid is like a pill that numbs the pain, if you get it to often you get addicted." ~ President of Eritrea President Isaias Afwerki~

~The vision and sacro-sanctional right of Eritrean people for liberation was not bestowed to us as a gift or favor on a silver platter. It was achieved after 50 long years of arduous toil and unparalleled sacrifice. ~ President of Eritrea President Isaias Afwerki

~"Resistance is a matter of both culture and heritage. And culture is narrated by intertwined value system. A value system takes time; it does not crystallize abruptly or by a chance of a fleeting moment"~ President of Eritrea President Isaias Afwerki

~" The opportunities that stand before us today are substantial. We must accordingly brace ourselves physically and mentally to implement robust programs of our development objectives with more vigorous power and greater pace. This is not an option; it is a necessity "~President of Eritrea President Isaias Afwerki

~"The priceless importance and value of liberation and freedom, the significance of sovereignty, augment and gain more luster with time as years go by. This does not only engender satisfaction and Fulfilment; but it also reinforces our resilience and determination"~ President of Eritrea President Isaias Afwerki~

~" Our society rejected outlaws and abusers. The Eritrean people do not accept crime. they respect law and justice." ~ Bitweded Abraha Eritrean Hero

~" Before it was for independence and country, now the struggle is for human liberty, so that fellow men would not exploit and abuse us." ~ Bitweded Abraha Eritrean Hero

~" I do not dwell on the past; I look forward to the future. This is a fraction of the lengthy, collective struggle we must wage for human liberty." ~ Bitweded Abraha Eritrean Hero

~" I can be promoted; I can benefit from it, but it would be at the expense of the nation. I will never betray my country." ~ Bitweded Abraha Eritrean Hero

~" I have not done anything except standing against those willing to sell the country." ~Bitweded Abraha Eritrean Hero

~" No one can stand in front of me and say Bitweded has committed any crime, all I said is that I would rather die than give our ports to our killers and murderers." ~ Bitweded Abraha Eritrean Hero

~" I was held in solitary confinement for 74 months, but now I stand here free and victorious. What I was saying then, they are saying it now." ~Bitweded Abraha Eritrean Hero

~" On this occasion, in the presence of my elders, of brothers and sisters, I express my readiness to seek no revenge and punishment

267

against those who wronged me. I forgive them all." ~Bitweded Abraha Eritrean Hero

~" Even those who have wronged me, now I consider my friends. Not focusing on the future grudges and I will not accept any monetary restitution, as to the descendants of Adkeme Miliga receiving compensation is an insult." ~ Bitweded Abraha Eritrean Hero

~" Fighting, acrimony and destruction only leads to turmoil. In a struggle for democracy, compatriots must choose to live together in harmony." ~Bitweded Abraha Eritrean Hero

~" Setting an example for others, I have decided to forgive them from the bottom of my heart, as forgiveness, peace and reconciliation are superior to everything." ~Bitweded Abraha Eritrean Hero

~" All humans, including me, seek forgiveness. on the other hand, it takes courage and bravery to forgive. let us forgive and we shall be forgiven." ~ Bitweded Abraha Eritrean Hero

~" Conflict, divergent views, and fights will always be there, but the best solution is achieved by sitting around the table." ~Bitweded Abraha Eritrean Hero

~" Peace is costly, but prison, muzzling and isolation are illegal and therefore wrong means to solve conflicts. They will never lead to a solution." ~ Bitweded Abraha Eritrean Hero

~" I am speaking as I stand on the graves of our martyrs, 65,000 of them have died. Settling divergent views through due process and in a peaceful manner will yield solid and lasting peace, but there is a small price to pay. I was wronged, but the gain was bigger. Compromising and solving conflict amicably is not a loss. Do not think that I have been defeated because I have forgiven." ~Bitweded Abraha Eritrean Hero

~" Some may think that going to the wilderness with a gun, fighting and killing people is victory. if you kill your brother, you are hurting your own self. When you seek revenge, you are also hurting yourselves. I reject this" ~ Bitweded Abraha Eritrean Hero

~" Those who genuinely believe in forgiveness, trust me, will never be prisoners of past grudges, or Acrimony. For the sake of peace and reconciliation I have completely forgiven them." ~ Bitweded Abraha Eritrean Hero

~" It is best to think about the long term. Let us focus on our children and grandchildren, on the long journey ahead of us leading to human liberty." ~ Bitweded Abraha Eritrean Hero

~" To preserve and protect peace, independence, justice, democracy. Let us think how we will preserve and protect the peace we have, let us not squander it." ~ Bitweded Abraha Eritrean Hero

~" The fool takes up arms because they have been wronged, but the wise instead chooses to sacrifice its ego for the sake of the people and the country." ~ Bitweded Abraha Eritrean Hero

~" Ideals of modernity, development, prosperity, peace, and justice were our goal, our vision, our dream I have chosen to focus on them. The journey is still too long." ~ Bitweded Abraha Eritrean Hero

~" In this new year, 1998, I embark in my journey with a fresh mind, with a new spirit and constitution of Eritrea, I am embarking on this journey." ~ Bitweded Abraha Eritrean Hero

~ "Living together in peace is the result of forgiveness, reconciliation and wisdom." ~Bitweded Abraha Eritrean Hero

~ "Nowadays, we judge how a great politician or leader of a nation is by the maturity of the mind, the wisdom of his political strategy." ~ Bitweded Abraha Eritrean Hero

~ "I choose to proceed peacefully and peacefully. Let us choose this path." ~ Bitweded Abraha Eritrean Hero

~ "Those who say they bring peace with guns, are lairs." ~ Bitweded Abraha Eritrean Hero

~ "It will just lead to an even heavier price in human lives. We must avoid civil war." ~ Bitweded Abraha Eritrean Hero

~ "We can only give what we have, let us hand the peace we have down to our children, so they can hand it down to their children." ~ Bitweded Abraha Eritrean Hero

~ "The greatest blessing for a human being is living in peace. Choosing and preserving peace, always." ~ Bitweded Abraha Eritrean Hero

~ "Alone we cannot go far. I am telling you; peace is superior to everything." ~ Bitweded Abraha Eritrean Hero

~ "So, I repeat, commitment is necessary and the advancements of the National interest, the rule of law and justice are our collective responsibility." ~ Bitweded Abraha Eritrean Hero

~ "I am not saying he is the only person who asked about my whereabouts and advocated for me. Many were imprisoned and sacrificed because of my case." ~ Bitweded Abraha Eritrean Hero

~ "that is why I am telling to commit. Omar Hakito asked the President, the minister, and others…tens of times but he was never arrested because he was brave." ~ Bitweded Abraha Eritrean Hero

~ "hopefully, they will be wiser and will not repeat their mistake, but we should never be silent." ~ Bitweded Abraha Eritrean Hero

~" It is not by how many you have killed that makes you a hero, but by how many you have forgiven, by how he invites Armed adversaries to a peaceful competition, by how he consoles who is in pain and compensates who have been wronged and by the way he is able to turn his enemies into allies and friends, by how he brings those who are distant, closer, by how he admits his mistakes and openly asks for forgiveness with humility. We do not need someone who lead Arrogantly." ~ Bitweded Abraha Eritrean Hero

Good afternoon. Today, as we watch freedom and liberty under attack abroad, I am here to fulfill my responsibilities under the Constitution to preserve freedom and liberty here in the United States of America. ~" Justice Brayer not only gave me the greatest job that any young lawyer could ever hope to have, but he also exemplified every day in every way that a supreme court justice can perform at the highest level of skill and integrity while also being guided by civility, grace, pragmatism, and generosity of spirit. Justice Brayer the members of the Senate will decide if I fill your seat, but please know I can never fill your shoes."~ Ketanji Brown Jackson United States Supreme Court Judge

~"Stated simply, the primary takeaway from the past 250 years of recorded American history is that Presidents are not kings. ...This means that they do not have subjects, bound by loyalty or blood, whose destiny they are entitled to control. Rather, in this land of liberty, it is indisputable that current and former employees of the White Housework for the People of the United States, and that they take an oath to protect and defend the Constitution of the United States. Moreover, as citizens of the United States, current and former senior-level presidential aides have constitutional rights, including the right to free speech, and they retain these rights even after they have transitioned back into private life."~ "~ Ketanji Brown Jackson United States Supreme Court Judge

~"Independence does not mean you decide the way you want."~ Stephen Breyer United States Supreme Court Judge

~"It doesn't help to fight crime to put people in prison who are innocent."~ Stephen Breyer United States Supreme Court Judge

~"There are loads of Countries that have nice written constitutions like ours. But there are not loads of Countries where they are followed. "~ Stephen Breyer United States Supreme Court Judge

~"Every citizen should figure out what kind of government he or she wants."~ Stephen Breyer United States Supreme Court Judge

~"It is important to every American the law protects his or her basic liberty."~ Stephen Breyer United States Supreme Court Judge

~ "The question is not whether everything thing is a risk or not, the question instead is what in this life is not a risk." ~

~"Change will not come if we wait for some other person or some other time. We are the ones we have been waiting for. We are the change we seek"~ 44th President of United States President Barack Obama"~

~" If you are walking down the right path and you are willing to keep walking, eventually you will make progress"~ 44th President of United States President Barack Obama"~

~" The future rewards those who press on. I do not have time to feel sorry about myself. I do not have time to complain. I am going to press on"~ 44th President of United States President Barack Obama"~

"An asset puts money in my pocket, liability takes   money out of my pocket "-Robert Kiyosaki

~"Money is not the only answer, but it makes a difference"~ 44th President of United States President Barack Obama"~

~"I think when you spread the wealth around it is good for everybody."~ 44th President of United States President Barack Obama"~

~"The thing about hip-hop today is it is smart, it is insightful. The way they can communicate a complex message in a very short space is remarkable."~ 44th President of United States President Barack Obama"~

~"Now, as a nation we do not promise equal outcomes, but we were founded on the idea everybody should have an equal opportunity to succeed. No matter who you are, what you look like, where you come from, you can make it. That is an essential promise of America. Where you start should not determine where you end up"~ 44th President of United States President Barack Obama"~

~"If the people cannot trust their government to do the job for which it exists-to protect them and to promote their common welfare-All else is lost" 44th President of United States President Barack Obama"~

~" I am the President of The United States, I am not the Emperor of the United States"~ 44th President of United States President Barack Obama"~

~"I just miss-I miss being anonymous"~ 44th President of United States President Barack Obama"~

~"The internet did not get invented in its own. Government research created the internet so that all the companies could make money off the internet. The point is, is that when we succeed, we succeed because of our individual initiative, but also, we do things together."~ 44th President of United States President Barack Obama"~

~"If you were successful, somebody along the line gave you some help...somebody helped to create this unbelievable American system that we have that allowed you to thrive. Somebody invested in roads and bridges. If

276

you have a business- you did not build that. Somebody else made that happen." ~ 44th President of United States President Barack Obama"~

~" Understand, our police officers put their life on the line for us every single day. They have a tough job to do to maintain public safety and hold accountable those who break the law."~ 44th President of United States President Barack Obama"~

~"It was not a religion that attacked us that September day. It was al Qaeda. We will not sacrifice the liberties we cherish or hunker down behind walls of suspicion and mistrust. ~~ 44th President of United States President Barack Obama"~

~"You have young men of color in many communities who are more likely to end up in jail or in the criminal justice system than they are in an excellent job or in college. and you know, part of my job, that I can do, I think, without any potential conflict, is to get at those root causes." ~ 44th President of United States President Barack Obama"~

~" Trayvon Martin could have been me 35 years ago." ~ 44th President of United States President Barack Obama"~

~"There is not a liberal America and a conservative America- There is a United States of America. There is not Black America and a white America and a Latino America and Asian America- there is the United States of America."~ 44th President of United States President Barack Obama"~

~"The fact that my 15 minutes of fame has extended a little longer than 15 minutes is somehow surprising to me and completely baffling to my wife."~ 44th President of the United States President Barack Obama"~

~"Focusing on your life solely on making a buck shows a certain poverty of Ambition. It asks too little of yourself. Because it is only when you hitch your wagon to something larger than yourself that you realize your true potential. ~" 44th President of United States President Barack Obama"~

~"We did not become the most prosperous country in the world just by rewarding Greed and recklessness. We did not do it just by gambling and chasing paper profits on Wall Street. We built this country by making things, by producing goods we could sell. ~~ 44th President of United States President Barack Obama"~

~"It took a lot of blood, sweat and tears to get where we are today, but we just begun today we begin in earnest the work of making sure that the world we leave our children is just a little better the one we inhabit today."~ 44th President of United States President Barack Obama"~

~"Where the stakes are the highest in the war on terror, we cannot possibly succeed without extraordinary international cooperation. Effective international police actions require the highest degree of intelligence sharing, planning and collaborative enforcement."~ 44th President of United States President Barack Obama"~

~Americans...still believe in an America where everything is possible-they just do not think their leaders do."~ 44th President of United States President Barack Obama"~

I know my country has not perfected itself. At times we have struggled to keep the promise of Liberty and Equality for all our people. We have made our share of mistakes, and there are times when our actions around the world have not lived up to our best intentions."~ 44th President of United States President Barack Obama"~

~" In my views, even though the race of humankind will not perish to exist by world wars, it is time for super powerful countries to prevent World War three before it happens. The idea of superpower is a very bad idea, and that very idea of Superpower is and will always be the main idea why our world Wars start. The competition for power of who become a superpower will always lead our world to a vicious cycle of World wars now and then. In my views, the only solution that will end World wars from not starting is when   all countries become equally super powerful. "~ Zerit Teklay

~" We need to internalize the idea of excellence. Not many folks spend a lot of time trying to be excellent."~ 44th President of United States President Barack Obama"~

~"My job is not to represent Washington to you, but to represent you to Washington."~ 44th President of United States President Barack Obama"~

"~ In my views, even though the race of mankind will not perish to exist by world wars, it is time for super powerful countries to prevent World War three before it happens by understand the root causes of World Wars and solving the puzzles embedded in the history of First World War and Second World war."~ Zerit Teklay

~"Dictating other Countries fait without the consent of their people is the highest and truest form of pure dictatorship. It is not only individuals who are dictators, but also there are Countries which are Global dictators. In my views Being a Superpower is the same as being a Global Dictator. If Global Super powerism or global dictatorship continues our world will always have world wars. The idea of Superpower is a synonym for Global dictatorship. The end of global dictatorship is the only solution left to save humanity from World wars. "Zerit Teklay

~"I think that the first people who should read this book are our brothers and sisters in the United States. Because their threat is in their own house. The devil is right at home. The devil is right at home, the devil himself is right in the house. The devil came here yesterday. Yesterday the devil came here. Right here! It smells of sulfur today. This table that I am standing in front of, yesterday ladies and gentlemen from this podium the President of the United States the gentlemen whom I referred as the devil came here talking as he owns the world. Truly as the owner of the world. I think we could call a

280

psychiatrist to analyze yesterday's statement made by the President of the United States. The spokes men of Imperialism came to share his nostrums to try to preserve the current pattern of domination, exploitation, and pillage of the peoples of the world. An Alfred Hitchcock movie could use as a scenario. I would even propose a title "the devil's recipe'. As champzi says here clearly in depth, the American empire is doing all it can to consolidate its Hegemonistic system of domination, and we cannot allow them to do that. We cannot allow World dictatorship to be consolidated."~ Hugo Chavez Venezuelan President speech at United Nations General Assembly on 20 September 2006

~"Man's freedom is lacking if somebody else controls what he need, for need may result in man's enslavement of man."~ Muammar Gaddafi President of Libya

~"I am a Bedouin warrior who brought glory to Libya and will die a martyr."~ Muammar Gaddafi President of Libya

~"Even if there comes a time when you do not hear my voice, do not give up. Do not stop fighting for your freedom until you have victory."~ Muammar Gaddafi President of Libya

~"To force a human being to learn according to a set curriculum is a dictatorial act."~ Muammar Gaddafi President of Libya

~"We believe America is practicing all kinds of terrorism against Libya. Even the accusation that we are involved in terrorism is an act of terrorism. "Muammar Gaddafi President of Libya

~"Somali maritime violence is a response to greedy western nations, who invade and exploit Somalia's water resources illegally. It is not piracy, it is self-defense. It is defending the food of Somali children's food. "Muammar Gaddafi President of Libya

~"The type of education now prevailing all over the world is directed against human freedom. State controlled education deprives people of their free choice, creativity, and brilliance. "Muammar Gaddafi President of Libya

~"All the great prophets of modern times have come from the desert and were uneducated: Mohammed, Jesus and me." Muammar Gaddafi President of Libya

~"Once a ruler becomes religious, it becomes impossible to debate with him. Once someone rules in the name of religion, your lives become hell."~ Muammar Gaddafi President of Libya

~ "Americans are good people. They have no aggressions against us, and they like us, and we like them. They must know I do not hate them. I love them. I hear it is a complex society inside. Many Americans do not know about the outside world. The majority have no concern and no information about other people. They could not even find Africa on the map. Americans are good, but America will be taken over and destroyed from the inside by Zionist lobby.

282

The Americans do not see this. They are getting decadent. Zionists will use this to destroy them."~ Muammar Gaddafi President of Libya

~"Let the free people of the world know that we could have bargained over and sold out in return for a personal secure and stable life. We received many offers to this effect, but we choose at the vanguard of the confrontation as a badge of duty and honor. "Muammar Gaddafi President of Libya

~"When everyone is part of the people's congress, what need is there for opposition? Opposition to what? You oppose a government! If there is no government, and the people govern themselves on their own, what are you going to oppose? Something that is not there."~ Muammar Gaddafi President of Libya

~"During my term in AU, I will initiate an organized compensation claim for Africa and I will fight for a greater voice for Africa in the United Nations Security Council. If they do not want to live with us fairly, it is our planet, and they can go to another planet."~ Muammar Gaddafi President of Libya

~" Whoever does not miss Soviet Union has no heart. Whoever wants it back has no brain." ~ Vladmir Putin President of Russia

~ "sometimes it is necessary to be lonely to prove that you are tight." ~ Vladmir Putin President of Russia

I am the wealthiest man, not just in Europe, but in the whole world. I am wealthy in that the people of Russia have twice entrusted me with leadership of a great nation such as Russia- I believe that is my greatest wealth." ~ Vladmir Putin President of Russia

~ "We are all different, but when we ask for the lord's blessings, we must not forget that God created us equal." ~ Vladmir Putin President of Russia

"~We need business to understand its social responsibility, that the main task and objective for a business is not to generate extra income and to become rich and transfer money abroad, but to look and evaluate what a businessman has done for the country, for the people, on whose account he or she become so rich." ~ Vladmir Putin President of Russia

~ "Nobody should pin their hopes on miracle." ~ Vladmir Putin President of Russia

~ "Those who fight corruption should be clean themselves." ~ Vladmir Putin President of Russia

~ "I don't read books by the people who betrayed the motherland." ~ Vladmir Putin President of Russia

~ "The United Nations founders understood that decisions affecting war and peace should happen only by consensus, with America's consent, the veto by Security Council members was enshrined in the United Nations Charter. The profound wisdom of this has underpinned the stability of international relations for decades." ~ Vladmir Putin President of Russia

~ "Terrorism has no nationality or religion." ~ Vladmir Putin President of Russia

~ "There are both things in the international law: the principles of territorial integrity and the right to self-determination." ~ Vladmir Putin President of Russia

~ "History proved that all dictatorships, all forms of Authoritarian government are transient. Only democratic systems are not transient. Whatever the shortcomings, Mankind has not devised anything superior." ~ Vladmir Putin President of Russia

~ "The point of conservatism is not that it prevents movement forward and upward, but it prevents movement backward and downward, into chaotic darkness and a return to a primitive state." ~ Vladmir Putin President of Russia

~ "The transfer of power is always a test of the Constitutional system, a test of its strength." ~ Vladmir Putin President of Russia

~ "I would never want Ukraine to be a piece on the map, on the chessboard of big global players, so that someone could toss us around, use us as a cover, as part of some bargain." ~Volodymyr Zelensky President of Ukraine

~ "Politics is not an exact science. That is why in school I loved mathematics. Everything in Mathematics was clear to me." ~Volodymyr Zelensky President of Ukraine

~ "let us find those people whose names do not cause controversy in our present and in our future. Let us name the monuments and the streets for those people whose name does not provoke conflict freedom Squares." ~Volodymyr Zelensky President Ukraine.

~ "We will never allow anyone, any organization, or any political party, at any time or in any form, to separate any part if Chinese territory from China." ~ Xi Jinping President of China

~ "I like the Dreams of the future than the history of the past." ~ Thomas Jefferson Third President of the United States of America

~ "A bill of rights is what the people are entitled to against every government, which no just government should refuse, or rest on inference." ~" Thomas Jefferson Third President of the United States of America

~ "tell me and I forget. Teach me and I remember. Involve me and I learn." ~ Benjamin Franklin founding father of the United States

~ "By failing to prepare, you are preparing to fail." ~ Benjamin Franklin founding father of the United States

~ "Early to bed and early to rise makes a man a healthy, wealthy and wise." ~ Benjamin Franklin founding father of the United States

~ "Money has never made man happy, nor will it, there is nothing in its nature to produce happiness. The more of it one has the more one wants." ~ Benjamin Franklin founding father of the United States

~ "Well done is better than well said." ~ Benjamin Franklin founding father of the United States

~ "Either write something worth of reading or do something worth of writing."
~ Benjamin Franklin founding father of the United States

~ "In this world nothing can be said to be   certain, except death and taxes." ~ Benjamin Franklin founding father of the United States

~ "Peace is much more precious than a piece of land...let there be no more wars." ~ Anwar Sadat third president of Egypt

~ "There is no happiness for people at the expense of other people." ~ Anwar Sadat third president of Egypt

~ "Fear is, I believe, a most effective tool in destroying the soul of an individual-and the soul of the people." ~ Anwar Sadat third president of Egypt

~"Great Minds discus ideas, average minds discuss events, small minds discuss people." Eleanor Roosevelt

~"By ensuring that no one in government has too much power, the constitution helps protect ordinary Americans every day against the abuse of power by those in Authority "~ John Robert's United States Supreme Court Judge

~"Judges are like umpires. Umpires do not make the rules. They apply them. The role of an umpire and a judge is critical. They make sure everybody plays by the rules. But it is a limited role. Nobody ever went to a ballgame to see the umpire. "John Robert's United States Supreme Court Judge

~"you cannot fight for your rights if you do not know what they are. "John Robert's United States Supreme Court Judge

~"The way to stop discrimination on the bases of race is to stop discriminating on the bases of race."~ John Robert United States Supreme Court Judge

~"I will be vigilant to protect the independence and the integrity of the Supreme Court, and I will work to ensure that it upholds the rule of law and safeguard those liberties that make thus land one endless possibilities for all Americans. ~John Robert United States Supreme Court Judge

~"People for reason of their own, often fail to do things that would be good for them or good for society. "John Robert United States Supreme Court Judge

~"President Ronald Regan used to speak of the soviet constitution, and he noted that he purported to grant wonderful rights of all sorts to people. But those rights were empty promises, because that system did not have an independent judiciary to uphold the rule of law and enforce those rights."~ John Robert United States Supreme Court Judge

~"If children do not understand the Constitution, they cannot understand how our government functions, or what their rights and responsibilities are as citizens of the United States. ~John Robert United States Supreme Court Judge

~"The ins United States is not and will never be at war at war with Islam."~44th President of United States President Barack Obama"~

~"My fellow Americans, we are and always be a nation of immigrants. We were strangers once, too."~ 44th President of United States President Barack Obama"~

~"

~" The immigration issue is, I recognize the one that generates a lot of passion, but it does not make sense for us to want to push talent out."~ 44th President of United States President Barack Obama"~

"~ Let us be honest- tracking down, rounding up, and deporting millions of people is not realistic. Anyone one who suggests otherwise is not straight with you. It's also not who we are as Americans." ~ 44th President of United States President Barack Obama"~

~"No other country in the world does what we do. On every issue the world turns to us, not simply because of the size of our economy or our military might-but because of the ideals we stand for, and the burdens we bear to advance them."~ 44th President of United States President Barack Obama"~

~" When 44th President of the United States President Barack Obama became the First African American president for the first time in the history of America, it ignited my Ambition and hope to one day see a Naturalized American citizen to become the President of the United States of America regardless of his birthplace."~ Zerit

~" If the United States of America was truly the land of equal opportunities, why is that a naturalized American citizen cannot be the President of the United States of America? Why does the birth certificate of a Naturalized American citizen have to matter whether a

Naturalized American citizen can or cannot be the President of the United States of America?" ~ Zerit Teklay

"Those who deny freedom to others, deserve it not for themselves" - Abraham Lincoln

"The independence of Ghana is meaningless unless it is linked-up with the total liberation of the African continent"

- Osagyefo Dr Kwame Nkrumah

"It is clear we must find an African solution to our problems, and that this can only be found in African Unity. Divided we are weak; united, Africa could become one of the greatest forces for good in the world"

- Osagyefo Dr Kwame Nkrumah

" I believe strongly and sincerely that with the deep rooted wisdom and dignity, innate respect for human lives, the intense humanity that is our heritage, the African race, united under one federal government, will emerge not as just another world bloc to flaunt its wealth and strength, but as a great power whose greatness is indestructible because it is built not on fear, envy, and suspicion, nor won at the expense of others, but founded on hope, trust, friendship and directed to the good of all mankind" - Osagyefo Dr Kwame Nkrumah

"The result of neo-colonialism is that foreign capital is used for the exploitation rather than for the development of the less developed parts of the world. investment under neo-colonialism increases rather than decreases the gap between the rich and the poor countries of the world" -Osagyefo Dr Kwame Nkrumah

"Revolutions are brought about by men, by men who think as men of action and act as men of thought"

"Action without thought is empty. Thought without action is blind" - Osagyefo Dr Kwame Nkrumah

"There will come a time when it's my phone spying on me through my phone anymore. It will be my phone spying on me.'

"The journey of a one thousand miles begins with one step." - Lao Tzu.

"I have a dream that my four little children will one day live in a nation where they will not be judged by the color of their skin but by the content of their character."

-Martin Luther King Jr.

Chapter 32

What do the American People and the Eritrean People have in common?

Both the American people and the Eritrean people have history of bravery, heroism, resilience and reaching for the stars for the independence of their people and their country from colonizers. Both the Eritrean people and the American people won on the long excruciating battle for freedom and for independence of their country and their country. Both The American people and the Eritrean people defeated the Idea of Colonization and Slavery.

Both American and Eritrean freedom fighters fought for what is right to free their people from the former oppressive British colonialist and former oppressive Ethiopian regimes led by Haile Selassie and Mengistu Hailemariam and the Former British Colonialist country, respectively.

The American people freed themselves from the former British colonizers, oppressors, torturers, and dictators. Likewise, the Eritrean freedom fighters fought to free their people from oppressive, former

294

dictatorial regimes of Ethiopia of Mengistu Haile Mariam and Haile Selassie. All dictators inevitably fall, and soon, all dictators in the world will fall. The clock is ticking for people to be free from dictatorship, tyranny, oppression, and unlawful imprisonment.

Chapter 33
Democracy

Justice Scalia, United States of America's Judge of the Supreme Court once said that 'Words have meanings and their meanings do not change." In other words, the word 'democracy' has a meaning, and its meaning does not change. We, the United Countries of the World confirm that as of yet, there is no such thing as true democracy anywhere in the world. No country in this entire planet can boast of practicing true democracy. Neither powerful governments nor non-powerful governments understand the meaning of the word "democracy." In one way or another, all superpower countries violate democracy laws written in their constitution. The greatest tragedy is that the powerful government leaders accuse other countries' presidents, calling them dictators, while they themselves are the greatest dictators of all time. We the people of the United Countries Government say, "Enough is enough." We must peacefully rise up, so the constitution of our countries is implemented. No government is as powerful as we the people. We are the only hope left to recreate true democracy based on the book of the constitution of our countries.

We have the following evidence to prove that there is no true democracy anywhere in the world:

Evidence 1a: The fact that the author of this book is incredibly careful not to write a lot of secrets of Governments, even with names withheld so as not to offend them so much that they may raid his home and follow him everywhere.

Evidence 1b: Genuine democracy does not have any sign of dictatorship in any of its actions. Another name for today's democracy is "Artificial Democracy."

Evidence 2a: True Democracy does not have agents invade foreign lands and does not dictate foreign lands' internal and external affairs.

Evidence 2b: True democracy does not bomb cities of innocent civilians.

Evidence 3: True democracy does not allow for spying on private citizens' smartphones, laptops, computers, and homes 24/7 and 365 days a year.

Evidence 4: True democracy does not exploit the natural resources of poor continents such as the continent of Africa (Eritrea) where the author of this book was born in 1981.

Evidence 5: True democracy does not tolerate killing other countries' legitimate presidents and remotely bombing their homeland with highly advanced technological drones.

Evidence 6: True democracy does not eliminate rising stars of revolution for true democracy on the grounds of mere suspicions.

Evidence 7: True democracy does not violate the laws of the land's constitution.

Evidence 8: True democracy does not tolerate discrimination.

Evidence 9: True democracy does not allow for the brainwashing of other countries' presidents and exploiting them as an extension of selfish gains - power and glory.

Evidence 10: True democracy does not allow for spending billions of dollars on expanding military bases in foreign lands and foreign seas of other autonomous and legitimate countries' lands.

Evidence 11: True democracy does not allow for the grand scheme of divide, rule, and exploit. **Evidence 12:** True democracy does not tolerate spending billions of dollars on sending spy agencies abroad to commit the crimes of interfering in internal and external affairs of foreign countries.

Evidence 13: True democracy is not aimed at being super powerful.

Evidence 13-91 are not written in this book so that

the author of this book can avoid trouble from some powerful countries. He understands that all super powerful countries have one thing in common, and that is eliminating anyone they think is a threat to their grand masterplan that border on Superpowerism. The author once said 'Rising stars for the pursuit of true democracy such as Martin Luther king, Malcom X, Abraham Lincoln, and J.F Kennedy were suddenly assassinated while in their quest to create true democracy. This cannot happen to this author because he already succeeded in publishing this book. There nothing as joyful as dying a good death in the name of True Democracy. Let the upcoming generation fight the good fight to defeat the so-called "Artificial Democracy" in order to achieve genuine democracy in the entire world. Let them follow peaceful and non-violent protests for the sake of replacing the Existing "Artificial/False Democracy" with "True genuine Democracy."

Chapter 34

Experience

Experience is the highest level of education. There nothing absolutely nothing in this world as important as and as valuable as experience in the world of constant learning and education. The main headquarters of experience can be seen everywhere in the world, in this university called life.

University of life is self-taught in all lands and seas of the world we are living in today. The experience here is the best teacher in the history of university learning and in the history of education. This university is the greatest, and most prestigious university in the entire world. Get the experience first, and then you will be the most educated person you will ever know in the history of your life.

Getting formal education does not and will not get you real life experiences. In my views, to be literate is the only thing you need to be successful. History shows hard evidence that the world's inventions and innovations are invented by college dropouts and high school dropout such as me. When you are self-taught, you get the 100% freedom and liberty to expand and nurture your highest true potential to be expressed by the University of life and by the University of experience. This form of learning marks the beginning of all experiences.

The only benefit of going to school is to be able to read and write. Schools do not teach you experience; they only teach theories, histories, and formulas, which means that no level of education, including PhD level of education can match an actual experience of the world of reality checks. The ups and down of life is the highest and truest form experiential education. Why? Because education without experience is null and void. Besides, history shows and proves that all the inventions and great ideas innovations created in the world today are the byproducts of brilliant minds who drop out of schools and colleges and pursue a dream or an idea that can change the world.

Experience + Defining your Purpose = Success.

Last Chapter
Success

~ "Success becomes a habit once you become successful in something. Simply put, the key to success is solving a problem of any magnitude. Solving a problem of any magnitude is what all successful people have in common. Focus, avoid distractions, and set a specific timeline on the problem you wish to solve, and your success will be inevitable. The level of your success depends on how big of a problem you try to solve. If you solve a personal problem, your success is limited to personal achievement. If you solve a global problem such as World Wars, your success becomes the biggest success one can hope to achieve in the history of the world of success. When you apply the keys to success, problems of any magnitude can be solved." ~ Zerit Teklay

~ "Sanctioning a country is the highest and truest form of global dictatorship our world has ever seen. The greatest tragedy of sanctioning a country is that it is not the government of the sanctioned country that suffers, but the innocent people. The question is not whether sanctioning a country is a problem or not, but that who suffers as a consequence of the sanction? The innocent people suffer. Sanction is more of a problem than a solution." ~Zerit Teklay

~ "Invading an autonomous country is the highest and truest form of dictatorship. Who suffers when a country invades another autonomous country? The innocent people of the country being invaded of course. Invading an autonomous country is more of a problem than it is a solution." Zerit Teklay

~ "Sanctioning a country or invading an autonomous country are part of the problem, not part of the solution to maintaining peace. Where there is a sanction and invasion of autonomous country, there will never be true peace, for generations to come, until the problems of sanctioning/invading an autonomous country stops." ~ Zerit Teklay

~ "Government-sponsored torture of innocent individuals is the highest form of cruelty in the history of humankind. The greatest tragedy of torture occurs when torture happens to an innocent individual who knows nothing about the reasons behind his or her torture. Trying to get an information which may not exist by torturing an innocent individual to the highest degree of inhumane treatment anyone can get. It is a tragedy that this still happens in today's world. Can you imagine how brutal it is for a human being to torture another human being? Can you imagine if you were the one being tortured? Torturing an innocent individual is a problem." ~ Zerit Teklay

~ "The question is not whether information needs to be categorized as highly classified or unclassified information, the real question who does classified information harm or benefit? And why do countries hide their highly

304

classified information from citizens that they are supposed to serve and protect? Will our world be better off if there is no such thing as highly classified information? The idea of highly classified information is part of the problem." ~

~ "The justice system has always and still protected the rich who have powerful lawyers. The greatest failing of our justice system is that it does not protect the poor who cannot afford powerful lawyers to represent them. There is a famous saying, "the law protects the rich." The highest level of injustice is when an innocent person gets sentenced for a crime he or she did not commit." ~ Zerit Teklay

~ "The highest level of Self-Care is becoming the primary caregiver of your mind, your body, and your emotion. ~"

~ "World War is the biggest problem of our World today. Solving a major big World War is not only the duty Governments, but also the duty and responsibility of ordinary citizens. Let us prevent any major World War from happening before it happens by taking a peaceful approach and applying diplomacy instead of using arms, nuclear bombs, and cyber-attacks. As we demand that TV news and social media platforms desist from generating and circulating hatred, likewise, we should do same. My heart goes out to victims of on-Going Wars. In my views, even though the race of humankind will not perish by world wars, it is time for super powerful countries to prevent World War three before it happens. The idea of superpower is a very bad idea and is mostly the main reason why World Wars start. The competition for who can emerge world power always leads to wars every now and then.

In my opinion, the solution that can bring an end to World Wars is when all countries become equally super powerful. Together, let us succeed in preventing a major World War from happening by our words, by our deeds and by our actions. Let us form a new form of superpower which we can call, "Global Constitution equalizer of all powers for the sake of everlasting Global eternal peace." Let working for peace be the duty and responsibility of each one of us. Together, we can succeed in preventing a major World War from happening. Using the four keys to success, any kind of problem of any magnitude can be solved." ~ Zerit Teklay

~ "Checks and balances among the Legislative, Executive and Judicial branches of the United States government is the greatest equalizer of power balance among the three branches of U S Government. What makes the United States Constitution the best constitution of all time is this system being applied throughout the three branches of government. This system states that "No person, nor government official is above the supreme law of the land." Everyone must obey the law of the land. This is the solution to abuse of power, and it is our collective duty to ensure that excesses from the government are being checked." ~ Zerit Teklay SEBHATLEAB

~"The highest level of success is not when someone one becomes a President of a country, but when someone one with a team of others solve major global crises such as wars, famine, crime and civil unrest on a global scale."~ Zerit Teklay SEBHATLEAB

This blank pages in this book above

and below this page are deliberately left as is, so that you, the reader, can author an essay on this book.

Amazoxa Peace University The home of True Education

Infinite Solutions: A Solution to everything:

One World. One Flag. One Currency. One Constitution. One University

Eritrean-born ZERIT TEKLAY SEBHATELAB

the founding father, CEO, and President of

318

Amazoxa Peace University the home of true education

BOOKS BY THIS AUTHOR

Follow Yourself: Become Your Own Role Model

ISBN 978-1-7375372-1-2

Https://Fys-Followyourself.com Llc

ISBN 978-1-7375372-2-9

Dedication To No Person, No Government Officail Or Government Is Above The Law. Every One Must Obey The Law.

ISBN 978-1-7375372-3-6

Summary Encyclopedia Of 51 Pages Long Zerit Teklay Sebhatleab Personal And Business Success Master Guidelline Refernce

Notebook A K A Hello, Wiseman Message Reader

ISBN 978-1-7375372-0-5

Lightning Source UK Ltd.
Milton Keynes UK
UKHW050811160223
417122UK00009B/1026